Freedom's Frailty

SUNY series in Chinese Philosophy and Culture
Roger T. Ames, editor

Freedom's Frailty

Self-Realization in the
Neo-Daoist Philosophy of Guo Xiang's *Zhuangzi*

CHRISTINE ABIGAIL L. TAN

With a Foreword by
BROOK ZIPORYN

Cover: Fish 群魚戲水圖 (detail). c. 1400. China, Ming dynasty (1368–1644). Hanging scroll, ink and slight color on silk. Cleveland Museum of Art.

Published by State University of New York Press, Albany

© 2024 State University of New York

All rights reserved

Printed in the United States of America

No part of this book may be used or reproduced in any manner whatsoever without written permission. No part of this book may be stored in a retrieval system or transmitted in any form or by any means including electronic, electrostatic, magnetic tape, mechanical, photocopying, recording, or otherwise without the prior permission in writing of the publisher.

For information, contact State University of New York Press, Albany, NY
www.sunypress.edu

Library of Congress Cataloging-in-Publication Data

Name: Tan, Christine Abigail L., author.
Title: Freedom's frailty : self-realization in the neo-Daoist philosophy of
   Guo Xiang's *Zhuangzi* / Christine Abigail L. Tan.
Description: Albany : State University of New York Press, [2024] | Series:
   SUNY series in Chinese Philosophy and Culture | Includes
   bibliographical references and index.
Identifiers: ISBN 9781438497464 (hardcover : alk. paper) | ISBN 9781438497488
   (ebook) | ISBN 9781438497471 (pbk. : alk. paper)
Further information is available at the Library of Congress.

10 9 8 7 6 5 4 3 2 1

For Sigrid

Contents

Acknowledgments — ix

Foreword — xi
    Brook A. Ziporyn

Chapter 1   The Question of Freedom — 1

Chapter 2   A Flattened Ontology and the Logic of Convergence — 25

Chapter 3   On the Self: Limits and Expanse — 67

Chapter 4   Freedom as Autonomy: Independence and Dependence — 95

Chapter 5   Freedom as Self-Realization: Dimensions of *Zide* 自得 — 115

Conclusion: "Freedom In" and Social Change — 141

Notes — 157

References — 187

Index — 195

Acknowledgments

So many people have been instrumental to the completion of this book, which took more than half a decade. Among everybody, however, two people stand out most: Professors Alan K. L. Chan and Brook Ziporyn, whom I thank for the gift of their mentorship in general, and the discussions about Guo Xiang in particular. Professor Chan's patience in reading the Guo Xiang commentaries with me, as well as his insightful comments on the earlier drafts of this study, have been the foundation of this work. Professor Ziporyn's earlier works on the subject have been the inspiration for this work, and I would not have been able to navigate through Guo Xiang's philosophical system if not for his comments and the many interesting discussions we have shared. There are more people than I can count who have given me their generous time and insights. Professors Li Chenyang, Lisa Raphals, Hans-Georg Moeller, So-Jeong Park, Dennis Schilling, Richard J. Lynn, Jeeloo Liu, and Winnie Sung are some of the established scholars who have graced me with their help. However, I have also had the good fortune of working with peers and mentees who contributed to the completion of this work, such as Kevin Roque, Wang Xinghao, and Eran Ranatunge. I also have to thank Yale-NUS College for providing me with a book manuscript workshop grant, and Professor Rajeev Patke for helping me secure this funding. This has allowed me the privilege and space to run a workshop discussing the contents of this work in an in-depth manner with some of the scholars mentioned above. Finally, I want to thank my husband, Anders Moeller, who has lived and suffered through the discussions of the ideas here, effectively becoming my sounding board, patiently deciphering these ideas, suggesting ways to improve my stylistic choices, and diligently proofreading the manuscript.

All errors in this book are the sole responsibility of my nosiest cat, Junjun, because my other cat, Sesame, is an angel who can do no wrong. Finally, I would like to thank you, the reader, for your interest in this topic. Any comments or questions about the manuscript are welcome and should be sent to my institutional e-mail.

Foreword

Brook A. Ziporyn

Guo Xiang is arguably one of the most important philosophers in human history, and yet he is also one of the least well known. His influence is vast, but it is of a certain subterranean kind that, precisely because melded so thoroughly and pervasively into the thinking of those that come after him, is camouflaged by its own ubiquity. It is true that the range of this influence is limited to the history of East Asian thought; he was unknown in the great premodern philosophical traditions of India and Europe, or anywhere outside the traditional Sinologosphere of East and Southeast Asia. But his influence flows like an underground stream into almost all subsequent Confucianism, Daoism and East Asian Buddhism, feeding them all and transforming them all. And yet in spite of this limitation of his influence to East Asia, the justification for venturing the seemingly outrageous claim that he is one of the most important thinkers *in all human history* considered globally is that this tradition is itself one of the most sustained, extensive and influential worlds of thought to have emerged within human history so far—and while this tradition has been deeply embattled over the past two centuries, it is nonetheless perhaps gradually gathering sufficient force and notice to play a major role in the philosophies of the future. This book by Professor Christine Tan, the book you hold in your hands, is surely an important step toward making that happen.

One of the reasons the name Guo Xiang is not more widely known is that all of his surviving writings are in the form of a commentary, camouflaging his revolutionary new brand of thinking as the explication of a great ancient predecessor: Zhuangzi. Even Zhuangzi is still not all that widely known outside East Asia, and Guo Xiang as a thinker has hidden himself behind this more prominent figure living about half a millennium before his own time, compared with whom he is thus bound to be the less well-known. Still, this piggybacking camouflage is also why almost all literate people in the traditional Sinologosphere have had some contact with the thinking and vocabulary Guo developed in that commentary. But that is not why I find it nonridiculous to make such an outlandish claim for Guo's importance. Rather, it is because a case can be made that locates a crucial turning point in the entire direction of East Asian thought in the work of Guo Xiang. I will call it the turn toward *antifoundationalist immanent apophatic mysticism*. What does this mean?

By "antifoundationalist," in Guo's case, I mean something very thoroughgoing indeed: I mean the denial of any source or ground, any overriding first principle or underlying original substance—for the world, for the person, for morality, for one thing happening rather than another, for anything at all.

By "apophatic mysticism," I mean the claim that there is a ubiquitous dimension of experience that is beyond all predicates, that cannot be grasped by thought or speech, and that there is something very important about realizing or communing with this dimension or considering one's existence in relation to it, because this dimension is beyond all oppositions and conditions, beyond all characterizations.

These two claims may strike some readers as directly contradictory to one another: on the one hand the denial of anything "beyond" whatever happens to happen, and yet on the other hand the affirmation of the ubiquity of something "beyond" all predication. But that is precisely where Guo's genius lies, and it is here too that we see one of his most influential insights. For what I have called a dimension of experience is not the same as an actual entity. It is not that there is some other entity beyond what happens that is beyond comprehension; it is that the very fact of "happening" is in a certain important sense beyond comprehension, and cannot be attributed to anything beyond itself—or even to itself. There is a sense in which "attributing" or "reducing" anything to anything else is nonsensical. This "sense" is what I am calling a "dimension"—and this dimension is a "mystical" dimension in that it is beyond all predicates and therefore beyond all oppositions between self and other, life and death, good and bad. There is nothing beyond the happening of whatever happens, but whatever happens itself is beyond definite explanation and beyond finitude. In being untouched by finite predications, this ubiquitous dimension of all experience is thus also the locus of what Professor Tan calls a "logic of convergence," a nonduality of apparent opposites, that is crucial to living well, that might even be the solution to the greatest existential problems of human life, that in some sense not only allows for the transcendence of all the contradictions and conflicts to which life is heir but is also beyond the reach of time and death.

I therefore call this apophatic mysticism "immanent" in Guo Xiang's case because unlike what is the case for most apophatic mysticisms, in this case that the locus of this dimension of experience that is so importantly beyond all possible predication and explication is not God, not the One, not Brahman, not the Dao, not Heaven, not Substance, but *each particular event happening anywhere at any time*. Every single event is seen to be absolutely valuable, not because it is rooted in a pure substance, not because it was designed and created by a benevolent deity, not because it serves a divine purpose, but precisely because it is not and it was not and it does not: it represents and rests on nothing beyond itself, it does not come from any divinity either good or evil, and it does not serve any purpose, nor is it the epiphenomenon of a neutral material substratum (e.g., "Nature") that has some claim to priority or reason to be celebrated by virtue of its role as the generative root of all existence. Each event is an absolute good not because it is a manifestation, an effect, or a cause of something that is Good, but rather because it is none of the above. Its goodness comes not from its relation to something else, but is rather just what is left when all interference from alien valuations are removed from our perception of it: it is good because its own inexplicable and unjustifiable existence is another word for its goodness *to itself*. For Guo, for an event to be what it is just *is* the establishment of its affirmation of its own value, indeed it is the only source of any meaningful sense of the idea of "value" itself. When freed from erroneous and superfluous attempts to ground it, to explain it, to justify it, to relate it to some value it may have as part of a larger whole, as working within a system, as contributing to a higher good, as caused by a divine intention, as serving some higher purpose, it is simply its own self-rightness, the only kind of rightness there is.

In other words, this ubiquitous dimension beyond all description is not only itself nondual; it also converges with its own apparent opposite, the complete denial of any metaphysical truths. Absolute skepticism allows of no duality, and is indistinguishable from the nonduality typical of absolute mysticism. Absolute nihilism and absolute affirmation "converge."

In more provocative moods one might call this not merely antifoundationalist mysticism but precisely *atheist* mysticism. But although that term sounds more controversial, it is actually the less radical of the two: a thorough antifoundationalism also entails a denial of a creator God, but an atheist might still admit the existence some other kind of metaphysical or ethical absolute beside a deity, something that is not active or conscious but nonetheless serves as a universal ground and source (Nature, matter in motion, the Absolute Idea, the One, Brahman, Substance, or the like). Guo Xiang denies every kind of foundation or ground—we might say that he denies the possibility of *founding* or *grounding* itself. Others in the Chinese tradition had certainly denied the existence of a creator God, or a providential conception of *tian* 天 (Heaven), and some had done so quite thoroughly and outspokenly. Many others, among them the elite ideologues of the preceding Han dynasty, had posited a vague and distant but morally relevant sort of guiding divinized Heaven that had at least some residual sense of conscious interest in the world, and which was the ultimate source of the order in the universe and in the empire. To be sure, as a third alternative, some thinkers in early China had pushed on the contrary toward a denial of any determinable source for things like identity, morality, the world, while nevertheless redefining *tian* in a way that pointed toward this very indeterminability . . . among them, arguably, some of the writers of the *Zhuangzi* itself. But that position was always at best ambiguous before Guo. That is to say, there were a few clearcut atheists, like Xunzi and Wang Chong, but their atheism tended toward pragmatic secularism and naturalism, rather than mysticism as defined above. Even in the case of the most antifoundationalist thinkers, in whom there is undeniably a powerful mystical dimension, such as many of the writers of the texts that make up the *Zhuangzi*, there is considerable ambiguity: it is more than possible to read even the contents of the *Zhuangzi*, considering it in its entirety, to be ultimately a foundationalist, even a fairly conventional one—and indeed, many have read Zhuangzi in just this way, and still do. That is precisely why Guo's intervention focuses on just this point: to disambiguate the *Zhuangzi* and spin it toward its more radical—that is to say, antifoundationalist, thoroughly atheist, immanently apophatically mystical—direction. And this tweak changed the course of Chinese intellectual history, becoming arguably the default assumption of much mainstream thought for at least the next millennium, which drove whatever theists and straightforward (nonparadoxical) foundationalists may have still survived into the nearly silent margins of the culture. And because this turn is so little developed at any length elsewhere in the world, and gained such spectacular developments in subsequent East Asian thought, Guo's importance for human history really cannot be exaggerated.

Anglophone scholars formerly used the English term "Neo-Daoism" to speak of Guo Xiang and other thinkers who are characterized in Chinese as belonging to a movement known in Chinese as *Xuanxue* (玄學, literally, "Dark or Abstruse Studies"), of which Professor Tan gives an insightful overview in the pages that follow. This English term was modeled on the term "Neo-Platonism" used by scholars for the past several centuries to refer to the thought of Plotinus and his followers in Western intellectual history. Both terms have justifiably fallen out of favor, for both are misleading labels, underselling at the same time the originality of the movements they name and also their syncretism. Plotinus is certainly a devoted exegete of Plato, and presents himself as such, but he conceived the secret oral teachings of Plato to converge with more widespread Pythagorean, Aristotelian and Stoic ideas. Figures like Wang Bi and Guo Xiang were also enthusiastic syncretists; indeed, both could justifiably be described as much Confucian as Daoist. But in spite of this welcome recent reconsideration of such terminology, there was something insightful about echoing the name of the Plotinian episode in Western thought when finding an English name for the thought of Guo Xiang. For Plotinus plays a role in Western intellectual history that is not unlike the one I have ascribed to Guo Xiang in East Asia. He is immensely but clandestinely influential, folded into much of what happens for the next millennium to such an extent that his name is rarely mentioned. And in both cases, for both Plotinus and Guo, these commentators hiding behind their primary ancient sources, their influence was most pronounced in a newly arrived religious realm: Plotinus became a key influence on the direction of mystical theology in Judaism, Christianity and Islam, but with his ideas renamed and reconfigured so as to fit the specific theological requirements of these revealed religions. Analogously, Guo's influence on the development of Chinese Buddhism, and from there all post-Buddhist forms of Confucian metaphysics, not to mention Daoist thinking and commentary thereafter, can hardly be overstated. In the case of Plotinus, it was the introduction for the first time of a true apophaticism, one only ambiguously gestured at in Plato and haltingly developed in Middle Platonism (another term that has fallen into disfavor) without quite managing to break through the glass ceiling of a demiurgic *Nous*. There had been some sprinkling impulses to push against the prevailing Hellenistic preference for *limit* and *form* and *intelligibility* over *limitlessness* and *formlessness* and *unintelligibility* to posit something that might be beyond form and intelligibility *and yet not therefore something horrible and chaotic and evil*, as the limitless and formless and unintelligible had always hitherto been thought to be in this tradition, *but rather the grounding of all intelligibility*: Plato's Form of the Good, and sometimes (e.g., in Alcinous's *Didaskalikos* of the second century CE), "God" as Nous, thinking itself or a thinking thing, which is nevertheless (rather problematically) also considered beyond all thought. Plotinus cuts the Gordian knot and makes the unnamable and unknowable One, beyond being and beyond thought, the very centerpiece of his system—the unthinkable that is the source of all thought, the unknowable that motivates and grounds all knowing, the hyperdivine void around which all divine Nous circulates. From that moment on, the divine darkness has a new role to play in theology; the *prohibitions* on naming God in the revealed religions can now be read as colorful invocations of the *impossibility* of naming God. Things might have gone quite a different way without the breakthrough of Plotinus, for the scriptural sources in all those religions leave plenty of room for a much more concrete and literal understanding of their deity, one with a much more straightforward and less paradoxical ontological profile than we find in the more sophisticated theologies of each tradition.

The parallel here is this: Without Guo Xiang, Confucianism could very possibly have been generally read as a *Tian*-based moral system, rooted in the idea that there was an at least semiconscious and vaguely personal deity called *Tian* (Heaven) that intervened to oversee dynastic change when morality declined beyond a certain point, and that had deliberately implanted moral values and demands in the human nature along with an expectation and imperative that they be brought to fulfillment. Instead, the Neo-Confucians of the Song dynasty from whose work was forged a new institutional orthodoxy for the last millennium of Chinese imperial history, as well as the Confucian dissenters among their contemporaries and through the succeeding Ming and Qing dynasties, all agree, pretty much without exception, that the shadowy deity still discernible lurking in the corners of early Confucian texts, in spite of its clear stand even then against the full-blooded theism of Mohism, is really just another name for a certain aspect of something that operates entirely without intention and purpose: Li 理 (the patterning, coherence, principle, or compossibility of all things), or Qi 氣 (spontaneously congealing and dissolving vital material force) or Xin 心 (heart-mind, the immanent affective and evaluative awareness constantly functioning in all human experience and relationships). The operations of whichever of these the later Confucians came to choose as the true meaning of the ancient metaphor *Tian* "Heaven" have one thing in common: Whether Li or Qi or Xin, it is not any particular entity existing outside our own present experience, and its workings are not the result of anyone's conscious intention, are not in any being's control, are not created by anyone. Its mode of existence and all of its effects and all of its attributes are, to use Guo Xiang's most central term, *ziran* 自然: self-so.

Without Guo Xiang, the Daoism of both the *Daodejing* and the *Zhuangzi* could have been read as a foundational mysticism or contrarianism, rooted in the idea that there was an invisible impersonal force of some kind at the base of the world or at the origin of the world or present everywhere in the world, called Dao (meaning "the Way" or "the Course"), which though having a slippery relationship to any and all naming and all determinate attributes, in the manner of monotheist negative theologies or Upanishadic apophaticism, was nonetheless the real objective entity or hyperessence at the root of all reality, contact and accord with which brought health, spiritual satisfaction, successful action, and which warranted and enabled a transcendence of social conventions. Instead, while we get still get plenty of Daoist writers who regard Dao as a metaphysical entity of sorts, and as the immanent source of all that exists, we consistently find levels of ironic underminings that go far beyond standard apophaticism and negative theology, underminings that many might feel verge uncomfortably close to outright skepticism or nihilism. As an example, we find in the Daoist canon the text *Guanyinzi*, attributed to a personal acquaintance of Laozi himself though actually a post–Guo Xiang creation, that opens with the following sentence: "It is not that there is a Dao that is inconceivable; inconceivability is itself the Dao. It is not that there is a Dao that is indescribable; indescribability itself is the Dao" (非有道不可言，不可言即道。非有道不可思，不可思即道).

And without Guo Xiang, Buddhism, even Mahayana Buddhism, could have been read only as a program for ultimately transcending the mundane world of life and death, even if that transcendence was long delayed on the Bodhisattva Path and had to undergo many conceptual twists and turns, or was accomplished by dispelling the idea of accomplishing it, or that there was anything to accomplish. The stress still could have been on the ending of delusion, understood as entailing the disappearance of life as ordinarily lived, the attainment of supernormal powers and faculties, and the ultimate goal of universal literal nirvana as the end of samsara, or at least of the illusion of there ever having been samsara. Instead, we find again and again in East Asian Buddhism, in one form or another, piggybacking on the uncompromising eschewal of metaphysics in Indian Madhyamaka, a concerted effort to eliminate any hint of anything truly outside of samsara, anything that in any way transcends experienced reality—whether above the world as its source, within the world as an essence lying below the surface of appearances, or as a transcending of the world in the form of eventual Buddhahood. This is true even where seemingly foundationalist concepts like Buddhanature and Alayavijnana were embraced, for they generally met with extensive redefinitions and reconceptualizations within the East Asian systems, almost always tending to qualify and limit their foundationalist and transcendent implications. Buddhahood, in Chan as in Tiantai and Huayan, is not merely available *within* life in samsara; it *is* life in samsara—and all aforementioned Chinese schools gesture, with various degrees of thoroughgoingness, to push the frontier of this immanence ever further, so that the true nirvana, "great" nirvana, not only implies that Buddhahood includes samsara, or is identical to samsara *if and only if the latter is seen correctly*. Rather, Buddhahood or Buddhanature is truly ubiquitous to all experience in Guo Xiang's sense, *prior* to any confusions imposed by delusions and *inextricably operating in and as all those delusions*. Samsara is nirvana, just as in prior Mahayana Buddhist theory, but much more importantly, delusion is itself Buddhahood: the very fact of misperceiving nirvana as samsara is itself Nirvanic, in a way explained differently, to be sure, by each of the above named schools. One approach was to compare the presence of enlightenment in delusion to the way in which it is just the purity of the reflectivity of the mirror that allows it to be obscured: the clearer the mirror, the more it reflects whatever is put before it, and thereby appears as something *other than* a mirror. The fact that it appears as such a non-mirrorlike thing is proof of just how much of a mirror it is. In the same way, the delusion and clinging and confusion of the samsaric mind, which misperceives nirvana as samsara, is itself the operation and verification of the purity and unobstructedness and nonattachment of the always immanent Buddhanature, the mind of pure awareness that precisely because of its purity never remains blank, and thus is truly pure precisely because never "pure" in the first-order sense of being unsullied by anything heterogeneous to itself. Its purity is seen in its always appearing as something *other than* awareness, *other than* purity. Other approaches up the ante of identity between nirvana and Samsara to the identity between delusion *about* nirvana and samsara and enlightenment about them, between correct and incorrect perception of reality, through redefinition of correct and incorrect in terms of theories of *upāya* (skillful means), epistemologies stressing the identity of the Two Truths or even the Three Truths, and Buddhahood redefined as the eternity of the Bodhisattva Path, constantly appearing in all possible forms in response to all possible delusions and attachments, dismantling them by means of an opposed and opposite delusion or attachment, rooted in the unconditionality and interpervasion necessarily implied in the structure of dependent co-arising as such, the unconditionality of the two opposed forms of one-sided conditionality. But what streams beneath all the sophisticated technical Buddhalogical moves made by these various Chinese schools is the central insight of Guo Xiang, for whom even entanglement and alienation in the morass of the "traces" that gives rise to erroneous attempts to ground and explain and give purpose to existence is itself eternally and inalienably *ziran*: we may act deliberately, we may make decisions, we may spin metaphysical theories, but even such attempts to erase the self-so-ness of things are themselves entirely self-so. When we engage in making decisions and claiming knowledge, the very antitheses of *ziran*, we are still inescapably *ziran*. However much we alienate ourselves from *ziran* through our attempts to control and explain and decide and understand, we never control our ability to control, we can never explain our ability to explain, we never decide to decide, and we never understand how we are able to understand. Our being there controlling and explaining and deciding and understand is something that happens without being controlled or explained or decided or understood—by ourselves or by anyone else, whether Buddha or God or human.

The relentless forefronting of *ziran*: this is Guo Xiang's great contribution that echoes throughout subsequent Chinese thought. What is *ziran*? The term survives in vernacular modern Chinese with the meaning of "naturally," in the sense of "without special effort." When modified by *da*, "great, vast," it is sometimes used to mean "Nature, the natural world." But literally, as Professor Tan explores in detail in these pages, it means "self-so": what happens not due to deliberate intention, not to attain any preconceived purpose, not even due to any discernible causal precedent or source. This is closer to the heart of Guo Xiang's usage of this term, which is found scattered here and there in the *Zhuangzi* and the *Daodejing*, but becomes truly the centerpiece of Daoist thinking only with this unremitting hammering on the idea, and development of its most radical implications, in the hands of Guo Xiang. And everything without exception is, according to Guo Xiang, ultimately *ziran*. The contemporary relevance of this idea is as compelling as its implications in the historical records are vast. For it is this uncompromising and relentless drilling down into the implications of *ziran* that opened a path toward what might be described as, to borrow a phrase, *the self-overcoming of nihilism*. Enfolded in this idea is a stunning implication. It is not just that nihilism is compatible with the nihilism-ending attainment of ecstatic mystical experience and liberating new ways of experiencing the interactivity between persons and persons, and between persons and their worlds: it is through the radicalization of nihilism that these salutary new modes of experience come about, and these liberating new modes of experience remain forever inseparable from and coextensive with the radicalized nihilism—or perhaps even identical to it. The kernel of this idea can be turned in many different directions, developed to many different depths and degrees of detail, associated with many different premises and implications, and the history of East Asian thinking might well be considered the story of the various ways in which it has been approached and processed and handled. But this core idea, the "logic of convergence," as Professor Tan describes it, applied to the seeming opposition between the nihilistic denial of all value or meaning to existence (insofar as these require the linkage of a thing to anything outside its actual manifestation) and the affirmation of the inviolable value of everything (insofar as this is conceived as a synonym for the self-affirmation that is embodied in its very manifestation)—this can be traced to the ancient intervention of Guo Xiang, the subject of this book, the denier of the validity of any and all traces of attributability. With the help of Professor Tan's capable guidance in the pages that follow, the reader is invited to drink deeply of all the vast implications of this idea, and thus see the immensity of Guo's historical contributions to expanding the possible modalities of human experience—as well as joining her in tracing out the immense practical and philosophical implications this tracelessness may yet come to have in the future.

1

The Question of Freedom

The concept of freedom, both metaphysical and political, is possibly one of the most elusive concepts in the history of philosophy, and it has definitely been a controversial one in relation to China. There is no literal translation for it in classical Chinese, and the Chinese word for it, *ziyou* 自由 (lit., self-cause), was not treated as a philosophical term until much later when Chinese liberal scholars such as Liang Qichao and Yan Fu promoted it as a political ideal.[1] This fact has thus led to the dominant view that this notion has never really developed in China, at least not until it was imported from the Anglo-European world. We shall go back to that claim later, but for now it is worth pondering this issue in a philological sense. Does it only occur in largely different languages that have different linguistic ancestries, such as English and Chinese? If so, what does that say about the kinds of issues each were concerned with? We will try to answer the latter question in the next section, but the former question recalls the very philosophical French term *jouissance*. In English, the literal translation is "enjoyment," yet the latter is not really treated as a strongly philosophical term. Why is this so? Unlike in the English world, France had a strong tradition of psychoanalysis, which transformed a word that has now entered conventional language into something philosophical, related to desire, pleasure, sublimation, and even suffering.[2] That said, do Americans not experience *jouissance* if they have no word for it? This would be a strange argument. Similarly, harmony is a very important concept in Chinese philosophy,[3] but it does not really carry much philosophical meaning in Anglo-European languages. This does not mean, however, that exploring what harmony means—in a philosophical sense—in Anglo-European philosophies is not a worthwhile task. Of course, we could not deny that there is a reason why certain terms are treated philosophically in certain cultures, as each time and place have their own unique concerns. However, this is the same for the concept of freedom, yet there are those who claim that freedom, specifically the freedom that in the liberal sense and as a basis for human rights is a universal value that China should adopt for itself. I do not disagree. Such an understanding of freedom, as we will see in the next section, however, is also a culturally situated one. Nonetheless, we live in an increasingly global world, and "freedom" is something that many global and international institutions seek to protect and/or champion. As such, it is worth having a conversation about, examining, and perhaps reshaping according to our needs, or to everyone's needs.

Nonetheless, there are those who argue that such a demand is a remnant of "Western" imperialism and chauvinism, because the Chinese have historically developed characteristically distinct traditions that had led to championing other values as more significant than, for instance, democracy. This is not helped by the fact that there are scholars who do say that freedom did not and does not exist as a concept in China, such as contemporary sinologist W. J. F. Jenner, who suggests that—despite its extensive cultural history—"the Chinese world" only came to realize the existence of such a concept as political freedom due to armed intervention by the West.[4] In the same work, Jenner only builds his claim from here and continues to say that "colonial rules gave many opportunities for new social, economic and political values and institutions to emerge."[5] He claims, moreover, that authority had always had a primal importance in the history of China and blames Confucianism for this, saying that "the need to remove an extremely bad ruler or, even more drastically, to overthrow an incurably decadent dynasty is one about which Confucian thinkers from Mencius onwards have felt very uncomfortable."[6] Framed this way, it is thus no wonder that an opposing position that comes from the same premise of difference also emerges as pushback from the former view. For instance, Daniel Bell points out that the ideal of harmony, which Confucians value most significantly, is shared among many civilizations including those in sub-Saharan Africa and Latin America; that the wider array of world cultures, ethical systems, and religions have prioritized the value of harmony above values like freedom, which the West supposes as universal, and that since Western societies are the outliers in terms of assuming freedom as a universal value, their devaluation of harmony as an ideal is controversial in the rest of the world.[7] Because of such differences, David Kelly notes that this denial of freedom as a concern in Chinese philosophical traditions is a "wedge issue," meaning that there can possibly be no point of overlap between what "Westerners" regard as "universal values" and what scholars such as Bell regard as "Chinese values." Nonetheless, Kelly examines a few modern Chinese thinkers who advocate for freedom in order to highlight "China's potential contribution to global social theory as a very live and fruitful field of inquiry."[8] While I share Kelly's goal, as well as agree with him when he points out the essentializing tendencies of Bell's position, I find myself uncomfortable with his enthusiasm for absolute or universal values that are based on liberal standards, as Jenner seems to take for granted. In fact, not only is Jenner wrong in claiming that freedom is something that only "Western" colonialism has brought to China as a sort of gift, but he is also making an erroneous claim when he purports that Confucians, especially Mencius, feel uncomfortable dethroning despots. As Tu Weiming points out:

> The significance of the concept of virtue (*te* 德), which features prominently in Confucian political thought, is that since "Heaven sees as the people see and Heaven hears as the people hear," the real guarantee for the well-being of the rulership lies in its acceptable performance rather than in its preconceived mandate. *The right of the people to rebel against a tyrannical dynasty*, the right of the aristocracy to remove an unjust imperial household, the right of the imperial clansmen to replace an unsuitable king, and the right of the bureaucrats to remonstrate with a negligent ruler are all sanctioned by a deep-rooted conviction that political leadership essentially manifests itself in moral persuasion and the transformative power of a dynasty depends mainly on the ethical quality of those who govern.[9]

Indeed, China has had a long history of revolutions,[10] from as early as the Zhou dynasty (1046–256 BCE), to the Qin (221–206 BCE), all throughout the dynasties stretching to the Qing dynasty (1644–1912), which had the famous Taiping Rebellion and Boxer Rebellion, up until the recent ones under the Republic of China (1912–1949). Among these rebellions is possibly one of the earliest peasant rebellions in the world, the Yellow Turban Rebellion or *Huangjin zhi luan* 黃巾之亂 (184–205 CE), which had ties with religious Daoism. In the early Zhou dynasty, moreover, the "Mandate of Heaven," or the idea that a ruler's legitimacy is sanctioned by Heaven as manifested by the people, has been used to justify ousting tyrannical rulers, as in the justified overthrow of the Shang dynasty (1600–1046 BCE) by the Zhou. More particularly during the Wei through Jin (266–420 AD) dynasties, there had been a unique wave of individualist thinkers,[11] as well as the emergence of one whom Étienne Balazs refers to as "China's first political anarchist,"[12] Bao Jingyan 鮑敬言 (ca. 200–400 CE).[13]

As such, while it is true that there is no direct equivalent in Chinese to the term "freedom" in classical Chinese philosophy, as shall be discussed in more detail later, it would suffice for now to say that it would be strange, if not simply erroneous, to claim that China did not know of political freedom, or at least had some idea of it—even if not corresponding to the liberal idea—before it had any exposure to Anglo-European traditions. Nevertheless, I do not wish to establish here that the Confucian alternative of freedom or a Chinese value of freedom that is similar to a liberal one had existed in ancient China, nor do I wish to claim that there is a singular unique notion of freedom that Chinese philosophy puts forward, because there is a plurality of arsenals from which the concept of freedom—in the basic sense of self-determination—is ripe for interpretation. I will cover such plurality shortly, but for now, it is more important to note that this book demonstrates that, notwithstanding the diachronic evolution of languages and terms, the concept of freedom is hardly a liberal invention, and so perhaps if we are to strive for more inclusive frameworks of freedom, then we need to reexamine and reshape this ideal in order to address the different needs, concerns, and circumstances of different peoples.

In order to achieve such an aim, I examine a specific Chinese philosopher, who may perhaps present us with a fruitful resource to better understanding and evaluating our notions of freedom, both ontological[14] and political. This work thus explores the potential of Guo Xiang, a commentator and philosopher from the Jin dynasty (266–420), and his philosophical enterprise to contribute insights toward a comprehensive account of freedom. More specifically, this book zeroes in on his notion of self-realization (*zide* 自得), using this as an anchor to explore its surrounding concepts of independence, agency, and causality (among others), as well as the implications of these unique ideas for how we understand the concept of freedom. Emerging at a chaotic but also syncretic time in the development of Chinese philosophy, his philosophical enterprise introduces a unique notion of freedom that is largely ontological and epistemological in nature yet shows considerable potential for deriving social and political aspects to this same concept of freedom. I suggest thus that Guo Xiang's philosophy allows us to conceive of a type of freedom that is as metaphysically necessary as it is contingent, and where freedom, while also having the radical potential to shed light upon the question of freedom in the sociopolitical arena, is both individual and collective. This is because unlike our dominant notions of freedom, Guo Xiang establishes an ontological and epistemological system that places the self as part of the empirical world of radical causality. By "freedom," moreover, I refer here to the basic understanding of it as self-determination and necessity (i.e., uncaused) that, as I shall demonstrate, is inevitably intertwined with freedom as self-realization. From the perspective of a philosopher like Guo Xiang, for whom the self has no fixed metaphysical grounds, what then might self-determination and self-realization look like? This is the question that we are going to pursue.

Moreover, it is important to note that for Guo Xiang, like many other Chinese philosophers, as we shall later discuss, freedom is not a given, as it is in Rousseau, wherein "man is born free."[15] Ideas develop differently in different historical contexts, and it is so with freedom, which does not emerge in identical ways through different traditions of thought. Although there are some dominant overlaps with the conception of freedom as self-determination among differing traditions, there are also differences and debates that are unique within traditions.

While Guo Xiang's notion of freedom can indeed be considered in terms of self-determination, I would like to demarcate his conception of freedom from the mainstream understanding of it in Anglo-European discourse. This is because Anglo-European discourse on freedom is deeply embedded in the problem of free will. While it is true that the free will problem has different concerns than that of political freedom, the concerns of ontological freedom—as this book will demonstrate—permeate the origins of our mainstream ideas on freedom.

In what follows, I show how the free will problem has developed throughout history, its relation to political freedom, and why, even though it cannot be applied to a Chinese philosophical context, that might not be a bad thing nor does it imply that there are no conceptions of freedom in Chinese philosophical discourse. I demonstrate the latter by surveying different Chinese philosophical conceptions and terms used to conceptualize Chinese notions of freedom, but I ultimately explain why looking at Guo Xiang for a reconstruction of a more holistic and comprehensive account of freedom, built on a different ontology, is likely to prove more fruitful.

A Brief History of the Free Will Problem and Its Metaphysical Foundations

Famous philosopher of freedom Daniel Dennett notes that free will is "an almost exclusively Western preoccupation."[16] As noted by Wenzel and Marchal later in this section, this is acknowledged by most philosophers. Political freedom, however, that is the absence of oppression, remains to be treated as a universal problem. Philosophers often distinguish metaphysical freedom from political freedom, and even Dennett himself, conceding the existence of free will simply for the fact that nihilistic determinism is a negligible position,[17] tells us: "There are real threats to human freedom, but they are not metaphysical. There is political bondage, coercion, the manipulation inducible by the dissemination of misinformation, and the 'forced move' desperation of poverty and hunger."[18] While this split might be convenient for philosophers, I argue that this is not so simple and the two are, more often than not, not mutually exclusive. In, fact, the concept of free will serves a very specific function in the development of Anglo-European philosophy. It is closely tied and inseparable to the problem of moral responsibility. There are different accounts about where the free will "problem" originated, but it was, originally, framed as a question of whether freedom of choice, and therefore moral responsibility, was compatible with fate, and more specifically, the foreknowledge of the gods and their divine providence. Democritus (460–370 BCE), for instance, desired to take control from the gods, and to challenge the idea that it is the gods who define our fate. Instead, he wanted to rest the responsibility of man's life within himself, saying: "People ask the gods for health in their prayers, but do not realize that the control of their health lies with them; through lack of self-control they act in opposition to it and so themselves betray their health to their desires."[19] Democritus famously favored the physical world over that of the gods, seeking to assign more responsibility to humans rather than the gods through his materialist philosophy. Even though he never outright denied the gods' existence,[20] Democritus made the first bold step toward the insistence on acquiring knowledge only through empirical observation. Ironically, however, Democritus instead came up with a theory that is closer to modern-day physical determinism[21] than being able to ascribe moral responsibility to humans. One of the more well-known claims of the atomists, the school to which Democritus belonged, is perhaps understood in Leucippus's description of fate in *On Mind*, where he says that "no thing happens in vain, but all things happen for a reason and from necessity."[22] Nevertheless, Democritus's attempt to ascribe responsibility to humans had, in turn, influenced Aristotle (384–322 BCE), and a generation after, Epicurus (341–270 BCE).

It was Epicurus, according to Pamela Huby,[23] who was finally able to provide a first account of a solution to the free will "problem." Huby says that Epicurus was able to do this because "he took over the atomic theory of Democritus almost unchanged, but introduced one significant new point, the swerve of the atoms, a slight change of direction that could occur without any cause."[24] Cicero (106–43 BCE), in his *De Fato*, criticizes this but also gives us our closest account of Epicurus's attempt to salvage free will from the determinism of the atomists. He says:

> But Epicurus thinks that the necessity of fate can be avoided by the swerve of an atom. And so a third kind of motion appears, in addition to weight and collision, when an atom swerves by a minimal interval (he calls it an *elachiston* [smallest]); and he is forced to concede, in fact if not in his words, that this swerve is uncaused. For an atom does not swerve because it is struck by another atom. For how can one be struck by another if the atomic bodies are moving, owing to their weight, downward in straight lines, as Epicurus thinks? It follows that, if one atom is never displaced by another, then one atom cannot even contact another.
>
> From which it is also concluded that if an atom exists and it does swerve, it does so without cause. Epicurus introduced this line of reasoning because he was afraid that if an atom always moved by its natural and necessary heaviness, we would have no freedom, since our mind would be moved in such a way that it would be compelled by the motion of atoms. Democritus, the founder of atomism, preferred to accept that all things happened by necessity than to tear from the atomic bodies their natural motions.[25]

While there is no clear account of how exactly this swerve accounts for free will, we know that Epicurus adopted the materialism of Democritus in order to ascribe responsibility back to man. Cyril Bailey, in his book *The Greek Atomists and Epicurus*, says that because Democritus wanted to get rid of the notion of divine guidance, his materialistic atomism had to compromise his ethical inclinations in order to make room for the logical uniformity and rigorous science of cause and effect, even if it had to lead to strict determinism. Epicurus, however, was not willing to make the same compromise, but he did not want to abandon his materialism either.[26] Epicurus thus saw it as necessary to continue to include the existence of the gods in order to defend the existence of free will and responsibility. He does this by saying that the gods do see our future, but that they simply do not care.[27] Thus, we ought to be held responsible for our actions, and our fates depend, to a point, on our own actions. In his *Letter to Menoeceus*, he says:

> As to [Fate], introduced by some as the mistress of all, "he is scornful, saying rather that some things happen of necessity," others by chance, and others by our own agency, and that he sees that necessity is not answerable [to anyone], that chance is unstable, while what occurs by our own agency is autonomous, and that it is to this that praise and blame are attached. For it would be better to follow the stories told about the gods than to be a slave to the fate of the natural philosophers. For the former suggests a hope of escaping bad things by honouring the gods, but the latter involves an inescapable and merciless necessity.[28]

However, Susanne Bobzien[29] challenges the claim that Epicurus "discovered" the free will "problem," and sure enough, there are many other contenders as to where the problem originated. Nonetheless, such early formulations were all still in relation to whether a divine being controls our choices, and if so, to what extent. For instance, Michael Frede claims that it is actually in Epictetus, during the first century CE, that we find the first notion of a free will.[30] Meanwhile, Dihle claims that "the notion of will, as it is used as a tool of analysis and description in many philosophical doctrines from the early Scholastics to Schopenhauer and Nietzsche, was invented by St. Augustine."[31] On one hand, Epictetus says that this ability *to do otherwise* is a faculty shared with us by Zeus. According to Epictetus, Zeus would have said: "We have given thee a certain portion of ourself, this faculty of choice and refusal, of desire and aversion, or, in a word, the faculty which makes use of external impressions."[32] On the other hand, Dihle tells us that St. Augustine, basing his conception of free will on the belief that man was created according to the image of God, as manifested in the existence of a human soul that was, as it were, "the obvious interpretation of Genesis 1:27 for a Roman or Greek intellectual about A.D. 400."[33] Either way, the notion of free will as framed by Epictetus and Augustine alike, pushes forward the claim that we are free precisely because we are made in the image of god. This then allows for a singular event that gives birth to our independent will.

At this point, it would not be a stretch to say that the origins and emergence of a concept of free will as we know it today in Anglo-European scholarship has always had its roots in theological inquiry, guided by anthropomorphic versions of a god or gods. Most apparently, the concept of free will gets picked up and brought to the fore by monotheistic religions, specifically in theodicy. In Christianity, for instance, God is supposed to be omnipotent and omniscient, but also omnibenevolent. However, we see in the Gospels that God would punish humans to be damned in hell for eternity.[34] As such, the only way for God to be omnipotent and omniscient, while being omnibenevolent (and not unjust), even while damning humans—the creation of whom He is solely responsible for—is to create a stopgap for the purpose of ascribing blame to humans instead: free will.[35] Without this anthropomorphized God, there would have been much less motivation to problematize the issue of human free will, as well as the need to conceive of it as a denaturalized absolute metaphysical faculty for uncaused agency—for starting a new causal chain ex nihilo and thus having full responsibility for it—because only if it is truly uncaused can the blame be kept off of God's shoulders.

It is perhaps for this reason, as previously mentioned, that Dennett points out the problem of free will as "an almost exclusively Western pre-occupation."[36] Yet ultimately, he also points out that "what we want when we want free will is the power to decide our courses of action, and to decide them wisely, in the light of our expectations and desires. We want to be in control of ourselves, and not under the control of others. We want to be agents, capable of initiating, and taking responsibility for, projects and deeds."[37]

This need for power, according to Dennett, is a "natural product of our biological endowment, extended and enhanced by our initiation into society."[38] So whether it is the external pull of something akin to the Greek *moira*, or even *telos*, when we are caused to move in a certain direction beyond our control, or the push of going back to a Christian god that is the precise cause for our free will—it is the power of that metaphysical or ontological ground zero that allows for free will, or in Dennett's words, for the "elbow room," that we seek. Dennett repackages this problem as scientific, yet acknowledges that this is an exclusively Anglo-European concern. This repackaging thus reflects how a specific idea, borne from a specific context, and serving a specific purpose, can easily be taken for granted as universal, as Dennett does. Moreover, he is not the first philosopher to do this, as there were countless others before him, replacing God with a different metaphysical *logos spermatikos*.

Immanuel Kant is perhaps not only the most famous but also the most influential example of this substitution. He replaces God, as the primal cause for the soul and will, with Reason, saying that "Reason therefore provides laws which are imperatives, that is, *objective laws of freedom*, which tell us *what ought to happen*, although perhaps it never does happen therein differing from *laws of nature*, which relate only to *that which happens*."[39] In other words, freedom as freedom of the will remains as necessity, that is, a primal cause. Metaphysical freedom, which Kant refers to as transcendental freedom, thus is, in a practical sense, "an unconditioned causality which begins to act of itself,"[40] or "the will's independence of coercion through sensuous impulses,"[41] which means that it is a *self-determination* of Reason.

Later after Kant, G. W. F. Hegel disagrees with much of Kant's claims regarding freedom and its compatibility with Nature, but he retains freedom as the freedom of an inherent will, possessed by a rational agent.[42] If freedom is necessity, and what is necessary is objective, then freedom is an objective Truth or Rationality. This is why Hegel says that "when we hear it said that freedom in general consists in *being able to do as one pleases*, such an idea [*Vorstellung*] can only be taken to indicate a complete lack of intellectual culture [*Bildung des Gedankens*]; for it shows not the least awareness of what constitutes the will which is free in and for itself, or right, or ethics, etc."[43] He endorses, instead, a freedom of will that is, not unlike that of his predecessors whom we have mentioned here, related to a higher and more universal entity. This line of reasoning thus is what allows Hegel to claim: "Man is free, this is certainly the substantial nature of man; and not only is this liberty not relinquished to the state, but it is actually in the state that it is first realized. The freedom of nature, the gift of freedom, is not anything real;

for the state is the first realization of freedom."[44] Nonetheless, this *logos spermatikos* or, to borrow a semiotic term, *final signified*, has had many shapes and forms throughout the history of Anglo-European philosophy. From God, Reason, Will, Soul, they are derived from universals, and are transcendent entities outside the world of causality, because to be free means to necessarily be the primary cause, and that can only be possible through a Soul or Will arisen from God or Reason. What this looks like differs and is a cause of debate for many philosophers after these two and those before them, but as we might guess, this becomes quickly problematic after the advent of totalitarian regimes such as the Nazis, with many postmodern philosophers questioning the objectivity of such a Reason with which to align our individual wills.

It is at this point, in this juncture of the historical development of this idea, that we encounter Isaiah Berlin's brand of liberalism. For Isaiah Berlin, it is precisely this kind of marriage that metaphysical freedom has with the practical and empirical world, that is a threat to our real and concrete political freedoms. In one of his renowned essays, *Historical Inevitability*, he makes the claim that "one of the deepest human desires is to find a unitary pattern in which the whole of experience, past, present and future, actual, possible and unfulfilled, is symmetrically ordered."[45] This kind of metaphysical coherence, the promise of the One and final truth, he says, is "an image which has often appeared in the history of mankind, always at moments of confusion and inner weakness."[46] Elaborating its dangers, Berlin continues:

> It is one of the great alibis, pleaded by those who cannot or do not wish to face the fact of human responsibility, the existence of a limited but nevertheless real area of human freedom, either because they have been too deeply wounded or frightened to wish to return to the traffic of normal life, or because they are filled with moral indignation against the false values and the, to them, repellent moral codes of their own society, or class, or profession, and take up arms against all ethical codes as such, as a dignified means of casting off a morality which is to them, perhaps justifiably, repulsive. Nevertheless, such views, although they may spring from a natural reaction against too much moral rhetoric, are a desperate remedy; those who hold them use history as a method of escape from a world which has, for some reason, grown odious

to them, into a fantasy where impersonal entities avenge their grievances and set everything right, to the greater or lesser discomfiture of their persecutors, real and imaginary. And in the course of this they describe the normal lives lived by men in terms which fail to mark the most important psychological and moral distinctions known to us. This they do in the service of an imaginary science; and, like the astrologers and soothsayers whom they have succeeded, cast up their eyes to the clouds, and speak in immense, unsubstantiated images and similes, in deeply misleading metaphors and allegories, and make use of hypnotic formulae with little regard for experience, or rational argument, or tests of proven reliability. Thereby they throw dust in their own eyes as well as in ours, obstruct our vision of the real world, and further confuse an already sufficiently bewildered public about the relations of morality to politics, and about the nature and methods of the natural sciences and historical studies alike.[47]

Berlin thus associates this kind of historical and scientific determinism[48] with the traditional belief in God's providence,[49] which ultimately allows free will through an uncaused cause, whether it be from being shaped in *Imago Dei*, or replacing God as a final signified with new referents such as Rationality, Absolute Knowledge, or even Emancipation. Berlin would repeatedly criticize this hope and dependence on a remote and distant single narrative, finally culminating in his seminal work, *Two Concepts of Liberty*. In this work, he claims that there are two types of liberty: "1) the *'negative' sense*, is involved in the answer to the question 'What is the area within which the subject—a person or group of persons—is or should be left to do or be what he is able to do or be, without interference by other persons?'[50]; and 2) the *positive sense*, is involved in the answer to the question 'What, or who, is the source of control or interference that can determine someone to do, or be, this rather than that?'"[51] As in much of his works, he goes to lengths to call out different varieties of positive liberty for their inevitable tendencies toward being oppressive and self-contradictory. Berlin argues that positive liberty divides the self into two, the real one and false one, the rational and irrational, and that according to these theories, we must strive toward the real one, because for someone who subscribes to positive liberty, one is free only if one's will is what influences one's life and principles, for it is in understanding the necessity of things that one wills things to be so, and so "knowledge liberates not by offering us more open possibilities amongst which we can make our choice, but by preserving us from the frustration of attempting the impossible."[52] For those who subscribe to positive liberty, moreover, free will is only free if it wills what is true, what is rational, and hence correct. Berlin says that this comes from an overarching metaphysical principle: "This is the belief that somewhere, in the past or in the future, in divine revelation or in the mind of an individual thinker, in the pronouncements of history or science, or in the simple heart of an uncorrupted good man, there is a final solution."[53] This theologically charged idea of the freedom of the will consists in aligning our will to that final solution, final truth, which some authority wields. Such is the case, Berlin says, when liberty and authority become mutually interrelated (as in the eighteenth century) despite their supposed incompatibility. Thus, the notion of the "rights of man" and its corresponding outlook on society was thought and spoken of at the time as designed by rational laws brought about by nature, history, or even by the "Supreme Being."[54]

And so, Berlin suggests that against "the absolute values of our primitive past,"[55] we ought to follow a definition of freedom as negative liberty instead, that is, the freedom to choose according to our pluralistic values. However, in order to make this possible, Berlin seems to preserve the notion of a transcendental self that is exempt from causality. Indeed, Aileen Kelly, in the introduction to Berlin's book *Russian Thinkers*, says that the idea that penetrates all of Berlin's works is simply "that men are morally free and are (more often than the determinists who hold the field believe) able to influence events for good or evil through their freely held ideals and convictions."[56] This is a conviction that is central to liberalist conceptions of freedom, but unlike John Locke, from whom we get the now-dominant idea of inalienable rights (including liberty) as given by God, Berlin attempts to get rid of the final signified. Yet he nonetheless preserves the immediate referent: the soul or, as it were, the Self—a floating individual emerged from nowhere, in possession of *freely held* ideals and convictions. He does not, in other words, fully abandon transcendence, nor does he give up faith in the Self as inherently valuable and powerful, able to influence the world around, and external to, it. As Daniel Dennett points out, this Self is leftover from an anthropomorphic god, and that "we can and should replace these sacrosanct but brittle traditions with a more naturalistic foundation. It is scary letting go of such honored precepts as the imagined conflict between determinism and freedom, and the false security of a miracle-working Self or Soul to be the place where the buck stops."[57]

While this account of the origins of the free will problem is far from comprehensive, it is sufficient to show that it has strongly theological origins rooted in Western philosophical and religious thinking. Thus, it forms itself in the shape of a problem that shouldn't be expected to appear in entirely different traditions and societies that do not rely heavily on anthropomorphic gods, such as that of the Chinese. Of course, it would be naïve to say that, in Chinese culture, there did not exist any such notions of anthropomorphic gods, or even that the mandating force of the world, Heaven (天 *Tian*), was not itself anthropomorphized,[58] but it had nowhere near the same sense in which Greek and Abrahamic conceptions of god were seen—as "unmoved mover."[59] In Chinese culture, even naturalistic manifestations of divine unsatisfaction are often considered to be caused by human choices that are considered to be problematic, and not because a god had Divine plans that only he was capable of comprehending. From this cosmological viewpoint of the Chinese, the self is thus far from being a soul or a transcendental being shaped in the image of a wholly transcendent Knower. Rather, it is generally a relational self that is always already within a material and social world, existing in the midst of a complex network of interconnections.

"Freedom" as framed in the free will problem therefore did not exist in classical Chinese philosophical discourse, as some scholars have already noted,[60] and so neither was there a word equivalent to freedom. In an article entitled "Chinese Perspectives on Free Will," Christian Helmut Wenzel and Kai Marchal examine the existence of the notion of free will in Chinese philosophy and suggest that there are discussions of concepts that are related to it, such as "fate, predetermination, agency, moral responsibility, choice, and chance."[61] As such, if we are willing to expand our mode of inquiry to these problems, they might just contribute to contemporary discussions on free will and moral responsibility. Nonetheless, "the [free will] problem seems to be absent in Chinese thought,"[62] so they conclude their exploratory study with the suggestion that

> we cannot exclude the possibility that free will might not be a real problem at all. Then the Daoist or Confucian account might be more appealing. We should also notice that some of

the questions debated by Western philosophers do not appear to be very meaningful to philosophers in East Asia. Broadly speaking, many Chinese and other East Asians do not share the Western belief in free will. But they often still explain, through the language of *xin*, *xing*, and *ming*, and other terms and ideas, why they feel responsible and ascribe responsibility to others.[63]

Indeed, I have also tried to suggest here—following Daniel Dennett's criticism of the "sacrosanct but brittle traditions" surrounding the free will problem—that while there is indeed no discussion of free will in Chinese philosophy, that might not be a bad thing at all, and it certainly does not mean, as some might have us believe, that Chinese philosophers were unconcerned with the problem of human freedom.

Be that as it may, these same concepts that hover around the free will problem may well lend themselves to understanding alternative conceptions of freedom in Chinese philosophical discourse. After all, as Wenzel and Marchal point out, "we should open ourselves to the idea that, in a global world, there are very different styles of reasoning, and human freedom is certainly among the problems which should not be discussed in terms of Western traditions alone."[64] It is thus in this regard that many studies, including this one, tackle the question of freedom in classical Chinese philosophical discourse, which, while taking into account and considering similar problems such as those of Western philosophical discourse, are not limited by their parameters. This is because as I have shown, the roots of the free will problem (which in turn informs conversations on autonomy and political freedom) as we see it in mainstream philosophical discourse are Abrahamic and theological in nature, and so expecting the same distinctions in Chinese philosophical discourse will be futile. After all, as Hegel says, "each individual is a child of his time; thus, philosophy, too, is its own time comprehended in thoughts."[65] A historical grounding therefore enables us to set aside our preexisting epistemic biases about Chinese philosophy and is an invitation for philosophers to be open to the transformative possibility of considering that there are alternatives of conceiving freedom as autonomy. One of these alternatives is Guo Xiang's conception of freedom, understood as autonomy (self-rule), but both as self-determination and self-realization, while not being beholden to the same theological roots.

The Problem of Freedom in
Classical Chinese Philosophy and Guo Xiang's *Zhuangzi*

Contemporary Eurocentric notions of freedom have proven elusive in Chinese philosophical discourse, since freedom in Chinese philosophy cannot be understood in the same terms as the free will problem in Anglo-European philosophy. How then can we frame our contemporary understanding of freedom in the context of Chinese philosophy?

Whenever there is talk of freedom and individuality, one text/philosopher never fails to crop up: Zhuangzi. Among Chinese philosophical texts, the *Zhuangzi* has enjoyed a relatively privileged position in the Anglophone sphere, as it is often seen as an alternative to the (mistakenly) perceived tyranny of Confucian philosophy. Whereas Confucianism is typically seen as rigid, Daoism, and more specifically Zhuangzi, is often seen as more carefree, more "unfettered." Whereas Confucianism fits neatly into "positive liberty" given that there are certain rights and wrongs in this framework, Daoism tends to be a bit more vague. As such, many herald the *Zhuangzi* as a guide for preserving one's individuality and personal liberty from external interference within the canon of Chinese philosophy.

Most of the time, however, this takes on a mystical form. Many scholars, both in Anglophone and Sinophone scholarship, interpret Zhuangzi's notion of freedom as something that is spiritual or transcendent. In turn, some scholars have argued that this type of freedom is not political in nature and therefore has little to no social value. A leading Zhuangzi scholar in particular, Jiang Tao, raises a challenge to scholars of the *Zhuangzi* via Isaiah Berlin, arguing that Zhuangzi scholars need to expand their intellectual horizons and explorations, and take into consideration the influential work of Berlin on freedom, to remain relevant in the contemporary world. He says that Berlin's negative freedom on its own would be self-defeating because it would be substantially empty as there is nothing it could strive toward or realize. Meanwhile, what he calls Zhuangzi's spiritual freedom hinders the larger project of pursuing negative, individual, liberty.

This is a shame, Jiang says, because Berlin and Zhuangzi have much in common "with regard to moral monism, social conformity, and political tyranny and share their advocacy of value pluralism and epistemic humility."[66] The difference, however, is that "for Berlin, the political should be the ultimate arbiter for any spiritual claim whereas for Zhuangzi the spiritual should be vigorously pursued whereas the political is to be put up with."⁶⁷ Jiang uses the story of the fasting of the heart-mind in the *Zhuangzi* and points to the expression "Roaming Free Inside the King's Cage (*You qi fan* 遊其樊)," where Zhuangzi advocates for a more effective way of engaging with a wayward king but ultimately ends up "accepting the king's cage as an unalterable, if hopeless, political reality."⁶⁸ Jiang argues that while Zhuangzi does not actively advocate for a "retreat to the inner citadel" here, it does exhibit some of the aspects of the retreat that Berlin critiques.⁶⁹ This is especially demonstrated in other passages of the text where Zhuangzi outright refuses to engage with politics at all.⁷⁰ As such, Jiang accuses the philosopher of being unquestioning, citing the fasting of the heart passage where Confucius tells Yan Hui to "play within the ruler's cage (*you qi fan* 遊其樊)."

Other sinologists and philosophers have adopted a similar stance. Renowned scholar of Chinese philosophy Bryan Van Norden finds in Zhuangzi the advocacy for a pluralistic acceptance of others that encompasses lifestyle, social class, gender, and physical deformity. However, he also concludes that Zhuangzi's metaphysical stance is "the night in which all cows are black," meaning that it eventually undermines all ethical and political values. Van Norden claims that this undermining contradicts Zhuangzi's supposed pluralism, noting: "Zhuangzi's advice seems to be to avoid political engagement if possible, and to avoid confrontation with authorities and the status quo when political engagement is unavoidable."⁷¹

This "night in which all cows are black," that is, the kind of spiritual or even psychological freedom that can fall into what Berlin critiques as a "retreat to the inner citadel," is not an uncommon interpretation. For many, there is merit to this kind of freedom. For instance, in his book *Liberation as Affirmation*, Ge Ling Shang compares Zhuangzi with Nietzsche, and says that both of them are neither nihilistic nor antireligion. On the contrary, the affirmation of life is central to Zhuangzi's philosophy, that this affirmation of secular life as religiously sacred is the ultimate liberation. This, according to Shang, is because "spiritual transcendence is possible by affirming life 'religiously' as sacred and divine."⁷² He claims that Zhuangzi is "a free dancer who was beyond ordinary language, rational knowledge, social norms, and political parties. Without this transcending spirit of liberation, according to Zhuangzi, a complete life of *xiaoyao* would be impossible."⁷³ What is there to transcend, though? According to Shang, Zhuangzi's view was that "society is a form of mass manipulation in which morality attempts to fix human life into prescribed social roles and thereby suppresses human freedom, which flows from the spontaneity of all things."[74] Thus, we need to transcend from, and rise above, these norms—abandon societal obligations, even—to be able to wander far-reaching and unfettered (*xiaoyaoyou* 逍遙遊), here considered as a state of personal liberty.

Zhao Guoping, incidentally comparing Zhuangzi to Nietzsche's antipode Levinas, nevertheless takes on a similar interpretation, saying that "Lévinas' subjectivity and Zhuangzi's non-being self have shown a radically different notion of freedom, as breaking away from our own confines and going beyond—a freedom located in spirituality, rather than in domination."[75] Eske Møllgaard argues that it is the "transcendental life" that is behind Zhuangzi's conception of *you* (wandering), and that this transcendence is Heaven's "act of pure grace. To be released into transcendental life is a second birth. As the *Zhuangzi* says, once we have left human life behind and are no longer entangled in its misery."[76] Similarly, Alan Fox argues that Zhuangzi advocates for *wuwei* (nondoing), which ultimately "takes the path of least resistance and does not rush or confront."[77] Fox claims that Zhuangzi shows us the image of a sage as "someone who is perfectly at *ease* in all situations."[78] Franklin Perkins argues that the goal of the *Zhuangzi* is to teach us to be "*beyond the human*," that is, to instruct us on "how we can alter our desires in order to enjoy the world as it is. In place of a prudential concern for following nature, we have free and easy wandering, *xiaoyaoyou* 逍遙遊 (carefree wandering, wandering far and unfettered, going rambling without a destination)."[79] Like many others, Perkins says that "Zhuangzi points toward a radical transcendence of being human and a total alignment with heaven and the myriad things."[80] This radical transcendence, Perkins then ultimately points out, "presents human beings as distinctive in having something like freedom in our ability to change perspectives and alter our reactions and emotions, this freedom is just what makes it possible to overcome tragedy, allowing us to accept the world as it is."[81]

This is not to say that the aforementioned interpretations of the *Zhuangzi* are all the same. Simply, they are all versions of interpreting Zhuangzi's notion of freedom as a kind of spiritual, albeit sometimes immanent, transcendence. This is to say that these interpretations are none other than what Jiang refers to as "spiritual freedom," or Berlin's "retreat to the inner citadel." Recognizing this, Liu Xiaogan yields and argues for the validity of the "retreat to the inner citadel" as a type of freedom that should be valued like any other. He says that according to Zhuangzi, "detaching from common society and going to a realm beyond it is a radical and ultimate way to deal with unavoidable troubles of the lived world."[82] He refers to this view as "Zhuangzian transcendent freedom."[83] More specifically, in an article describing the notions of freedom in Zhuangzi and Guo Xiang, Liu Xiaogan tells us that their notions of becoming far-reaching and unfettered (*xiaoyao*) share the same form as what Isaiah Berlin criticizes as the "retreat to the inner citadel." Although Liu says there are key differences between Zhuangzi's and Guo Xiang's notions of becoming far-reaching and unfettered (*xiaoyao*), he nonetheless admits that they are both "only an adaptation, acceptance or escape from reality."[84] In other words it does not have the power for social change and transformation. Nonetheless, he argues that "this is in fact a question of choice and preference in values, not a question of whether spiritual and mental freedom is [philosophically] sensible."[85] Liu thus points to the possibility that if an agent is consciously and fully aware of her motivations and actions, with values freely internalized, would it really be unfree to retreat into an inner citadel when social resistance proves to be futile? After all, the reality is that "if modern people cannot completely avoid fixed circumstances that cannot be changed, then they must reflect on how to live better, with more ease, and nobler, in this unpleasant but fixed circumstance." As such, he makes a plea toward the philosophers of freedom of our time, saying that "the pursuit of pure personal spiritual satisfaction should gain understanding or sympathy, or at the least, should not receive condemnation."[86] This is an affirmation of the kind of pluralism that Isaiah Berlin ultimately advocates for.

Like many of Zhuangzi's leading scholars, Liu seems to believe that this retreat does not harm society and so its adherents should be left alone to pursue their own happiness. For Berlin, however, the "retreat to the inner citadel" is narcissistic at best, because it deprives freedom of its political subversiveness, preventing it from manifesting its powerful ability for social transformation, and hence, ultimately harms everyone. Indeed, turning inward to escape from one's horrible external state not only distracts from social and political action, but it also splits one's inner world from that of the external political reality—similar to that of positive liberty as self-realization, which Berlin provides a powerful critique against. However, does the *Zhuangzi* really advocate such self-abnegation? Not according to its leading commentator, Guo Xiang (252–312).[87] In this work, thus, we will explore how Guo Xiang transforms some of the ideas originally found in the *Zhuangzi*, so as to give rise to a systematized framework for a philosophy of freedom, making the text a political treatise of his own.

There are two related reasons for this choice: 1) the first one is because Guo Xiang provides Zhuangzi a systematic framework for exploring a comprehensive account for both ontological and concretely political freedom, understood and interchangeable here as autonomy; and 2) the second is because of the historical context that has allowed for this to happen—an age of heightened individualism that emerged from the amalgamation of Confucianism and Daoism, a political age.

What this means for us is that Guo Xiang's philosophical enterprise contains a notion of freedom more robust than the simple dichotomy of negative and positive freedom, or *freedom from* and *freedom to*, respectively. Whereas classical Confucian notions of freedom resort to defending certain notions of positive liberty as self-realization,[88] Daoist notions of freedom are often construed to be positive liberty as self-abnegation, including the aforementioned dominant interpretations of the *Zhuangzi*. Guo Xiang, however, presents us with a third alternative that is not beholden to Berlin's dichotomy of liberties, which are both nonetheless beholden to the pseudo-problem of free will.

That is to say that in Guo Xiang's philosophy of causality, which I call a *logic of convergence*, there is the potential of a philosophy of freedom that has an alternatively more cohesive notion of the self (as opposed to being an atomistic individual or simply being a member of a higher whole), as well as the operations of the world around it, which we shall refer to as a *dependence-based autonomy*—a notion of freedom that is largely ontological and epistemological in nature, while also having the potential to be understood in social and political contexts. Unpacking this promising theory of freedom, therefore, is the task of this work.

The task, however, starts with a radical premise: there is no reading Zhuangzi's notion of freedom without Guo Xiang's commentaries. It just wasn't the core text's main concern. Moreover, given that it was Guo Xiang who edited and compiled the extant text, we may never really know what it was originally. I therefore maintain that the best way to read it systematically is with Guo Xiang's commentaries, and that if we are to expect the text to yield fruitful political and social ideas, we must treat it as mainly Guo Xiang's work, rather than the other way around. Just as we may never know whether Plato tweaked Socrates for his own agenda, the case is hermeneutically the same with Guo Xiang and Zhuangzi. I shall, therefore, treat the *Zhuangzizhu*, which is the *Zhuangzi* with Guo Xiang's comments, as a single whole, and as that of Guo Xiang's.

Although there are questions as to what else in the text Guo Xiang has tweaked, however, we do know that that he did politicize the *Zhuangzi* through his comments. This makes sense, considering the time in which he lived. Guo Xiang is often referred to as a "Neo-Daoist," and this movement is comprised of scholars from the Wei-Jin 魏晉 period whose study is often referred to as *Xuanxue* 玄學, meaning the study of something that is far and dark, in the sense of being fuzzy, or perhaps more aptly, the profound.[89] This time is often associated with the height of individuality[90] and the discussion of abstract concepts, which is perhaps most evident in the practice called *Qingtan* 清談 or "Pure Conversation." Pure Conversation is a practice of philosophical, often abstract,[91] discussion that was performed in public, making a display of aesthetic and argumentation skills, which brought about a type of "celebrity scholar" culture. Among these scholars was Wang Bi, a prodigy in his early twenties, founder of the *Xuanxue* movement, and responsible for coining the term for what is now understood as "ontology," *benti* 本體. He was not alone, however. After Wang Bi came many other brilliant scholars who partook in this cultural performance. Among them were He Yan, Wang Bi's close friend and stepson of the famous general Cao Cao, Ji Kang, Ruan Ji, Pei Wei, among others, most of whom were from noble families.

Guo Xiang, however, was historically described as only "second to Wang Bi"[92] in his debate or oratory skill. As Richard Mather points out, his work is "probably the most consistent effort to reconcile the opposing claims of activism and quietism,"[93] referring to the tension between social order (*mingjiao* 名教) and natural spontaneity (*ziran* 自然), commonly associated with Confucianism and Daoism, respectively, which was a defining feature of the period. The success of his amalgamation[94] lies at the very heart of his philosophy of freedom, which, if we dare delve further into, shows us a profound image of the individual self who is, at the same time and *on equal levels*, both self-sufficiently independent but also has a unified sense of oneness with the universe through a materially grounded dependence. Guo Xiang thus shows us a logical connection that challenges our preconceived notions of, as William James put it, "whether a man is a decided monist or a decided pluralist,"[95] or as Berlin put it, whether he is a hedgehog or a fox.[96]

Nonetheless, it is important to stress that it was not only Guo Xiang who had revolutionary ideas. As mentioned earlier, Wang Bi effectively invented metaphysics. Some scholars, such as Jana Rošker, even go as far as claiming that Wang Bi made the first step in the formation of what later became known as *mingli* (the study of names and structure).[97] This move is significant because it allowed for the systematic discussion of philosophical concepts and their relation to each other, making a systematic study of metaphysical concepts using symbols (whether through language or images) possible. Rošker thus says that, thanks to Wang Bi, "words and symbols were seen as codes that could gradually, level by level, decipher the particular meanings from this structural network."[98] It is a bold claim, but one that she supports by demonstrating how such a systematicity made a more effective discussion for concepts such as nonbeing (*wu*), structural coherence (*li*), and oneness (*yi*).[99] It is thus in this same vein that I make the radical claim that Zhuangzi's notion of freedom can only be systematically read through Guo's comments, especially if we were to have any attempt at conceiving of a coherently metaphysical and political notion of freedom. After all, *Xuanxue* thought lies mostly in the attempt to show that metaphysics cannot be divorced from political and even ethical concerns lest we stumble into the pitfalls of their time when, as Xinzhong Yao would note, "hypocritical politicians and warlords made an immoral use of Confucian virtues, particularly *Zhong* and *xiao*, to strengthen their own positions"[100]—precisely because they had little ground and ontological basis to fully comprehend the philosophical magnitude of such concepts.[101] Moreover, the Wei-Jin period saw the height of conversations that centered on human nature, feelings,[102] individualism,[103] the downright rejection of traditionally Confucian doctrines such as filial piety and social rituals,[104] revolt against despotic regimes in favor of the underdogs,[105] and even escapism or nihilism.[106] All these are important markers that this movement, and era, was one that was concerned with freedom.

As such, my aim in this work is to thus show that not only is there a plethora of diverse notions of freedom in Chinese philosophy, but there is also a unique and sophisticated one that can be found in Guo Xiang's *Zhuangzi*, which we can only glean if we look at it systematically. Indeed, as I have demonstrated earlier, we would be bound to fail in finding this out if we insist on looking for what is within the ballpark of a type of freedom that is rooted in metaphysical free will and its theological foundations. However, if we are willing to set that aside and look at this Neo-Daoist philosopher's work on its own terms, then deriving a new and innovative perception on the notion of freedom might be possible. Moreover, this study aims to build on such nonbinary logic that has allowed for Guo Xiang's notion of absolute causality and the logic of convergence. It brings forward a notion of freedom that is neither absolute nor deterministic yet is also both absolute and deterministic; neither pluralistic nor monistic but also both pluralistic and monistic. The possibility of this, as I would argue, can only be arrived at from Guo Xiang's ontological and epistemological import, which brings forth a self-organizing, self-transforming, image of the cosmos. This, in turn, not only allows but necessitates an account of a more inclusive, holistic, and irreducible account of ethics and politics. This, moreover, is significant to our modern sensibilities, because philosophy, if it endeavors to have significance in the contemporary intellectual arena at all, should confront the nagging issues of society, such as the pitting of one faction against all others—as a consequence of the reductionism of our time,[107] while drawing from ontological and epistemological foundations. This study thus aims to confront the issue of the fragmentation of consciousness rampant in our time, which leads to considerable conflicts both political and ethical.

More specifically, this book aims to break down the dichotomous divides between one and many, particular and universal, necessity and contingency, and by extension, the self and other. This will show, in Guo Xiang's philosophical enterprise, a comprehensive and holistic notion of freedom that can finally escape the trap of a split self as found in both positive and negative notions of freedom. Thus, it will not have their idealistic tendencies of conceiving identities that are removed from others around it and their causes, whether it be negative freedom's radically independent subject[108] or positive freedom's tug of war between the real self and false self.

2

A Flattened Ontology and the Logic of Convergence

One of the most important moves in Guo Xiang's rendering of the *Zhuangzi* is the systematization of causality. At the heart of this philosophical system is an underlying convergence of opposites, similar to the unity of *mingjiao* and *ziran* that Guo Xiang, as Neo-Daoist, had successfully amalgamated. I call this the *logic of convergence*.[1] One of the most important manifestations of this logic can be seen in Guo Xiang's comment when, in the *Zhuangzi* text, Confucius tells Zigong that he does his "roaming in the internal realms." Guo then describes how the external and internal realms eventually become one anyhow. It is in this passage that the unity between *mingjiao* and *ziran* becomes most apparent, while simultaneously demonstrating how such an amalgamation can achieve a consistent and coherent ontological ground:

> When the coherence of things reaches its full extent, the external and the internal merge into one. It can never be the case that someone ventures into the furthest of the external realm, but not [at the same time] also be fully immersed within the [affairs of the] internal realm. [Conversely,] it can never be the case that someone is able to be fully immersed within the [affairs of the] internal realm, and yet not [at the same time] voyage outside it.
>
> Thus, the sage constantly ventures outside the [internal world of] mundane affairs to merge fully with it. He empties his heart-mind to be in accord with the world of myriad beings

and affairs. Therefore, although the sage assumes different roles [and engages in different tasks, depending on circumstances] all the time, his spirit or *qi* essence [i.e., inner self] does not change. He watches over the myriad transformations of the world and responds to its affairs, but he is always calm and remains unaffected.

Now, the problem that persistently encumbers the world is precisely that people see mundane affairs but fail to reach [the point where they can see] the sage's [numinous] spirit. As such, when we see the sage mingling and engaging with the things and affairs of the world, it cannot be said that he has abandoned the world and parted from the society of men. When we see him embodying [the world's] transformations and responding to its affairs, we then cannot say that he has sat in forgetfulness and achieved self-realization [in isolation].

How could it be said that Confucius was not so? Rather it must be said that the ultimate principle is not such [that Confucius was only concerned with mundane affairs without spiritual accomplishment].

Therefore, Zhuangzi sought to illuminate the basis of the unity [of the external and the internal], in order to enable an understanding of the world. If he had just depicted Confucius to be thus, [with full convergence of both the internal and the external,] some might reject it on the basis of what they observed [of Confucius's appearance]. Thus, Zhuangzi went beyond the internal traces of Confucius, and transmitted [knowledge] through [transcendent] external occupations represented by these masters. It is better to forget Zhuangzi's metaphors to seek the general meaning of [what] the written work [tries to convey]. Then, the way of roaming beyond the [internal] mundane world and yet [being] fully immersed in it would become abundantly clear. [Therefore,] the incomparable discourse in the book of Zhuangzi is after all still a perusal of [the issues within] the mundane world.

夫理有至極，外內相冥，未有極遊外之致而不冥於內者也，未有能冥於內而不遊於外者也。故聖人常遊外以冥內，無心以順有，故雖終日見形而神氣無變，俯仰萬機而淡然自若。夫見形而不及神者，天下之常累也。是故睹其與群物並行，則莫能謂之遺物而離人矣；睹其體化而應務，則莫能謂之坐忘而自得矣。豈直謂聖人不然哉？乃必謂至理之無此。是故莊子將明流統之所宗以釋天下之可悟，若直就稱仲尼之如此，或者將據所見以排之，故超聖人之內跡，而寄方外於數子。宜忘其所寄以尋作之大意，則夫遊外冥內之道坦然自明，而莊子之書，故是涉俗蓋世之談矣。[2]

This passage lays down quite clearly that Guo Xiang intended to read the *Zhuangzi* as an ultimately social and political text. However, in order to do that, he must also clarify the ontological aspects of the philosophical system. This is exactly what he does here, primarily through utilizing the concept *li* as a member or several interrelated core concepts in his rendition. So, what he tells us here is that *li*, the coherence of things, is such that it is not simply found within the concept of nature itself, as though there was somehow some world external to ours, but also within social engagement. Guo Xiang thus builds his argument with the premise that the internal and external, the mundane and the transcendent, are one and the same when *li* reaches the extreme. Philosophically, one might think that social affairs can purely be so, or that ontological statements can be taken out and treated as separate from our social reality, but this is not so, and one who can truly understand one realm and/or the other knows this. In the rest of the text, Guo Xiang expands on Zhuangzi's famous line, that "outside the limits of the human world, the sage exists but does not theorize, inside the limits of the human world, the sage theorizes but does not debate" (六合之外，聖人存而不論；六合之內，聖人論而不議).[3] Guo Xiang tells us that Confucius is such a true sage who truly embodied sagacity, and that it was in him that the internal and external realms were truly united. The point that Guo Xiang is making here is thus to say that when one is truly transcendent or one with the nature of the cosmos, having an empty heart-mind and a full *qi*, then he will be in accord with the society of men and its transformations, because ultimately, they are one and the same. To emphasize, Guo Xiang's argument here is not simply that internal and external are complementary, but that the fulfillment of one depends on (and results in) the fulfillment of the other. Confucius, whom Guo Xiang and other Wei-Jin philosophers considered to be the ultimate sage, was a man who had achieved self-realization, as though sitting in forgetfulness (of the mundane world), but achieved through fully immersing within the mundane affairs of the world, as well as mastering it by becoming one with it. This absolute convergence of the external and internal can indeed be said to be the overarching theme of Guo Xiang's philosophical enterprise, albeit hidden beneath the *Zhuangzi*.

Guo Xiang is likely the first Chinese philosopher who introduced this concept of the ontology of complete convergence, and it is this logic of convergence that allows Guo Xiang to posit the argument that the height of the (internal) mundane is, at its core, (external) transcendence, and vice versa. Because one realm enables the other, the true sage and the emptiness of his heart-mind is what allows him to simply be in accord with the thousand changes and transformations of the world within his grasp, that is, to laugh as ordinary people laugh, and to mourn as ordinary people mourn, for in those fleeting moments he holds on to nothing and that is ultimately what allows him to be fully present within each moment, feeling, change, and the entirety of the world. This, according to Guo Xiang, is what it truly means to let go and no longer hold on to anything, not even one's own solitude or self.

To elucidate this even further, the following passage is from an earlier commentary that Guo Xiang made when he described the sage's role in the larger picture:

> All this is simply metaphorical language. The "divine man" is what we now call a sage. Though the sage is in the imperial hall, yet his heart differs not from when he is in the mountain forests. How would the world know this! They merely see his dwelling within a yellow canopy and wearing the seal of jade at his girdle, so they speak of it as sufficing to bind his heart; when they see him walking beside mountain streams and taking part in the life of ordinary people, then they speak of it as sufficing to sadden his spirit. How would they understand that those who have attained the ultimate is unwaning![4]

> 此皆寄言耳。夫神人即今所謂聖人也。夫聖人雖在廟堂之上，然其心無異於山林之中，世豈識之哉！徒見其戴黃屋，佩玉璽，便謂足以纓紱其心矣；見其歷山川，同民事，便謂足以憔悴其神矣。豈知至至者之不虧哉！

The sage's perfect unity and embodied harmony demonstrate the unity of the mundane and transcendent. This is why in the previous passage, Guo Xiang says that the ultimate principle (*li*) is no different and operates in the same way of convergence. While the burden of the common people is that they are stuck in the mundane, Guo Xiang's sages can operate fully and devotedly within the mundane precisely because they are profoundly in touch with transcendence; simultaneously though, they are able to go beyond the mundane and into the transcendent precisely because they are masters of the mundane. Furthermore, Guo Xiang says, "all this metaphorical language," and repeatedly insinuates as much in other passages as well, because more than the specific details of the passages in the text, he is concerned about the motivation behind them, which is "to illuminate the basis of the unity [of the external and the internal], in order to enable an understanding of the world." In other words, Guo Xiang wishes to clarify that while the Zhuangzi may seem like a text about transcendence, it is as much talking about the mundane world as it is about the world beyond.

It is in this vein that wu 無 and you 有 are treated by Guo Xiang, that is, as not simply complementary to each other, but necessary. In this sense, they are necessary to the constitution of each other. We must note, however, that Guo Xiang provides a new understanding of wu or "nonbeing" here in order to make nonbeing here take up its literal sense—nothing, pure lack, emptiness. Here, we see that the definition of nonbeing as purely nothing is made possible by the definition of pure being as pure manyness. This logically amounts to nothingness while, in turn, such pure nothingness is the very possibility of being as being.

Nothingness and Being

Not surprisingly, the issues that Guo Xiang tried to grapple with, such as the role of nothingness in social and political reality, emerged from a social context, just as most ideas do. Apart from the rediscovery of Daoist texts such as the Zhuangzi and Laozi during the Wei-Jin period, the era was also marked by Wang Bi's metaphysical shift from Han cosmology into what is possibly the first systematic metaphysics in Chinese intellectual history. In Wang Bi's philosophical comments and essays, the concept of wu 無 or nothingness and its relation to being (you 有) features as his central concern. This topic thus became one of the main points for contention among Neo-Daoist philosophers of the following generations. They were, after all, concerned with the metaphysical and ontological aspects of their social and political lifeworld.

During the beginning of the Wei-Jin era, Wang Bi and his friend He Yan were proponents of what became known as 以無為本 (taking nonbeing as the root). In his *Discourse on Dao* (*Dao lun* 道論), He Yan claims that "beings depend on *wu* in coming into existence, in becoming what they are. Affairs on account of *wu* come to fruition and become what they are."[5] Wang Bi takes on a very similar position, which is to integrate the concept of nothingness in the *Laozi* as the core of all things, into the social and political world. In his comment on the first verse of the *Daodejing*, Wang Bi plainly says that "anything that exists originates in nothingness [*wu*]."[6] In his preface to the *Daodejing*, moreover, he claims that "the original substance of Heaven and Earth consists of perfectly quiescent nonbeing [*wu*, nothingness]."[7] By taking nothingness as the root, and calling it the original substance (*benti* 本體), he invents what we now refer to as *benti lun* 本體論 (ontology). He Yan and Wang Bi thus formed an intellectual camp with the position that nothingness, or rather the featurelessness and emptiness, in all things is the means by which each and every thing exists. Wang Bi's work on the *Yijing* makes this even more evident, where he points out that each hexagram has its own master (*zong* 宗).

Later in the Wei-Jin period, however, this nothingness came to be interpreted as the lack of restraint, or at least the Confucian philosopher Pei Wei thought so. Pei Wei, a contemporary of Guo Xiang, thus sought to address the moral vacuity and pessimistic nihilism of the time by denouncing the idea of absolute nonbeing as a type of root or source to anything. This was the political motivation for his claim in "Chong you lun" 崇有論 (Discourse on Esteeming Being) that being (*you*) must be esteemed above nothingness (*wu*). Pei says that "that which is the substance of coherence [in the world], it is called being" (理之所體, 所謂有也),[8] meaning that it is in Being that the world finds order. Privileging nonbeing over being has dangerous implications because, Alan Chan notes, "once we embark on an intellectual path that devalues the actual, existent realm of beings, we would also be undermining the complex workings that bind society and the environment together."[9] Guo Xiang does share this concern, but he does not go as far as the absolute monism of Pei Wei, who believed that what made being transform are natural laws and principles that are universal. Rather than emphasizing wholeness and order, Guo emphasizes the singularity of beings, with nothing that makes them one stable and unitary whole. For this, Guo found the perfect weapon in Zhuangzi, who shared the view that the "piping of heaven" is nothing but "the gusting through all the ten thousand differences that yet causes all of them to come only from themselves,"[10] leaving no room for any single rouser nor set of laws and principles. Commenting on this passage, Guo says:

> *The music of heaven is not an entity existing outside of things.* The different apertures, the pipes and flutes and the like, in combination with all living beings, together constitute heaven. *Since non-being is non-being, it cannot generate being.* Before being itself is generated, it cannot produce other beings. *Then by whom are things generated? They simply spontaneously self-generate.* By "self-generation," it is not meant that there is an "I" to generate. The "I" cannot generate things and things cannot generate the "I." So "I" is self-so. Because it is so by itself, we call it natural (lit., heaven-so). Everything is what it is by nature (lit., heaven), not through taking any action. Therefore [Chuang Tzu] speaks in terms of heaven. The term "heaven" is used to explain that things are what they are spontaneously, and not to mean the blue sky. But someone says that the music of heaven makes all things serve or obey it. Now, heaven cannot even possess itself. How can it possess things? Heaven is the general name for all things. Heaven does not set its mind for or against anything. Who is the master to make things obey? Therefore each thing self-generates and thus has nothing that makes it emerge. This is the Way of Heaven.[11]

> 夫天籟者，豈復別有一物哉？即眾竅比竹之屬，接乎有生之類，會而共成一天耳。無既無矣，則不能生有；有之未生，又不能為生。然則生生者誰哉 塊然而自生耳。自生耳，非我生也。我既不能生物，物亦不能生我，則我自然矣。自己而然，則謂之天然。天然耳，非為也，故以天言之。〔以天言之〕所以明其自然也，豈蒼蒼之謂哉！而或者謂天籟役物使從己也。夫天且不能自有，況能有物哉！故天者，萬物之總名也，莫適為天，誰主役物乎？故物各自生而無所出焉，此天道也。

So, Guo Xiang tells us that all things, being what they are, are spontaneously so—they are naturally so. Nothing exists outside of them, and they mutually coexist to make each other exist. This is what is meant by the term Nature (*Tian* 天). In other words, because things mutually produce each other, they are simply self-so (*ziran*). This means two things: first, that no one thing causes another thing; and, secondly, that nothing governs any or all of them. Causality as well as creativity are both, as it were, flattened. In this scenario thus, nothingness, or the lack of a single governing principle, and being mutually coexist and become necessary to the existence of each other. Furthermore, this leads to the logical consequence that things are also absolute in themselves—everything exists, so therefore there is no One existence. That is to say, if things then produce themselves spontaneously, there is no principle that governs everything but their own principles of self-generation. This ontological oblivion[12] is the absolute lack of any primary being whatsoever. There are countless passages where Guo Xiang reiterates this, but in an earlier passage, Guo Xiang also says that everything is so by itself and is self-generating (塊然而自生). Commenting on the following portion of the "great clod" passage of the *Zhuangzi*,[13] Guo Xiang says:

> The Great Clod is not anything. So, how can that which belches out breath be anything? The breath is simply being belched out spontaneously. As for the production of things, there is nothing that is not so by itself and self-generating. Since the substance of that which is naturally so is [so vast and] great, it is therefore given the name Great Clod.[14]
>
> 大塊者，無物也。夫噫氣者，豈有物哉？氣塊然而自噫耳。物之生也，莫不塊然而自生，則塊然之體大矣，故遂以大塊為名。

This is perhaps one of the blatantly materialist passages in Guo Xiang's commentary of the *Zhuangzi*, highlighting that things are simply so. The metaphor for the great clod here shows us one cannot personify or esteem a mere lump of earth, because the great clod is simply that: a lump of earth. This lump of earth simply moves, belches, and things become what they are. The only thing "great" about this clod is the breadth with which it connects to everything else.

This flattening of a seemingly esteemed concept or figure is a recurring theme in Guo Xiang's *Zhuangzi*, but here it is emphasized how the generativity of all things is not a grand process by which things have fixed purpose: they simply are. They are self-generating and spontaneous: not anything else, nothing. Yang Lihua notes that this nothingness (*wu* 無) is what makes two other important concepts in Guo Xiang's philosophy, lone-transformation (*duhua* 獨化) and self-generativity (*zisheng* 自生), consistent with the rest of his ontological system. I would say that it is even simpler than that, boiling down to what I have called the logic of convergence. Either way, however, Yang does hint at this convergence, specifically nothingness and being here, and says: "Guo Xiang thinks that not only is 'nothingness' unable to produce 'being,' 'being' also cannot be completely dispelled as 'nonbeing.' Whatsoever exists, regardless of whether they undergo any sort of transformation, still cannot become 'nonbeing.'"[15] He continues: "Since 'nonbeing' cannot produce 'being,' it also cannot govern or control the myriad things."[16]

Yang Lihua points to a specific commentary of Guo Xiang, where the *Zhuangzi* text says:

> Who, resting inactive himself, gives the cause that makes it go this way?[17]

> 孰居無事推而行是？

Guo Xiang then comments:

> As nonbeing, it therefore does not have any capacity to cause [things to become what they are]; as being, then each has its own [sphere of] activity. In that case, who [or what] could it be that is without activity and yet causes and activates [other beings]? Each self-activates on its own, that is all.[18]

> 無則無所能推，有則各自有事。然則無事而推行是者誰乎哉？各自行耳。

According to Yang, since "nonbeing" is being simply such, it also cannot have any effect or influence that can occur toward things. There is no unified master and ruler behind the myriad things. Therefore, the cause and maintenance of things is but the result of "all things simply maintaining themselves" (各自行).[19] Nonbeing for Guo Xiang thus is simply the breakdown of linear causality through intercausality, resulting in necessity; it is the breakdown of linear dependence through the interdependence of all, resulting in independence. Further, it is important to reemphasize how Guo Xiang strips nonbeing of any transcendent role as first cause. In the following passage, Guo Xiang directly explains:

> Not only is it impossible for non-being to be changed into being. It is also impossible for being to become non-being. Therefore, although being as a thing undergoes infinite changes and transformations, it cannot itself become non-being. It cannot become non-being, thus even from old, there was never a time when being did not yet exist, as being is eternally existent.[20]
>
> 非唯無不得化而為有也，有亦不得化而為無矣。是以有之為物，雖千變萬化，而不得一為無也。不得一為無，故自古無未有之時而常存也。

The reason why being can undergo infinite changes and transformations is because being is infinitely diverse, not because of a nothingness as root as Wang Bi and He Yan claim, nor is it because of a set of universal principles as Pei Wei claimed. The myriad things are always transforming and changing, but never *become* a pure void. This is a scenario where interlinkages between different nodes are infinite because those nodes themselves are constantly being transformed by the interlinkages themselves. Thus, pure nothingness—nonbeing as the opposite of being—doesn't really exist as something primordial, it just is that: nothing. It cannot exist because at no point in time does being cease to exist; it simply transforms itself through intercausation. Isabelle Robinet draws a helpful insight from this concept of nothingness:

> At the origin of beings, there is nothing external to them that gives birth to them; beyond them, there is nothing either: "At the limit of beings, there is nothing, that is why words and knowledge cannot exceed beings; disappearance and emergence are spontaneous, there is no origin nor that which comes after"(27.43b): *wu* is not an entity which causes or surpasses the beings, it is not an external and transcendent origin to beings; the term *wu* is the negation of all this; "There is nothing that makes them" 未有為之者 (25.31b); the "creator" is "beings by themselves" ("each being is self-created") (3.47a).[21]

Because *wu* simply means nothing, being is absolute, hence her fittingly titled work "Kouo Siang ou le monde comme absolu." There is nothing external to the world that causes it to be so, meaning it is absolute and so in itself, which makes the term *wu* or nonbeing simply a reference to pure lack of a first cause or creator. There is no master, no grand narrative, for everything is simply so in and of itself. This is an apt articulation of Guo Xiang's conception of existence and the world as absolute. However, we must be careful not to tip the delicate balance between necessity and contingency here, as Robinet seems to have done due to going one slight step toward necessity. She says: "This noncontingent world 無分待 (3.47b), without master 無主 (3.47a), possesses all the fundamental attributes of the absolute: the eternal and necessary existence of itself. There is nothing outside of it, no creator, no reality. It is the supreme reality. It is one and all beings are consubstantial to it."[22]

While everything else in this passage is consistent with Guo Xiang's philosophy, it would nevertheless be misleading to highlight the noncontingency of the world as opposed to its contingency. This is because *ziran* 自然, the very spontaneity and being so in itself of the world, is pure contingency and such pure contingency is what is necessary to a world that is absolute. For Guo Xiang, spontaneity is itself necessity, making contingency a necessity, and necessity a contingency at once, as we shall see later. Indeed, this issue is further highlighted when Robinet continues:

> In this language, *wu* plays the simple role of negation and means "to have nothing"; the function of the word *wu*, for Guo Xiang, is to deny that there is an origin. Guo Xiang is probably the only Chinese thinker to use this term in this fashion, at least categorically so. "The *wu* is simply the *wu*, it cannot generate the *you*" (2.7a, 25.48a . . .). This obviously evokes Parmenides's "being is and nonbeing is not." For Kouo Siang, there is an impassable abyss between *wu* and *you*; "*wu* cannot change into *you*, *you* cannot be changed into *wu*" (24.38a).[23]

Here it becomes clear that Robinet views nonbeing and being as two opposite entities that are contradictory instead of necessary to each other. She continues in a later discussion: "This self-creation is self-identity, which is uniform in all; it is Guo Xiang's way of understanding 'the oneness of beings' 齊物 of Zhuangzi. This leads, of course, to monism, as in Parmenides, the premises being the same."[24]

While we can easily surmise the self-creative property of Zhuangzi's cosmos as rendered by Guo Xiang, the same cannot be said about the uniformity of all beings in the second inner chapter (*Qiwulun* 齊物論). It can only be so in a carefully qualified manner, such that self-identification won't necessarily mean uniformity of all the diverseness of being, but rather that things are all identical in being different or diverse. This is why, as previously mentioned, Yang Lihua points out that nothingness (*wu wu* 無物) is what makes lone-transformation (*duhua* 獨化) and self-generativity (*zisheng* 自生) consistent. It is precisely because there is no cause at all that they cause themselves to be so. Although Robinet compares Guo Xiang's ontological import to that of Parmenides's monism here, we have already pointed out that this is not the case as Parmenides's monism is more comparable to Pei Wei's.[25] In fact, Guo Xiang also makes several remarks that are contrary to arguing that there is only being and nothing else, as he acknowledges that both Laozi and Zhuangzi often talk about nonbeing, and indeed even makes arguments for the modification of action into stillness *via negativa* in several passages. Guo Xiang also says that "obscure, deep, dark, and silent, all of these are [means of conveying] total nonbeing"[26] (窈冥昏默，皆了無也).

Note here that, as this characterization shows, nothingness or nonbeing almost always has a positive meaning in Guo Xiang except when he is reacting to an interpretation of it as a kind of Ultimate. He repeatedly uses such imagery to describe how the self-generativity and self-activity of all things are possible through nothingness, as well as their mutual enabling. For instance, Guo Xiang says that "one who has an empty heart-mind, and abides by the self-generativity [of things], is worthy of becoming an emperor or king"[27] (夫無心而任乎自化者，應為帝王也).

And again, in a later passage, he says that "to gaze into nothingness, is to then bear one's lone-genesis"[28] (睹無則任其獨生也). Nonetheless, although Guo Xiang applies the notion of nothingness to the cognitive level here, the relation between nothingness or absolute lack and self-transformation as well as lone-genesis is clear: absolute nothingness is not simply what allows self-transformation and lone-genesis, but it also inevitably demonstrates self-transformation and lone-genesis. Guo Xiang does this in such a way that since there is nothing that governs anything, then everything depends on everything else. This ultimately leads to the conclusion that each and every particular thing is absolutely and irreducibly singular. Even when he talks about being able to rule things, as in the preceding passage about becoming an emperor or king, he notes that this is simply possible by being *wuxin* 無心 or having an empty heart-mind. As such, such singular beings are not caused and are therefore simply spontaneously so, and will transform spontaneously so. They can do so because nonbeing as nothingness—meaning the complete lack of any being—is the only thing that governs everything, so really nothing governs anything. All of this said, Guo Xiang does realize that he needs to account for when Laozi and Zhuangzi talk at length about nonbeing. So he tells us:

> Why is it that Zhuangzi and Laozi often call it nonbeing? To make it clear that that which generates things is no thing and that things simply generate themselves. Self-generation, simply, is not generated by action, so what act can be applied to what is already generated?[29]
>
> 夫莊老之所以屢稱無者，何哉？明生物者無物而物自生耳。自生耳，非為生也，又何有為於已生乎！

For Guo, nonbeing is simply a reference to the *zisheng* 自生 of all things, a blanket term for the nonexistence of anything that causes everything because everything causes everything, and therefore none does. Nonetheless, we must still be able to talk about the absence of something, so we use the term nonbeing to refer to such absence in a conventional way. To drive the point further, Guo Xiang also tries to account for "what came first" as found in the accounts of both Laozi and Zhuangzi. He says:

> What could exist before there were things? If I say yin and yang came first, then since yin and yang are themselves entities, what came before them? Suppose I say [the event of] spontaneity came first. But spontaneity is only things being self-so. Suppose I say perfect dao came first. But perfect dao is perfect non-being.
> Since it is non-being, how can it come before anything else? Then what came before it? There must be another thing,

and so on *ad infinitum*. We must understand that things are what they are spontaneously and not caused by something else.³⁰

They merely are self-so, thus [their] grace flows through a hundred generations and yet does not fall into neglect.³¹

誰得先物者乎哉？吾以陰陽為先物，而陰陽者即所謂物耳。誰又先陰陽者乎？吾以自然為先之，而自然即物之自爾³²耳。吾以至道為先之矣，而至道者乃至無也。既以無矣，又奚為先？然則先物者誰乎哉？而猶有物，無已，明物之自然，非有使然也。取於自爾，故恩流百代而不廢也。

Tang Yijie, a renowned Wei-Jin scholar, aptly explains this passage and breaks it down into logical steps. He says:

> Whatever exists are "things" (物), therefore the "myriad things" (萬物) are themselves the sole existence. "*Ziran*" is the state in which the myriad things naturally exist, it simply means to denote that the "myriad things" (萬物) are existing and transforming on their own, and that not one single thing causes them (它) to exist or transform in such a way. For instance, "dao" is also not a single entity, and is "ultimate non-being" (至無); since it is non-being it cannot exist before "being" (有), it simply is "things" (物), which is why it [dao] is in such a state of movement and transformation.³³

Following Tang's explanation, it is more than reasonable to say that *wu* 無 cannot become *you* 有 and vice versa, because things always already are what they are. We think one thing gives birth to another, but this is not the case. We simply are observing the phenomenon of movement and transformation, even though it might appear to us as if one thing has caused another. This would then translate into there being no absolute being, or one single thing that causes everything; precisely because there is not even one single thing that causes another thing that can result in linear causation.

This very structural phenomenon is what I refer to here as the logic of convergence, which converges while simultaneously breaking the dichotomy between being and nonbeing, cause and effect, subject and object, and so on. This is what leads to the ultimate destruction of logical and ontological dualisms. Such emphasis on the nonbinary is perhaps also why both Tang Yijie and even Isabelle Robinet[34] read Guo Xiang as a precursor to Buddhism, and indeed a kind of culmination of indigenous Chinese thought during this era.[35] While we have no historical basis as to whether Guo Xiang's logic of convergence influenced Buddhist thought, the other way around, or if there was any contact at all, some scholars have certainly proven the distinctive parallels in what would seem to be a logic of contradiction, and in the case of Guo Xiang himself, the convergence of such contradictions. It is in this vein that logician and Buddhist Graham Priest's enterprise that is Dialetheism, which he claims is an important import of Buddhist logic,[36] is perhaps worth evoking. In most of Priest's works, he argues that "our concepts, or some of them anyway, are inconsistent and produce dialetheias,"[37] a term that he coins in order to indicate "the Janus-headed nature of a true contradiction."[38] In a different work with Buddhist scholars Jay Garfield and Yasuo Deguchi, they note that contradictions are "a consequence of rationality itself."[39] The relationship of contradiction to intercausality, moreover, is explained by Priest in his work entitled *One: Being an Investigation into the Unity of Reality and of Its Parts, Including the Singular Object Which Is Nothingness*,[40] where he explains the concept of Interpenetration and Indra's Net[41] in order to show the true contradiction of **everything** and **nothing**.[42] Priest uses the example of a magnet to illustrate the concept of interpenetration and notes that the north pole of a magnet can only be what it is in relation to its south. In the following, Priest illustrates the structure of *n* (north pole) wherein *s* (south pole) is contained:

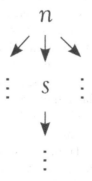

He notes that "what we see is that the tree for n contains the tree for s as a proper sub-tree. Metaphysically speaking, then, the ontological structure of n contains that of s."[43] In the same way, however, the node s will have the following structure:

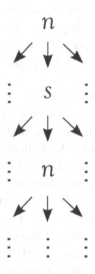

In other words, the tree for n is the tree for s, and the tree for s is the tree for n. Each contains the other as a necessary condition of being and thus *interpenetrate*. As such, Priest concludes that "every object then interpenetrates with itself, and interpenetration is an equivalence relation,"[44] and that this is the similar logic that goes on in the Net of Indra, where each jewel reflects the entire totality of the net, which means that "**everything** and **nothing** then interpenetrate. And since any thing interpenetrates with **nothing**, it interpenetrates with **everything**."[45]

Deguchi, Garfield, and Priest say that this dialetheism that we find in Buddhism is inevitable given the nature of the reality it tries to describe. They note: "In this respect, Buddhism is akin to any of a number of positions that claim that there is an ineffable reality, and then go on to explain why this is so, in the process, saying things about that reality. The phenomenon is to be found, for example, in Neoplatonism, in Advaita Vedānta, and in Heidegger on Being."[46] This is similar to what we find in Guo Xiang as well, where that ultimate reality is ineffable or unknowable because it is ultimately contradictory, in reference to nothingness, or in the case of Buddhism, to emptiness, which, as Deguchi, Garfield, and Priest note, is "identical with dependent origination."[47] Similarly, Guo Xiang says that "since knowing comes from nonknowing, nonknowing is always the source. Hence, the Genuine Human Being discards knowledge and thereby knows, does nothing and thereby does"[48] (知出於不知，故以不知為宗。是故真人遺知而知，不為而為). At this level of ultimate truth, we can accurately say that this is the same logic behind Guo Xiang's philosophy. However, unlike in much of Buddhist philosophy that separates Ultimate reality/truth from conventional reality/truth, and where contradictions are only true at the ultimate level, these distinctions do not occur in the same way in Guo Xiang. For Guo Xiang, contradictions do not simply occur at the ultimate level, but because everything at the conventional level already contains its ontological opposite, as is seen in the previous discussion on the boundaries between external and internal realms that disappear into each other. For Guo, everything is ultimately contradictory in that each thing is its own contradiction, which makes the contradiction of anything ultimately *nothing*. In this manner, Guo Xiang may be said to have a similar logic with dialetheism, but pushed to the extreme. A similar ontological position (when it comes to contradictions) worth evoking is that of Hegel, whom Priest considers a precursor for paraconsistency and dialetheism. In his book *In Contradiction*, which is one of the most important works on dialetheism, Priest explicitly says that "the main claim of this book [is] that Hegel was right."[49] Elsewhere, Priest argues that "Hegel's and Marx's dialectics is based on dialetheism."[50] Indeed, Hegel went so far as to scandalously proclaim that "everything is inherently contradictory"[51] and that speculative thinking, in other words philosophical exercise, in thinking about thinking, "consists solely in the fact that thought holds fast contradiction."[52] Hegel explains:

> It is one of the fundamental prejudices of logic as hitherto understood[53] and of ordinary thinking,[54] that contradiction is not so characteristically essential and immanent a determination as identity; but in fact, if it were a question of grading the two determinations and they had to be kept separate, then contradiction would have to be taken as the profounder determination and more characteristic of essence. For as against contradiction, identity is merely the determination of the simple immediate, of dead being; but contradiction is

the root of all movement and vitality; it is only in so far as something has a contradiction within it that it moves, has an urge and activity.[55]

For Hegel thus, contradiction is only immediately apparent when being is seen as dead—fixed. But due to the fact that being is indubitably organic, we can say that its root is contradiction, that is, its own negation. In this sense, Guo Xiang would agree that contradiction (between being and nonbeing) is the root of all movement and vitality. This is why, as discussed earlier, he says that "Zhuangzi sought to illuminate the basis of the unity [of the external and the internal]" by going "beyond the internal traces of Confucius, and transmitted [knowledge] through [transcendent] external occupations represented by these masters."[56] It is thus only by going beyond "ordinary thinking," in Hegel's terms, or "the internal realm" that true *comprehension* is possible.

Guo Xiang would disagree, however, that this is where the buck stops, for in Guo Xiang's view, Confucius was able to comprehend *and* embody that unity. For Guo Xiang, it is when one embodies nonbeing in the realm of being that one is self-realized. It is important to note, however, that this "going beyond" traces does not mean that there is no place for conventional truth in what Guo calls the "internal realm," which refers to the sociopolitical lifeworld. After all, to *embody* said unity, one must remain within the internal realm. As such, Guo does, in fact, acknowledge that ruling well and the existence of sages (Confucian values) are important. Sages, values, good government, and good teachings such as those of Zhuangzi's, thus become an ontological "raft"[57] that connects the internal to external, ordinary to ultimate. To be that raft is to embody the unity of nonbeing and being. This is given much more attention later on in the different types of Chinese Buddhism, but in Guo Xiang, we already see that to "discard" knowledge, one must first acquire knowledge. He says this of the sages as well, commenting:

> How true this statement is! But although this statement is true, we still cannot do away with the sages. Since all the knowledge in the world is not yet able to be completely obliterated, the way of the sages is still needed to subdue it. If everyone else's knowledge is allowed to exist and only the sages' knowledge is obliterated, this will harm the world

A Flattened Ontology and the Logic of Convergence | 43

even more than allowing the sages to exist. Thus although the harm caused by the sages is much, it is still better than the disorder of having no sages. But although it is better than having no sages, it is undeniably not as good as the total lack of harm there would be if all [knowledge] were obliterated.[58]

信哉斯言！斯言雖信，而猶不可亡聖者，猶天下之知未能都亡，故須聖道以鎮之也。群知不亡而獨亡於聖知，則天下之害又多於有聖矣。然則有聖之害雖多，猶愈於亡聖之無治也。雖愈於亡聖，故未若都亡之無害也。甚矣，天下莫不求利而不能一亡其知，何其迷而失致哉！

Here, the sages' knowledge or the accounts of it (the classics) are what Guo Xiang refers to as harmful, because they are fixed. It is thus what is immediately apparent, and what people take as a be-all and end-all. However, to be a sage, or to have ultimate knowledge through no-knowledge, one must "embody the world's transformations and respond to its affairs" (其體化而應務), as mentioned earlier in this chapter. This embodying of transformations is, ultimately, the same with embodying nothingness or nonbeing, since there is nothing that governs one's response to things, which is what allows the sage to respond to everything. The classics, the raft, is a tool, an example model, that has a use but must be discarded once its utility is fulfilled, *once full convergence is realized*.

Of course, this logic of convergence would have different consequences in dialetheism, Hegel, and Guo Xiang, even if merely as a result of the different determinations of their philosophical systems in their own historical contexts. Nonetheless, recounting these similar logical-cum-ontological dispositions helps us conceive of what Guo Xiang would have meant by affirming contradictions in contemporary terms. At this point, however, it is important to remind the reader that, as I have mentioned earlier, I do not intend to present Guo Xiang's way of reasoning as more valid than others, but simply to lay down the foundations of his philosophical system. As such, I present these other thinkers as an invitation to conditionally accept types of logical thinking that demonstrate how contradictions can be a fundamental ground of reality, for it is only then that we can begin to comprehend Guo Xiang's philosophy, which considers nonbeing as necessary to being. Moreover, it is this logic of convergence that leads Guo Xiang's philosophy into the ultimate destruction of linear causality and, in its place, the absolute independence and interdependence of all things, as grounded in the inherent contradiction of being as nonbeing.

This ultimate coalescence between independence and interdependence is not only, as Ziporyn puts it, "the ultimate breakdown of the concept of causality."[59] But also, and more pertinent to our purposes here, the ultimate collapse of any distinguishable binaries between particular and universal, and indeed, one and many. The result of the convergence, however, does not make them the same, but singularly different. What allows for this is the logic of convergence, but in more physical terms, this is made possible by the basic ontological premise of Guo Xiang on emergence and transformation. Indeed, if being does not come from nothing, and there is no time when being is not being, then how is it even possible for anything new to be created or born? This, according to Guo Xiang, is because everything is *zisheng* 自生 and *zihua* 自化 and therefore *dusheng* 獨生 and *duhua* 獨化.

Spontaneous Self-generation as Spontaneous Self-transformation: *Zisheng* 自生 and *Zihua* 自化

The concept of *zisheng* (spontaneous generativity or self-generation) is closely related to *wu* or nonbeing. Things are only self-generating because there is nothing that causes them, or no principle that governs them. Although things are also self-generating in the *Zhuangzi*, it is in Guo Xiang's commentaries that the concept is formalized and given a specific function in understanding what he rendered as Zhuangzi's system. One of Guo Xiang's clearest and most comprehensive explanations of the concept of spontaneous generativity is a comment on Zhuangzi's passage that follows:

> In the Great Beginning, there was nonbeing; there was no being, no name. Out of it arose One; there was One, but it had no form. From this, things came to be generated, and it was called Innate Power. Before things had forms, they had their allotments; these were of many kinds, but not cut off from one another, and they were called endowments. Out of the flow and flux, things were born, and as they grew they

developed distinctive shapes; these were called forms. The forms and bodies held within them spirits, each with its own characteristics and limitations, and this was called the inborn nature. If the nature is trained, you may return to Innate Power, and Innate Power at its highest peak is the same with the Beginning. That sameness is emptiness; that emptiness is great. It converges the cheeping and chirping—the convergence of cheeping and chirping, is in accord with the convergence of heaven and earth. Their convergence is wild and confused, as though they were stupid, as though they were demented. This is called profound Innate Power, it is the same as the greatness of acquiescence.[60]

泰初有無，無有無名；一之所起，有一而未形。物得以生，謂之德；未形者有分，且然無閒，謂之命；留動而生物，物成生理，謂之形；形體保神，各有儀則，謂之性。性脩反德，德至同於初。同乃虛，虛乃大。合喙鳴；喙鳴合，與天地為合。其合緡緡，若愚若昏，是謂玄德，同乎大順。

Guo Xiang clarifies, however:

Having no being, it thus had no means for being named. The One, the beginning of being, is the finest subtlety. As the finest subtlety, therefore, the One does not yet have the form of the principle of things. "Out of it arose One," means that it arises from the ultimate one, and not from nonbeing. But in that case what is the reason that Zhuangzi often says "there is nonbeing in the beginning"?

The beginning means something as yet ungenerated attaining generation. Even something as difficult as attaining generation was done without depending on nonbeing prior [to generation], nor on knowing [why] after, but just suddenly [self-]attaining (*zide*) this generation [in a spontaneous way]—so why should we try to manage the generated in its state of already-having-been generated and thus lose its spontaneous generativity (lit., self-generation)? Nonbeing cannot generate things, and it states that "things come to be generated [from the One]," in order to show **the spontaneous realization (*zide*) of the generation of things**. They rely on their own spontaneous realization (*zide*), that is why it is called "Innate Power." Innate Power forms endowed natures (*xingming* 性命), it causes transformations in rank and position, it is one and the same with being self-so. It is persistent by way of not doing anything and yet realizing itself (*zide*). It is not identical with the beginning, yet it acts in the midst of dao, that is why at the center of its bosom, things therefore come to exist; things exist yet the nourishing that Innate Power [provides] is [insignificantly] small! The heart-mind does not intend to speak of it, yet the words come about on their own, [and those words are] converging with cheeping and chirping. [In the same way,] heaven and earth simply has an empty heart-mind, yet it moves itself. It (Innate Power) is to sit in forgetfulness, and yet spontaneously [self-]converge [with heaven and earth], as opposed to observing the means by which they converge. Innate Power is profound and it is the means by which those who acquiesce become great.[61]

無有，故無所名。一者，有之初，至妙者也，至妙，故未有物理之形耳。夫一之所起，起於至一，非起於無也。然莊子之所以屢稱無於初者，何哉？初者，未生而得生，得生之難，而猶上不資於無，下不待於知，突然而自得此生矣，又何營生於已生以失其自生哉！無不能生物，而云物得以生，乃所以明物生之自得，任其自得，斯可謂德也。夫德形性命，因變立名，其於自爾一也。恆以不為而自得之。不同於初，而中道有為，則其懷中故為有物也，有物而容養之德小矣。無心於言而自言者，合於喙鳴。天地亦無心而自動。坐忘而自合耳，非照察以合之。德玄而所順者大矣。

Here, Guo Xiang explains that innate power (*de* 德) is that which allows one to embody nonbeing and become one with "cheeping and chirping"—the subtlety and smallness of such innate power is itself that which allows one not only to acquiesce but also to ultimately partake in the greatness of heaven and earth.[62] There is a subtle differentiation here between simply acquiescing, which is to say that one simply follows one thing or one morality whatsoever, and the act of acquiescing through innate power (*de*). By making use of the innate power that does not come from anything in particular, we make our surroundings *ours* and ours alone. This is the means by which *zide* is possible, and achieving this comes precisely through *wuxin* or an empty heart-mind. In other words, achieving innate power is possible through *wuxin*, which then allows one to converge with the transformations of heaven and earth. It is itself, through nonbeing, the possibility for spontaneous self-generation. Here we might recall what was earlier mentioned, which is that Guo noted how things simply self-generate, and that "by 'self-generation,' it is not meant that there is an 'I' to generate."[63] This is what having "innate power" is, that is, to recognize the immediacy of being, and thus merge one's "self" with it. Looked at more closely, we notice the semantic structure of this passage, as the terms nonbeing (*wu* 無) and spontaneous-X (自 *zi*-X) are repeatedly paralleled, highlighting the phenomenon of nonbeing as pointing to the existence of the myriad things that, in the main, is characteristic of a self-organizing and spontaneous generativity. In the simplest terms, this is what the logic of convergence is: it is such that nothingness (*wu*) is spontaneity (*zi*) at the same time. It is because there is nothing governing them, not even the "I," that they are altogether one. In this absolute oneness—because nothing is governing them—things are spontaneously generating. Because they are spontaneously generating, and these generations are interconnected to each other simultaneously, they are also spontaneously transforming each other through that spontaneous generation as a multitudinous but single and simultaneous process; conversely, it is because of spontaneous transformation or *zihua* that they are also spontaneously generating and that new things start to emerge through the process, leading to mutual generativity and transformation.

In another sub-story from the *Zhuangzi* where a metal being cast is seen in a circumstance where it hypothetically leaps up and says that it does not want to be anything but a sword like the Mo-ye, Zhuangzi likens the situation of the metal to that of men's, and says that it would be equally uncanny if a human were to say that he doesn't want to be anything but a man. Guo Xiang then comments and relates this scenario to argue both for the occurrence of *zihua* and *zisheng*, as well why we ought to simply let these be:

> "I don't want to be anything but a man! Nothing but a man!," is nothing but the ambition to become a man. So too it is the same with the leaping up of metal, for all in the world would consider the metal to be uncanny, as it is unable abide by its own self-transformation.[64]
>
> In the Course [道 *dao*] of change and transformation there is nothing that is not encountered sooner or later. Now

you have encountered the state of having a human form. How could this be anyone's deliberate doing? Generativity does not take place deliberately—**at any moment, it is simply [or spontaneously] self-generating**. Is it not misguided then to labor yourself attempting to possess and control it?⁶⁵

人耳人耳，唯願為人也。亦猶金之踴躍，世皆知金之不祥，而不能任其自化。
　　夫變化之道，靡所不遇，今一遇人形，豈故為哉？生非故為，時自生耳。務而有之，不亦妄乎！

Again, we see Guo Xiang arguing for the reliance of everything and everyone in the world on self-transformation (*zihua*). This is because relying on self-transformation leads to spontaneous generativity (*zisheng*). Being simply so, it will self-transform. Self-transforming, it is born, but always *in medias res*, and right at birth, always already transforming. Thus, Guo Xiang shows in this passage that deliberately wanting or desiring to become something else is a deviation from that self-transformation, because generativity itself is a spontaneous product of the transformative process. What this means is that everything is always within the process of transforming, and that we can never really map out an exact beginning to when everything truly started to exist; yet, somehow, within such an eternally moving and ever-changing world, new things always emerge, new things that themselves transform and lead to transformation, and so the cycle continues.

As we will recall, the logic of convergence is such that it is contradiction that is the foundation of all movement, vitality, and not least, transformation. This means that because of this contradictory nature, things are also always emerging from that constant transformation wherein one thing is not the same thing in the next moment, for even within the moment, something is always already in contradiction with itself, having nothing as its content, and simply being self-so.

Lone-Transformation as Lone-Generation: *Duhua* 獨化 and *Dusheng* 獨生

Because everything is self-so, each one is also its own cause, which now brings us to lone-generation (*dusheng*) and lone-transformation (*duhua*), which Ziporyn states is not interchangeable with self-transformation (*zihua*). I follow him in this regard, and he says that this is because self-transformation (a term that Zhuangzi himself uses) seems to suggest that "all are manifestations of a single spontaneity,"[66] while lone-transformation is a term that Guo Xiang invents in order to stress "uniqueness, particularity, and individuality."[67] Ziporyn thus gives an apt and succinct explanation here because this is simply the necessary consequence of everything causing everything. If everything is simply spontaneous and self-so, it necessarily leads to each thing being its own particular unique self. We now see the aspect of Guo Xiang's philosophy that pertains to self-determination, in that each thing manifests something that is not externally influenced; however, it must again be reiterated that this self-determination doesn't come from an inherent "I," as noted earlier—it is simply so, precisely because it acquiesces. This spontaneity is then what allows for true freedom, as we shall go back to later.

Nonetheless, the prefix term *du* 獨 in Guo Xiang's usage is ultimately in relation to a singular entity whereas *zi* 自 refers to the spontaneity of the whole. What this means is that though "lone-" (*du*) and "self-" (*zi*) are terminologically or semantically different, they are, in actuality, conceptually interchangeable. Similarly, generation (*sheng*) and transformation (*hua*) in Guo Xiang are, conceptually speaking, ultimately the same. For Guo Xiang, this means that what is many or pluralistic is no different from the one or the singular; each and every thing is absolutely singular, and yet everything else coherent because even though they are generating and transforming on their own, that is, singularly, they still belong to an interconnected network. Each is influenced not simply diachronically, but synchronically by everything else, which, by virtue of the logic of convergence, is ultimately nothing. What this means is that one thing has, in it, the rest of the "other" entities, eventually making none really "other." Each thing has a constitutive otherness to it that makes it what it is. That is to say, the whole is substantially comprised of many wholes, and so conversely the particular has, within itself, the essence and substance of the whole. In the same way, what his conception of transformation ultimately suggests is the same thing, conceptually, as with his conception of generation. Ultimately thus, generation and transformation no longer have a distinguishable Difference, because everything is already just there in an eternal movement of change and transformation and so are without any beginning whatsoever. As Livia Kohn has aptly suggested, it is the case for Guo Xiang that "the universe exists by itself and of itself; it is existence just as it is. Nothing can be added to or subtracted from it; it is entirely sufficient upon itself."[68] This is why in a passage where Zhuangzi says:

> The bright and shining is born out of deep darkness; the ordered is born out of formlessness; pure spirit is born out of the Way.[69]

夫昭昭生於冥冥，有倫生於無形，精神生於道

Guo Xiang comments:

> These [items in the *Zhuangzi* text] are all meant to show their lone-generation and that there is nothing by which they give and take.[70]

皆所以明其獨生而無所資借。

Such reflexive relationship of these things shows that the nondependence and independence of autonomous beings is how we can understand the intimate relations not only of opposites, and how they mutually generate each other, therefore having no external creator. It also shows, ultimately, the dialectic between micro and macro, individual and community, particular and whole. This is why for Guo Xiang the whole is more than the sum of its parts. Each of them are autonomous, and their autonomy is the condition of the others' autonomies, but these parts are, in themselves, whole. They are thus self-sufficient. In order to understand this better, we ought to look at another one of Guo Xiang's commentaries on one of Zhuangzi's more famous stories: The Penumbra and the Shadow. The *Zhuangzi* passage goes as follows:

> The penumbra asked the shadow, "Formerly you walked, and now you have stopped. Formerly you sat, and now you have arisen. Why is it that you have no fixed course of action?"
> The shadow said, "Do I have something I depend on (*dai*) in order to be as I am? Does what I depend on depend on something else to be as it is? Am I dependent on snake scales or cicada wings? How could I discern how and why I am as I am? How could I discern how and why I am not as I am not?"[71]

罔兩問景曰：「曩子行，今子止；曩子坐，今子起；何其無特操與？」

　　景曰：「吾有待而然者邪？吾所待又有待而然者邪？吾待蛇蚹蜩翼邪？惡識所以然！惡識所以不然！」

This is a short passage but it is packed with meaning and Guo Xiang presents a long commentary to explain the concept of causality that he thinks Zhuangzi presents in this story. It is also in this passage that we first see Guo Xiang introduce the concept of *duhua* in his comments in order to explain the conception of causality in the *Zhuangzi*. Though Zhuangzi does not use the concept here, Guo Xiang formalizes the concept of absolute independence as absolute dependence that is already present in the *Zhuangzi* through this term. According to Guo Xiang, even though it seems the penumbra is dependent on the shadow, and the shadow is dependent upon something else, it actually does not depend on anything. He notes:

> If we search for that which [each thing] is dependent on and seek out what [each thing] comes from, this searching will lead to an infinite regress, and in the end we will come only to the lack of dependence (*wudai*). Thus the principle of lone-transformation (*duhua*) becomes clear.[72]

若責其所待而尋其所由，則尋責無極，〔卒〕至於無待，而獨化之理明矣。

Guo Xiang thus goes a step further than Zhuangzi, which he sees as a necessary step in systematizing the text, and so presenting us with an attack against the very principle of causality as a linear phenomenon. The argument here is not simply that causality is a circular phenomenon, which places nonbeing as a central metaphysical concept. Guo goes against this argument precisely by radicalizing it. In the *Zhuangzi*, we are told that if we accept the idea that something else external to one thing is the cause of that thing, we will be led to an infinite regress without coming to a final creator, because every "final" creator must have been created externally. If it were not so, we must admit to the idea that such a creator was self-created. Yet, if self-creation was possible for a creator, there is no reason why it is also not the case for everyone and everything else. But since we know that we have this concept of self-creation, there is no longer a need for an external creator to create other beings, as they are self-creating as well. Therefore, it is impossible to point out specifically what the particular cause of a particular thing is, because creation comes simply from transformation of all things to all others. And without any particular cause, all things then are lone-transforming. Brook Ziporyn notes, moreover, that "Guo rejects the concept of causality itself; he cuts out the middle man entirely, and asserts that all things are unmediated, and transform in solitude."[73] If it was mediated, then we go back to linear causality. This is thus why it is difficult to discern any fixed course of action—because there is none. The shadow is neither dependent on snake scales nor cicada wings because it simply lone-transforms, *duhua*. Guo Xiang continues:

> Hence, of all things involved in the realm of existence, even the penumbra, there has never been one that did not lone-transform in the realm of dark vanishing (*xuanming*).... Now, if even in the case of the penumbra's following of the shadow we can still say they simultaneously come to be but without mutual dependence, then although the ten thousand things come together to collectively form the Heavenly, nonetheless each of them in perfect distinctness appears on its own in independent solitude (*liran duxian*). Thus, the penumbra is not controlled by the shadow, nor is the shadow caused.... Transforming and not transforming, being thus [or right, *ran*] and not being thus, following others or proceeding from one's own self, none are not self-so; how could we discern how or why they are so?[74]

> 是以涉有物之域，雖復罔兩，未有不獨化於玄冥者也。。。
> 　今罔兩之因景，猶云俱生而非待也，則萬物雖聚而共成乎天，而皆歷然莫不獨見矣。故罔兩非景之所制，。。。，則化與不化，然與不然，從人之與由己，莫不自爾，吾安識其所以哉！

Here we see the collapse of causes that are either external or innately internal (that is, the *authenticity* of something). In other words, the relation of cause and effect is one that is impossible to conceive because, as Ziporyn notes: "Everything and anything makes this particular thing what it is; thus it need make no distinction between what is necessary to it and what is not, for all things are equally necessary to it."[75] The concepts of *duhua* and *ming*, moreover, blur into each other because everything is caused by everything that everything disappears into everything; since all disappears into everything, we are left with the mere lone-transformations of things. That is, though we think it makes sense to talk about what causes what because we can say that X causes Y and W causes X, ultimately we can find no first cause, and thus ultimately there is nothing that causes W, and thus nothing that causes Y, and thus nothing that ultimately causes X. This, of course, is a gross oversimplification of the process of *duhua*, yet if we push the penumbra's logic to its ultimate, we get to see that the fact that there are many different causes for a certain effect, which in turn becomes a cause among a variety of other causes, which means that we are left with a vast network of infinitely interconnected points. In this way, we can thus conclude that everything causes everything, and if this is so, then nothing, or no one thing or even a specific set of things, can ultimately cause anything, because causes are always connected to other causes ad infinitum.

As such, when Guo Xiang says that "the ten thousand things come together to collectively form the Heavenly," he is not denying that the movement of reality is caused by everything, but that precisely because it is caused by everything it becomes radically contingent. This radical contingency wherein everything is caused by everything—everything being its cause as pushed to the extreme—means that it has everything inside something. When everything is inside something, nothing then is outside of it, which makes it perfectly distinct. In this sense, we see that when the transformation of the manyness of myriad things is pushed to the extreme, it becomes singular; hence, lone-transformation.

In sum, nonbeing or *wu* is an important signifier for the spontaneity (自 *zi*) that highlights the phenomenon of the whole, whereas it manifests as singular in the prefix of lone-X (獨 *du*-X). This, however, is offset by the suffixes of generativity (X-生 *sheng*), which highlight emergence as both nonlinear and singular, as well as transformation (X-化), which highlights the phenomenon of change as both spontaneous and basically uncaused. Indeed, it is through this denial of linear causation that Guo's philosophical commentary is able to smoothly maneuver for the complete fusion of one and many, necessity and contingency. This ultimately leads to the inseparability and interchangeability of one to the other in its radical extremity.

Absolute Necessity as Absolute Contingency

Guo Xiang thus draws from Zhuangzi a philosophy of absolute nothingness, which is pushed to the limits and hence becomes a philosophy of pure being collapsing into each other leading to a robust oneness of all. This is why it is only in those instantaneous moments of spontaneous and independent generativity as well as transformation that necessities[76] are fulfilled.

Of course, we must clarify that the distinction between physical/causal necessity and logical necessity does not occur as neatly in Guo Xiang or Zhuangzi, or any other indigenous Chinese philosophical thought for that matter, as it does in Anglo-European philosophy. Nonetheless, such "conflation" does not cause a problem in Guo Xiang's philosophy, because in such a system, traditional logic—or the very idea of logical abstraction itself—would be problematic, as we have touched upon earlier. If Guo Xiang were alive to see traditional logic and how it operates, we may again infer that he might understand it similarly to how Hegel saw it, which is "a multitude of detached necessities"[77]—forms separated from their contents.[78] However, in contrast to such traditional logic, Guo Xiang's system holds that everything is connected to everything, everything thus causes everything, and that is why each thing is an absolute necessity even if contingently grounded. We cannot say why something is so, it simply *is* so and self-generating (*zisheng*), because if everything is the cause, then no thing is the cause, and therefore it is necessary or uncaused because of its singularity in transformation and emergence; but even though there are no extant reasons why it could have been otherwise, it *could* have actually been otherwise, and therefore contingent. This self-generation, already found in the *Zhuangzi* but expanded by Guo Xiang, is a thoroughly dynamic process, but it simply returns to itself, by itself, and hence, is lone-generating (*dusheng*). Similarly, it is lone-generating (*dusheng*) because each thing contains within it its own antipodes, which means that it is always already "other." If we conditionally accept this process to be true, this will inevitably mean that it can only transform unto itself, that is, by lone-transforming (*duhua*). Everything is always already what each has always been and can be, yet these determinations or identities are not fixed, they are always contingent in as much as they could always be otherwise, as one could *vanish into* (*xuanming* 玄冥) another, because even though each thing is distinct, each thing's distinctness vanishes into another. However, there is also no reason for the way that they are so, they are simply self-so (*ziran* 自然) and therefore necessary in that sense. This includes knowledge, because Guo Xiang closes off his/

Zhuangzi's system of totality entirely that there is nothing that exists outside of it (such as a creator), and for that to work, he must admit to each thing being the cause (and also the effect) of everything else. In other words, there is nothing that is *other* to something, and being everything, it is entirely inaccessible to thought, which is only limited in its allotment (*fen* 分). Like things, knowledge is thus also self-so and is only within its own realm. Paul D'Ambrosio puts it aptly and simply, saying that, for Guo Xiang, "knowledge is always situationally dependent,"[79] and thus constantly transforming. In this sense, it is singular and without any *particular* cause, but caused by everything else, and is therefore emergent unto itself—simply so because they are so, and yet always changing. Thus, Guo Xiang's universe of absolute necessity is one of absolute contingency as well.

In sum, it is the case that in a singular object, we can find the wholeness of the reality that caused it to be so. Moreover, because everything caused this singular object to be so, then there is really nothing in particular that caused it. Hence, this and every other thing is spontaneous or self-generated, wherein such generativity that is spontaneous leads also to transformation that is spontaneous and emergent, wherein such emergence means that it is on its own, causing its own, and transforming its own. By being a whole in itself, moreover, each object acts by itself, in order to ultimately fulfill its role in the organic whole; by being a whole in itself and having the entirety of reality within it, the movement of each small thing thus becomes the movement of and for the whole. It is not therefore the case in Guo Xiang's *Zhuangzi* that nothing is necessary, and nothing is absolute—but rather, everything is necessary, and everything is absolute; Contingency is led to the extreme, that it becomes necessity, and the other way around. For Guo, only a necessity that's contingent is worth having, and only the type of contingency that is necessary is truly uncaused.

From an Anglo-European perspective, we see how even when we pull out the idea of a central *logos spermatikos* or that one thing that keeps everything together, such as a god, it does not necessarily follow that coherence and wholeness would collapse—there can and will still be meanings to the changes and transformations of the myriad things, even without one single grand narrative. This leads us to another important concept in Guo Xiang's philosophy, which again was only hinted at by Zhuangzi: 理 *li*.

Li 理: Coherence in the One and the Many

Another concept that was widely debated during the Wei-Jin period that did not come up philosophically before is the notion of *li*. This becomes an important concept in Neo-Confucianism and Chinese Buddhism later on but was actually first treated philosophically by Wang Bi. Strictly speaking, the term is meant as a reference to an overarching pattern, law, order, or principle—that is, how something is organized. In Neo-Confucianism, where the usage of the term is most pertinent, it is meant as "the unifying principle of the universe."[80] Like the term dao, it is used to denote an underlying order to the cosmos, though what that is exactly is a topic of debate in the history of Chinese philosophy from time immemorial. Brook Ziporyn has pointed out that there are the nonironic and ironic senses of the term.[81] In the philosophy of Guo Xiang, however, Ziporyn notes: "For the first time in Chinese thought, we can state directly that coherence [*li*] as such is incoherence as such, that determinacy and indeterminacy are strictly synonymous. The term *li* is central to this development, and here its two opposed directions converge: it means both absolute division and complete unity."[82] Indeed, in line with the rest of Guo Xiang's philosophy as previously discussed, it is not the case that opposites are simply complementary, but they are strictly necessary to the existence of each other and one cannot exist without the other, for one *is* the other. In other words, the only true *li* is non-*li*—that which is unbound by any actual pattern or law, because "the real principle (self-so) is the absence of all so-called principles."[83]

So what does it mean to be able to understand this ironic coherence,[84] this noncoherence that is Guo Xiang's *li*? From what we have seen so far, it is quite apparent that he wouldn't advocate noncoherence as a means for coherence, which is what a philosophical primacy of nonbeing would be. Indeed because of Guo Xiang's logic of convergence, which radicalizes the convergence of opposites instead of simply giving importance to nonbeing, or to being, for that matter, he makes coherence and incoherence synonymous, as noted by Ziporyn. This means that, instead of a withdrawn sense of acceptance or a kind of giving up as a means of escaping the disorder that results from the loss of dao for Guo Xiang (which, if we shall remember, can be found in vanishing into things rather than from), we see a kind of acceptance that is inward—one that is not defined by giving up, but rather, by a sense of belonging that takes a different kind of effort. As Ziporyn puts it: "To vanishingly merge with whatever one encounters is to vanishingly merge with one's own nature, with one's own limits, with one's own allotment. In this sense the term *the nature* or *the coherence* is an ironic empty term for Guo, just as 'Dao' or 'nothingness' is."[85]

Here it will be useful to recall our earlier discussion on causality, which explored the disappearance into each other of entities that cause each other leading to the breakdown of causality in *zisheng*, *zihua*, *dusheng*, and *duhua*. Ziporyn further notes that this is "a vanishing of the identifiable individual 'things' themselves—that is, of their traces [跡 *ji*],"[86] wherein such vanishing of traces is what is meant when Guo Xiang says that whatever it is that stems from the height of coherence is spontaneously self-so and has no traces [2.14.29G 至理之來，自然無跡。] precisely because it is a *merging into*.

This kind of understanding of coherence (*li* 理) is perhaps best seen in Zhuangzi's story of the cook in the third chapter of the text, where Guo Xiang once again relates coherence with the vanishing of traces, telling us that the cook has understood the 理 *li*. What this means, therefore, is that by being able to understand the 理 *li*, he has mastered his craft—his allotment (*fen* 分).

The following is a complete excerpt of the story of the cook (with Zhuangzi's passages in bold), followed line-by-line by Guo Xiang's commentary, which builds on the story:

Cook Ding was cutting up an ox for Lord Wenhui [King Hui of Liang] in such a way that with:
   Each stroke of the hand,
   Each thrust of the shoulder,
   Each stamp of the foot,
   Each jab of the knee,
   Matched a sharp sound of rending, as he played his knife, swishing in and out, always in perfect tune, right in step for the "Mulberry Grove Dance" and in perfect rhythm with the "Jingshou Melody."

庖丁為文惠君解牛，手之所觸，肩之所倚，足之所履，膝之所踦，砉然嚮然，奏刀騞然，莫不中音。合於桑林之舞，乃中經首之會。

That is, he exercises his skill with the greatest of ease and never fails to make absolutely the right cut. Since he has thoroughly grasped the principle [*li*] involved, not only is he in perfect harmony with the principle of the ox, he keeps in perfect rhythm [*he yinjie*].

言其因便施巧，無不閑解，盡理之甚，既適牛理，又合音節。

Lord Wenhui said, "Wow! Terrific! How could skill ever go so far as this?"

文惠君曰：「譆，善哉！技蓋至此乎？」

Cook Ding put his knife down and replied, "What I am good at is the Dao, for I have advanced beyond skill.

庖丁釋刀對曰：「臣之所好者道也，進乎技矣。

He simply lodged the principles of the Dao in his skill, so what he was good at was not the skill itself.

直寄道理於技耳，所好者非技也。

When I first began to cut up oxen, what I saw was nothing but the whole ox as such,

始臣之解牛之時，所見無非〔全〕牛者。

He could not yet see the interstices in its natural configuration.

未能見其理間。

but, after three years, I no longer saw the whole ox as such.

三年之後，未嘗見全牛也。

He only saw the interstices in its natural configuration.

但見其理間也。

And now, I encounter it with my spirit [*shen*] and do not see it with my eyes.

方今之時，臣以神遇而不以目視，

He arcanely fuses with its principle/natural configuration.

闇與理會。

When sense and knowledge stop, the divine is ready to act.

官知止而神欲行。

As the senses which govern scrutiny quit working, he loosen his mind and accords with principle/natural configuration.

司察之官廢，縱心而理〔順〕。

In accord with the natural principle [configuration, *tianli*],

依乎天理，

He does not cut arbitrarily. [lit.: I do not blow sideways so as to amputate it.]

不橫截也。

I strike at the gaps.

批大卻，

These are the places of juncture, which he follows to strike at the ox and so cause it to come apart.

有際之處，因而批之令離。

Following the large openings,

導大窾，

These are the empty places where the joints come apart, which he accordingly follows to cause it to sever.

節解窾空，就導令殊。

I follow where inherent certainty leads me.

因其固然。

The knife is not applied rashly.

刀不妄加。

It never happens that my plying encounters the joints,

技經肯綮之未嘗，

Such is the marvelousness of his technique that he always plies the knife edge in emptiness and never lets it come up against the slightest obstacle.

技之妙也，常遊刃於空，未嘗經概於微礙也。

So how much the less likely am I to encounter a big bone!

而況大軱乎！

Gu [big bone] here means to encounter a big bone, which would defeat the knife edge.

軱，戾大骨，衄刀刃也。

A good cook has to change his knife once a year, this because he cuts through [the meat].

良庖歲更刀，割也；

He fails to hit the interstices in the natural configuration.

不中其理閒也。

The ordinary cook has to change his knife once a month, this because he hacks.

A Flattened Ontology and the Logic of Convergence | 61

族庖月更刀，折也。

He hits bones and so breaks the knife.

中骨而折刀也。

Now, my knife has lasted nineteen years, and the oxen I have cut up number in the thousands, yet the edge of my knife is as if it had just left the whetstone.

今臣之刀十九年矣，所解數千牛矣，而刀刃若新發於硎。

Xing is a whetstone.

硎，砥石也。

The joints have spaces in them, but the knife edge has no thickness. To insert what has no thickness into what has a space means that it will be so spacious that there will be more than enough room to ply the knife. This is why even after nineteen years my knife edge is as if it had just left the whetstone.

彼節者有閒，而刀刃者無厚；以無厚入有閒，恢恢乎其於遊刃必有餘地矣，是以十九年而刀刃若新發於硎。

However, whenever I come to a grouping, I note that it presents difficulties,

雖然，每至於族，吾見其難為，

Where things intersect and come together is a "grouping."

交錯聚結為族。

fearfully take warning, my look stopped,

怵然為戒，視為止，

He no longer applies his eyes to anything else.

不復屬目於他物也。

my action slowed,

行為遲。

He slows down his hand.

徐其手也。

I just have to move my knife the slightest amount, and, with a sharp rending sound, it's already come apart,

動刀甚微，謋然已解，

Since he gets it just right, he has to use very little effort.

得其宜則用力少。

as if it had been dirt clumped into earth.

如土委地。

The natural configuration [理] comes apart yet there's no trace of the knife, as if it had been clumped earth.

理解而無刀跡，若聚土也。

Raising my knife and standing there, as a result I look all around and linger awhile filled with satisfaction because of what I have done.

提刀而立，為之四顧，為之躊躇滿志，

This indicates one self-fulfilled [自得] with all his sense of preeminence and feeling of pleasure.

逸足容豫自得之謂。

I set my knife right and put it away."

善刀而藏之。」

He wipes his knife clean and places it in its sheath.

拭刀而弢之也。

Lord Wenhui then said, "Excellent! I have heard Cook Ding's words and learned how to nurture life from them."

文惠君曰：「善哉！吾聞庖丁之言，得養生焉。」

Since one can do such nurturing with the knife, he realized that life too can so be nurtured.[87]

以刀可養，故知生亦可養。

In this passage, we are told how it is with ease (便 *bian*) that the cook is able to cut the right way. Specifically, Guo Xiang emphasizes that it is because the cook has understood the *li* involved in this particular ox. This is because the cook is in harmony with the pattern of this ox and thereby effectively vanishes and merges into it.

The *Zhuangzi* text, however, proceeds to describe how the cook was able to arrive at such expertise, which was something that is beyond skill. We may even think of this in terms of framing the height of skill as no-skill, that is, when thinking or deliberate understanding stops. What we are shown here when the cook describes his progress is that he was not born good at it, and instead it took him quite long to master his craft, and yet when he did finally master it, he ironically no longer thinks about it—a knowing that required no knowing, because according to Guo Xiang, he is in accord with the *li*. Similarly, developing a certain skill would generally entail a collection of knowledge, but here we see that this collection of knowledge, at its height, disappears or vanishes: there is the suspension of the cook's senses that pertain specifically to scrutiny. Beyond learning a specific set of skills, the cook merges with this *specific* ox and its specific configuration, he "fuses with its natural configuration" (*lihui* 理會). Such state, therefore, does not mean one can simply follow whatever one desires at any moment in time. The paradox here lies in the fact it actually takes effort in order to achieve supreme effortlessness. In the case of the cook here, his knife had been in use for nineteen years and unlike the simply good cook who misses the *li*, or the ordinary cook who ruins the knife by hitting the bones, he leaves no traces of the knife, because it has become one with the ox. This, however, was achieved not because of the lack of distinctions or division, for on the contrary, a good cook is only good and not great because he fails to see the interstices of spaces (*jian* 間) between the structural patterns of the ox. Indeed, the ability to see those distinctions and nuances is what makes this particular cook a master of his craft—that is, the ability to be able to comprehend what to do in exactly the right moment, at the place, in the right circumstance, which nevertheless always changes in fleeting moments that are always distinct and unique from each other, because that is what the *li* is: spontaneous and self-so (*ziran*). In this case, the cook was able to exercise the height of *li* through being self-so, which is to merge into what they are not, into their environment or what they encounter, which, in this case, is the ox. This is ultimately why he is self-realized (*zide* 自得) as a butcher of oxen.

Moreover, there is another layer to this story that is noteworthy. As one might know, butchering oxen is not a pleasant sight—carcasses, blood, organs—but this might be deliberate on Zhuangzi's part. The Confucian philosopher Mencius was roughly a contemporary of Zhuangzi and there are several metaphors that might be alluding to Mencius's philosophy, one of which is this passage on the cook or butcher Ding. In Mencius 1A7, we see an ox being taken for consecrating a bell with its blood. Meanwhile, the king spots it and feels sorry for it, then orders his men to spare it. He says, "Spare it. I cannot bear its frightened appearance, like an innocent going to the execution ground."[88] Mencius then says that this is the root of benevolence, and why gentlemen cannot bear to see animals die, cry, and then eat them. So, "gentlemen keep their distance from the kitchen."[89] In contrast, Zhuangzi takes us to a scene in the kitchen and shows us the manner in which this gory scene can teach us how to nurture life. Guo Xiang highlights this and explicitly says that the butcher fuses with and is in accord with the natural configuration (*li*) of being self-so (*ziran*). Thus, it is this butcher that is—just as how anyone else can be—self-realized (*zide*).

Thus, though it may look different in different circumstances, it is simply similar in life as with the knife: to understand the height of *li* is to assimilate with the patterns that one encounters by encountering situations with fusing oneself differently into different situations that are by no means a "one-size-fits-all" rule. One need not be a gentleman in the traditional and noble sense, for one can achieve being one with the natural configurations (*li*) by *vanishing into* things such that one *merges into* them, resulting in the radicalized breakdown of duality that, according to Guo Xiang, is what the realization of one's self (*zide* 自得) truly means. This is fitting in relation to the story of Guo Xiang, who rose from an economically ordinary family to a high position in government, based mostly on merit. In a way, then, both Zhuangzi and Guo Xiang are also telling us that it is not necessary for one to be born into nobility to be able to know the right way to live, and to assume so is an elitist and exclusivist stance, relying on moral education, the values of which are anyhow arbitrarily chosen. The butcher has his own way of living, and it can be just as nourishing as that of Confucius. Fundamentally, everything is the same in that they are all different from one another, that is the natural pattern (*li*) of things. That is why Guo Xiang says "of things, there is nothing that doesn't cohere; it is only right to follow along with it (*li*)"⁹⁰ (物無不理，但當順之). So, regardless of where one is or who one is in life, the secret is to "follow along with (*li*)." This *li* is the same spontaneity that is found in the singularity and uniqueness of all things. So, Guo says that the *li* that makes things cohere is always correct (*dang* 當), meaning that any existing coherence has things that *necessarily* make it cohere. However, since we know that *li* is *ziran*, we also know that this "rightness" is not a value judgment but simply means spontaneous. Thus, things could not have been otherwise, and whatever happens, they are always right, that is, they make sense, when seen in the context of everything else that also exists, in such a way that one might see the causalities from many angles, so, not only is there is no single cause for any one of them, but also everything exists against the backdrop of everything: no one thing is an isolated atom existing on its own. Here it is useful to recall Guo's constant parallelism of *wu* 無 and *zi* 自. If everything is self-so or *ziran*, it means that there is no reason for them being so. If there is no reason for things to be so, then any one thing that is self-so cannot be an accident that is isolated. Nothing is *not supposed to happen*, because there's nothing that *is* essentially supposed to happen. Being self-so, any one thing has no reason other than itself for its own reason for being so. So, there is no *one* thing that makes it right or correct, and as such, it is self-right. As such, they are right, but one angle is not solely right for one or a few specific reasons, as everything needs to be just as it is in that specific context, and is necessary and right in order for this to be this and that to be that at this very moment. This is an ontological statement that tells us that because each thing contains in it its own contradiction, its transformations will always simply lead unto itself. More precisely, in line with the discussion on necessity and contingency, an effect will always have the cause already contained in it, and the cause will always already have the effect contained in it. Thus, things would always already have been right, or what they are "supposed" to be: contingency is merged with necessity. The "rightness" (*dang*) of following along with the spontaneity of *li* is thus a reference to *both* the negation of deliberate volition (motivated by a desire to superimpose change) as well as an isolated spontaneity that is arrived at simply by chance. Just as it is for Zhuangzi, so also for Guo Xiang, that each thing is "that" because everything else is "this" and "that." The ground of each thing is its very groundlessness, which is also the spontaneous ground for everything else. Contingency becomes necessary and, thus, self-right. Seen in this dialectical way, nothing is indeed exclusive from anything, bringing its existence into full play, and thereby existing and transforming at the same time.

3

On the Self

Limits and Expanse

Now that we have discussed the absolute nature of existence, both as cause and effect, that is, radically contingent and therefore necessary, we can understand how the existence of each thing is dependent on everything else. As such, each and every thing is necessarily and independently just so in and of itself, by virtue of everything and therefore nothing as a *condition sine qua non* for existence.

This then leads us to the question, being that: if everything is self-right (*zidang*), how does the world not result into a deterministic, albeit random, system? After all, even though the world is constantly transforming and generating itself, it is unclear how we can exercise our agency. But where does this agency come from? If it is a distinct "self" where we want such agency to come from, then we must first consider what constitutes the self for Guo Xiang. These questions and issues are indispensable in rehabilitating Guo Xiang's ontology from misconceptions of him as determinist and fatalist. Further than that, Chinese philosophy and culture is often touted to Anglophone readers as having no sense of individuality and therefore freedom,[1] whereas Guo Xiang provides a stalwart account of a self that is no longer split, a self that is both is and not, which allows for an alternative account of freedom. Nonetheless, we shall now demonstrate in the following discussions how Guo Xiang's conception of the self is dynamic, and therefore cannot be reduced into a single set of principles.

Fen 分: On the Precise Distinction of Each Thing

The assumption that Guo Xiang's philosophy is fatalist and even deterministic is not entirely without basis. For instance, in the following passage, where he discusses the concept of allotment (分 *fen*), we find him saying:

> Now if officials and concubines each commit only to their lot, then they will never be inadequate to govern each other. The alternate ordering of each other, like hands, feet, ears, and eyes, the four limbs and all the body parts, each has what it regulates, and they alternate in making use of each other.[2]
>
> 夫臣妾但各當其分耳，未為不足以相治也。相治者，若手足耳目，四肢百體各有所司而更相御用也。

At an initial read, this passage seems to suggest that whether one is a minister or a concubine, master or servant, one should simply be content with whatever is given to them at any given point. In fact, it seems as though they should not even wish for more or want to become more. Some might read this passage as implying something more similar to the traditionally Western or Christian use of the body (i.e., when St. Paul speaks of the Church as the "body of Christ" wherein Christ is the head and hence main controller of the rest in a clear hierarchy), in which case Guo Xiang would be advocating for the political contentment even of those who are oppressed, discriminated against, or pushed into the margins, because the system works as a whole, and so there is no point in demanding to be treated equally.

If we follow along this fatalistic logic, then it will have more dangerous ethical and political implications than said oppression. In this case, Guo Xiang's type of freedom would not only have the tendency for, but would inevitably lead to, suppression and despotism. This seems to be why Livia Knaul would call such a view "depressing."[3] Seen in this way, Zhuangzi's original passage that Guo Xiang was commenting on does not seem to be any less depressing, with Zhuangzi lamenting how humans always try to live with a purpose or master in mind. Seen in another way, however, "alternate in making use of each other" can be seen to presuppose equality albeit in unorthodox ways—meaning the way the hand serves the foot when the foot focuses on having to do something like walking, but the foot also serves the hand when the hand is focused on having to do something like jumping toward a tree in order to grab something, and so on.[4] While Zhuangzi laments how the autonomy of specific parts and singularities are mistakenly taken to be foreclosed in completion (*cheng* 成), Guo Xiang highlights how to avoid what Zhuangzi is lamenting, which is the ability of one part to extend and use the other through regulation and performing a role flawlessly, even when acting only for its own self. Indeed, Zhuangzi's metaphors on the body never use or refer to one certain or specific part as having unilateral control over others, and often he explicitly denies any possibility of a creator or controller of things. Similarly, it follows well from the logic of convergence, which explains the interconnectedness and intercausality that is most apparent in Guo Xiang's philosophy. Moreover, the reading that understands this passage to mean one part dominating the other is a superimposition of a theistic reading of Guo Xiang, as in the secularized version seen in Thomas Hobbes's *Leviathan*, wherein the sovereign wields absolute power and assumes the position of Jesus Christ, with everything and everyone else functioning only as part of his own body. In this model, which is the same model that dictatorial systems like fascism adopt, society is treated as one body, and is thus arguably rehashed version of this Christian model. Guo Xiang, on the other hand, allows each part to take the lead as they "alternate in making use of each other." Of course, this is not to discount the fact that the very existence of concubines itself is problematic and essentialist in terms of the role of women in society, but this is a case of a loophole not uncommon to philosophers who contradict themselves in order to have their views accepted in their time. Alternatively, Guo (not unlike Zhuangzi) may just have taken the social context in this specific instance for granted. Either way, the point remains that if we translate Guo Xiang's ontological system into a political one, concubines should not exist in the first place as it is essentializing, but the main idea of the passage that is about the regulation of everything by everything still holds true.

Thus, it is safe to say that for Guo Xiang's ontological system, just as it is for Zhuangzi's, if one commits to an identity that is fixed, then that is already problematic as one does not self-transform or self-generate. To be satisfied with one's lot means that one ought to recognize one's situation, circumstance, in that specific time and place, and move only within those confines, for only in that way can one actually self-transform, or can change come to be. The more one clings, either to past or future, current role or desired role, the more one strays from one's lot. Moreover, it is this clinging to a fixed identity, or fixed ideals (rather than assuming one's evolving place in society), that leads to tyranny. This is because once one has an idea of something fixed, something that one ought to be or one ought to strive for, one inevitably violates his dao, which is spontaneous or self-so. In the following passage, Guo Xiang addresses the possibility of tyranny directly in a passage of the *Zhuangzi* where the text tells us of the evil tyrant whose insatiable greed must be stopped. Guo Xiang comments with an interpretation of why the tyrant is such, and he says:

> The tyrant does not only seek to indulge his desire, but also seeks glory, yet this very seeking violates his own dao.[5]
>
> 夫暴君非徒求恣其欲，復乃求名，但所求者非其道耳。

Thus, it is when one seeks something external that one violates his dao, something unique and particular to each. In other words, things go wrong out of deviation from the correct path of that moment, and when that violation happens, then we have tyrants who seek to fulfils their ideals. This is why Guo tells us that the correct allotment (*fen*) should be followed in contentment and satisfaction—anything other than this, discontent and dissatisfaction beyond the proper dao—leads to the violation of the entire order of the whole and indeed the dao. But this still does not directly answer the essentialist charge, for it may very well be the case that Guo Xiang simply thinks that human nature is intrinsically good when nourished, and thereby given free and spontaneous rein, so anything external to it that meddles with the internal purity is automatically bad by virtue of pushing one's nature into disorder. After all, it is not uncommon for Chinese philosophers to hark back to the "good old days" when everything was supposedly well and good.[6] If, however, we recall Guo Xiang's logic of convergence, especially with regard to the notion of *li* 理, then we would know that this is simply impossible as a natural consequence of an ontology that avoids immutability and is, at any given time, never fixed. To call Guo Xiang's philosophy a deterministic and depressing view of the world is but a consequence of thinking that his system subscribes to a logic of "either-or" instead of being "both-and," as in contingency as necessity, the one as many, or as it were, a logic of convergence. In other words, while it can be quite misleading to refer to political passages such that one mistakenly thinks he is an essentialist, it is with strong evidence that we can see how Guo Xiang's philosophy is one that is committed to change and transformation, as well as individuality and uniqueness, but at the same time, and to the same extent, to the whole, to order, and to structure. Such order, in the sense of dialectical unity, however, is something that is emergent, meaning that it comes from the individual things and their uniqueness rather than the other way around.

Another way to understand the concept of allotment (*fen* 分) is to turn to an epistemological angle rather than a purely political one. In what follows, Guo Xiang explains what one's allotted nature, or the limit of one's nature, is, in such a way that it becomes clearer to us what the relation between *fen* and *li* is:

> The self-becoming (*ziwei* 自為) of every allotted nature (*xingfen* 性分) all comes from the ultimate natural patterns (*zhili* 至理) and therefore cannot be dispensed with. Therefore the person who is good at nourishing life follows as well as relies on this self-becoming.[7]
>
> 性分各自為者，皆在至理中來，故不可免也，是以善養生者，從而任之。

If, therefore, we know that allotment (*fen* 分) comes from the natural patterns (*li* 理) that are themselves emergent and self-so, then we also know that it cannot be something that is essentialist or fixed in nature, for such natural patterns are always in the plural even as they are one in their plurality and transformation. Participating in and yielding to the distinctions and allotments for each and every being is to understand that our connection with the natural patterns is constituted by our differences with each other and our uniqueness. Recognizing that we are different from each other and how that is necessary, despite being able to participate only in our limited capacity, is what it means to fully maximize our capability to nourish life. Indeed, in an earlier passage, Guo Xiang says:

> All this shows that the reason why the Peng flies at such a height is simply that its wings are large. When that which things of small material require are not dependent on anything large, then that which things of large material use are not

obtained from anything small. Therefore, natural patterns have their precise distinctions, things have their certain limits (物有定極). Each is sufficient to perform its function and each makes equal accomplishments. Consequently, if one neglects the main issue, living a life of forgetting about [one's] life, and making plans for it beyond what best suits one—function thus not corresponding to strength, nor action to inclination—then even wings like clouds hanging down from heaven will not be able to avoid exhaustion, nor flights of a few moments' duration be without obstacles.[8]

此皆明鵬之所以高飛者，翼大故耳。夫質小者所資不待大，則質大者所用不得小矣。故理有至分，物有定極，各足稱事，其濟一也。若乃失乎忘生之生而營生於至當之外，事不任力，動不稱情，則雖垂天之翼不能無窮，決起之飛不能無困矣。[9]

Here, Guo Xiang highlights the complementarity and even necessity of the parts to the whole, and how important it is that each part recognizes its distinct role in the larger order of things. When he says that the natural patterns have very precise limits (理有至分),[10] it is to emphasize the necessary differences of each and every one. Moreover, his emphasis on suitability—as demonstrated in his argument about how the Peng is only able to fly such heights because it has large wings—serves to show how Guo Xiang does not mean to say that all views or rightness are equally valid at all times and places, but instead, that there is something that is suitable for every single circumstance and situation, even if that circumstance is always relative to everything else. This is why "even wings like clouds hanging down from heaven" would be insufficient if one does not correspond to the specific circumstances that require a recognition of limitations. This is also seen in Zhuangzi's story about the Earl of He (*Hebo* 河伯) who comes to Ruo of the Northern Sea (*Beihai Ruo* 北海若) thinking that there was none equal to himself, but then sees the boundless realms of Ruo. Guo Xiang says of Ruo:

He knows his smallness and that it cannot be made great, so the natural pattern of allotment has a [naturally worthy] simplicity, a feeling of overreaching esteem cannot operate within it.[11]

知其小而不能自大，則理分有素，跂尚之情無為乎其間。

In other words, our differences are naturally emergent and highly contingent, which is exactly why one must be completely in accord with them. Our limitations are something that we cannot control, even if and because they are always changing, so the best way to be in accord with them is to not do anything about them (*wuwei* 無為). It is important to maintain one's limits because acknowledging this limitation is an acknowledgment of the nontotalization of a single unchanging reality and pattern. Guo Xiang further notes:

> If you use your limited nature to seek knowledge that is boundless, how can anyone not find himself in difficulty?[12]
>
> 以有限之性尋無極之知，安得而不困哉！

Elsewhere, this epistemological angle of allotment (*fen*) is also captured:

> So [I say] those who divide fail to divide; those who discriminate fail to discriminate.[13]
>
> 故分也者，有不分也；辯也者，有不辯也。
>
> All things have their own allotment, all affairs have their own distinctions. And still they want to make such allotments and distinctions themselves, without realizing that all things naturally distinguish themselves.[14]
>
> 夫物物自分，事事自別。而欲由己以分別之者，不見彼之自別也。

Guo Xiang explains how, if we try to see things from the vantage point of wanting to deliberately make the differentiation ourselves, we will then fail to actually see things. Those who consciously and deliberately try to make differentiations about what's what don't realize that all things differentiate themselves naturally and in a certain way that cannot be differentiated any differently.

Furthermore, on the ontological level, Guo Xiang would suppose that interactions of their distinct natures are necessary for order to emerge, as was seen in the passage of concubines and ministers, yet these distinctions continuously change and transform not only themselves but everything else in a process of mutual emergence. While this may seem oppressive and politically regressive if taken out of context, we are able to see how, for Guo Xiang, if one thing changes, then so does everything else (whether positively or negatively), because that is what the natural patterns (*li*) of the world are. This is reflective of Guo Xiang's overall project, which is to merge *ziran* 自然 with *mingjiao* 名教; synthesizing ontology and morality, and to show that these are not mutually exclusive of each other.[15] Seen this way, we can assume that these *fen*, these allotments and distinctions, can only be treated as true in their own singular moments in time. Otherwise, it would become external to *fen* and is what Brook Ziporyn translates as "traces" (*ji* 跡), which refers to remnants of what once was, no longer what is, and as such, cannot be treated as a fixed model for what should be imitated—this is also Guo Xiang's argument for why we should not imitate past models.[16] Guo Xiang says:

> What leaves the traces is the true nature. For those following the true nature of things, their traces are the six classics. Today, when people deal with things, they should consider *ziran* to be the shoes and the six classics to be the traces.[17]

所以跡者，真性也。夫任物之真性者，其跡則六經也。況今之人事，則以自然為履，六經為跡。

Though we can't treat the political parts literally, it is appropriate to look at the concept of allotment or distinctions in Guo Xiang from a specifically epistemological vantage point. That is to say, that recognizing one's limits and the equal legitimacy of a different, even contradictory, perspective of seeing how things are and ought to be does not trump one's own, and is actually even necessary for the legitimacy of one's own. Knowledge is only complete if it recognizes that it is incomplete,[18] and sufficiency can only be achieved through the recognition of insufficiency, for it is in their incompleteness, their insufficiency, that they are singularly complete and sufficient.

From this understanding of allotment (*fen*), we can see what Guo Xiang meant when he said:

> These five, all of these are those whose sufficiency is injured by deliberate action; they cannot remain in their original nature as they seek the external without end.

The external cannot be sought and so seeking it is regarded like a circle trying to learn to be a square, or a fish that's longing to be a bird.

Although one hopes for the wings of a fabulous phoenix, intending to imitate the sun and moon, as "this" gets even nearer to "that," it gets even further from what is real, learning [to be something else] is increasingly obtained yet [one's] nature is completely lost. Therefore, equalizing things is to shackle away what is still one-sided.[19]

此五者，皆以有為傷當者也，不能止乎本性，而求外無已。夫外不可求而求之，譬猶以圓學方，以魚慕鳥耳。雖希翼鷙鳳，擬規日月，此愈近彼，愈遠實，學彌得而性彌失。故齊物而偏尚之累去矣。

That is to say, that original nature (*benxing* 本性) does not actually mean that it is unchanging and fixed, or that it is inborn, for it simply means unfettered, that is, unadulterated by deliberate action. When subjects are given the space to self-organize without deliberate intervention (*ziran*), only then can order (*xu* 序) actually emerge,[20] one's nature becomes self-right, or right at the exact place where one is at that exact moment in time. That in itself is liberating inasmuch as it is of equal importance to everything else, in our mutual transformation and collective unfolding. As such, it is actually when one is caught up in a single moment or stuck in a still frame that is supposed to be in flux, that is, to hold on to a fixed value in refusal to identify with the spontaneous nature of things, that things will start to go awry.[21]

If, therefore, we are not supposed to imitate others, such as the wings of a fabulous phoenix, and be fulfilled in our own natures, is it because our own natures are different and we should be content with what we have, or is it because it is the same, so there is no point in deliberately trying to be different? To be more specific, do what define our natures come internally either by inherent constitution or willful agency, or do they come externally, from a kind of universal source, whether divine or worldly? As is shown in previous discussions, these are not necessarily contradictory to each other and in Guo Xiang, difference and sameness are one—not simply because they are complementary or don't contradict each other, but because they are necessary to the fullness of each, and are each of the other's logical extreme that allows one to exist.

In the following discussion, we will look the two angles of nature (性 *xing*):[22] one is one's individual or distinct nature (性分 *xingfen*), which I shall translate as allotted nature or natural allotment, depending on the context; the other one is one's endowed nature (*xingming* 性命). We focus on these two aspects because one highlights the particularity of *xing*, whereas the other denotes a relation to the whole, or to a conception of order in the world. These two, however, are equally important to the philosophy of Guo Xiang and are mutually necessary for the logical consistency of the other.

On One's Nature as Distinct (*xingfen* 性分)

Although the compound *xingfen* 性分 never appeared in the *Zhuangzi*, Guo Xiang often used it to denote the singular nature of each and every thing in the world, an idea that once again was already present in Zhuangzi. This, however, suggests that Guo treated it as a core concept in his rendering of Zhuangzi's philosophical system. In the following passage, Guo Xiang provides a critique of deliberate learning. He says:

> "Outside the limits of the world" means outside the allotted natures of all things. What is outside a thing's own allotted nature may have its own natural patterns, but since it is outside one's own allotted nature, the sage is never affected by it and thus the sage never discusses it. For if he did discuss it, he would be leading all things to study that which is beyond their own capabilities. Thus he does not discuss their externalities, rather, the eight demarcations[23] are in unison with their self-realizations.[24]
>
> 夫六合之外，謂萬物性分之表耳。夫物之性表，雖有理存焉，而非性分之內，則未嘗以感聖人也，故聖人未嘗論之。〔若論之〕，則是引萬物使學其所不能也。故不論其外，而八畛同於自得也。

What this means is that the sage does not talk about things that are external to one's allotted nature, that is, what is outside the sage's own spontaneous purview. Guo Xiang thus emphasizes what is internal to natural allotment (*xingfen zhi nei* 性分之內) and denounces any trace of externality. This allotted nature is what he calls *xingfen*, and by internal allotted nature, he means the present and concrete. This is because whatever is external, which Guo Xiang also refers to as traces (*ji* 跡), will lead to one-sided dominance and ontological oppression, which means that it will pervert the natural allotment of a thing. Furthermore, what is external to one's nature is something that is deliberate, therefore a trace, and is unnatural, since it does not change. By natural here, Guo Xiang means that it is changing, as it follows the change and transformation of the natural patterns of the world, and yet it cannot be deliberately changed. We can see the contrast when, like in the following passage, he presents a contrast with what is external to natural allotment (*xingfen zhi wai* 性分之外). He says: "Those that cannot be known, are all external to natural allotment. Thus, [knowledge] stops at what is internal to knowledge and yet it is supreme"[25] (所不知者，皆性分之外也。故止於所知之內而至也). In this passage, we again see Guo Xiang's epistemological position, which is to highlight the limits of knowing and the argument that we must acknowledge that our position in the world would inevitably limit us from knowing about a fixed universal truth or principle other than the principle of self-so (*ziran*), while at the same time, that limited perspective is "supreme" as it nonetheless contains within it all other possible knowledge. In other words, the contrast between internal and external can be characterized in terms of a resistance against an overarching canopy of truth and reality, a metanarrative. The acknowledgment of one's knowledge and experience as limited is supreme because it is also the recognition that difference exists and is integral to the mutual existence and transformation of our knowledge about each other as well the interconnectedness of our epistemic transactions. This not only allows us to listen to others without owning or imposing on them, but further than that, we learn that we *understand* something only in relation to us, and that is a better understanding than trying to deliberately, *fully* understand something else. Another passage that captures this is when Guo Xiang comments on a passage of Zhuangzi and says that it is because of the specificity of events and circumstances that it is no use to apply fixed methods or principles to them. The *Zhuangzi* text says:

> Zeng, Shi, Yang, Mo, Master Kuang, Carpenter Chui, and Li Zhu all set their Virtuosities outside themselves, using their radiance to disorder the world. But the world is something for which standards are of no use.[26]

彼曾、史、楊、墨、師曠、工倕、離朱，皆外立其德而以爥亂天下者也，法之所無用也。

What this passage means is that while it is true that these people had their own virtuosities (*de* 德), they only ever applied to their own selves. They truly were radiant and bright (*yue* 爥), yet the moment they tried to universalize this brightness, it just disorders the world. They tried to use their brightness and virtuosity as "standards," methods, or rules (*fa* 法), but this makes those standards external to everyone else and their particularities, so they bring nothing but disorder, have no good use, and thus should not be held on to. Guo Xiang then comments:

> These people are people who have various kinds of endowments, thus causing all under heaven to leap over themselves to imitate them. Imitating them then I lose myself, I lose myself because of an other, then that other becomes the principal disorder. That which is the great calamity of all under heaven is losing myself.²⁷

此數人者，所稟多方，故使天下躍而效之。效之則失我，我失由彼，則彼為亂主矣。夫天下之大患者，失我也。

If for the standards they use, their looking does not exceed what they see, then the eyes of all are clear-sighted. If their listening does not exceed what they can hear, then the ears of all are sharp. If their tasks do not exceed what they can do, then the techniques of all are skillful. If their knowing does not go beyond what is known to them, then the natures of all are comfortable and fit.

If their virtues do not go beyond what they themselves obtain, then the virtues of all are right. What use is there for establishing what they cannot seize, outside of their natural allotments, thereby causing the world to gallop off, unable to turn back?²⁸

若夫法之所用者，視不過於所見，故眾目無不明；聽不過於所聞，故眾耳無不聰；事不過於所能，故眾技無不巧；德不過於所得，故群德無不當。知不過於所知，故群性無不適；安用立所不逮於性分之表，使天下奔馳而不能自反哉！

Guo Xiang thus highlights the equality of all things, and how a single governing principle cannot be applied to all, or put simply, how one size does not fit all, and how not a single one is exceptionally and inherently special in his or her experience, circumstance, knowledge, or even virtue—not because one is not different, but precisely because one's own, just like everything else, is different from each other and each has one's own standard that can only be applied to oneself. What use is there, then, in establishing a *fixed* set of rules for what cannot be categorically applied to each and every single one's natural allotment or disposition? In the same way, we cannot use the model of the past as a fixed standard for our present actions. Guo Xiang is again going against the traditions of Chinese philosophy here in modeling the present according to the past,[29] taking the past sages as standards of emulation. He does so, however, not in and of themselves during their time and their circumstance, as we see when he also talks about them with reverence,[30] but Guo does remind us how we need to acknowledge that all of history evolves according to the changing circumstances, and so nothing can really be fixed and unchanging. Therefore, if we try to imitate what was appropriate for a past or different time and scenario, that is something external to *this* scenario and will fail to work. Values or standards espoused by sages ought to be practiced not in and of themselves, but as a means of rightness in that situation, that exact place and time, and how that specific sage made things cohere (*li*), which ultimately changes inevitably and infinitely. Guo thus reminds us to work on our own selves according to our own standards brought upon by our own circumstances, for only then can "the natures of all be comfortable and fit." To do otherwise is to lose one's own self and singularity, a mere copy of something else, which is ironically caused by the desire for a stable identity. Indeed, when we chase after ideals set upon us by others, model ourselves according to an ideal person or sage, we lose and sacrifice our individual self, seeking something that cannot in fact be seized, for we can never truly see ideal sages for who or what they are—we only see their traces, and traces are not real. The world is not made up of these traces because the world is dynamic, always transforming, hence something for which "standards are of no use" (法之所無用也). However, we must also remember that these "standards" go both ways: 1) toward moral cultivation and progress, but also 2) back into some primitive "natural" state.

In another comment that relates to how fixed standards lead to the loss of self, Guo Xiang discusses this second "standard" using a controversial example:

The true determinacy of horses is not such that they reject the saddle and hate to be ridden; it is just that they have no desire for superfluous luxury and honor. . . . One who is good at riding them does so by actualizing their abilities to the utmost; the way to do this is to let them follow their own spontaneity (*ziren* 自任). But if when they would walk, one makes them gallop, seeking a function that exceeds their ability, some will be unable to bear it and many will die. If however we allow both nags and steeds each to accord with its own power, going along with and fitting to the distinct determinacies of sluggish and swift, then although they leave their footprints all over the world's wildernesses and beyond, the natural determinacy of each horse will be kept whole. But when the deluded hear (us say), "Allow the horses to follow their own determinacies," they say we should release them and not ride them; when they hear talk of non-activity, they say walking is not as good as lying down; how is it that they go so astray without turning back!? They grievously miss Zhuangzi's point.[31]

馬之真性，非辭鞍而惡乘，但無羨於榮華。. . . 夫善御者，將以盡其能也。盡能在於自任，而乃走作馳步，求其過能之用，故有不堪而多死焉。若乃任駑驥之力，適遲疾之分，雖則足跡接乎八荒之表，而眾馬之性全矣。而惑者聞任馬之性，乃謂放而不乘；聞無為之風，遂云行不如臥；何其往而不返哉！斯失乎莊生之旨遠矣。

Though it may be shocking to the modern-day reader how Guo Xiang can just so easily justify the domination of horses, and how this is a defense of oppression, according to Brook Ziporyn, what Guo is pointing at here is the problem that is in "making the weak and slow horses try to conform to the standard of the strong and fast, that is, to make the petty man conform to the standard of the sages."[32] Since the *Zhuangzi* passage criticizes a man named Bo Le for forcing horses beyond their capacity to the point of death, this is a reasonable and faithful interpretation from Zhuangzi's perspective. However, it does not account for the latter part of Guo's comment about "the deluded." Indeed, I think there is something more to his criticism of those who think that horses "reject the saddle and hate to be ridden," and that we ought to "release them and not ride them." This seems more likely to be a direct rebuke of the primitivist interpretation of this chapter in the *Zhuangzi*,[33] which assumes that there is a "natural" state of things, which is stable and primitive. But there is no one single "natural" state of the world. There is no natural state in which horses are "free" only if they are spontaneously roaming in the wild, because they do not exist apart from the rest of the world. On the contrary, horses are prey animals, meaning they would live in constant fear of being hunted by wolves and lions "in the wild." One cannot just create a world where domesticated animals like horses (or pet cats and dogs, for that matter) can simply just be released in "nature" and the wild, and assume that it will all of a sudden dissolve their oppression and domination. We are part and parcel to the same world where past, present, and future are always already intertwined, where we cannot simply and deliberately try to go back into the past and undomesticate horses as a one-stop quick solution. The world is not so simple and to believe it to be so is what Guo would claim a delusion.

His point, therefore, is that the opposite of "freeing them into the wild" would not necessarily simply be domination, as there is no such natural state where they are "free in the wild." The assumption that the opposite of domination, which Zhuangzi was criticizing in the passage, is necessarily "freeing in the wild" and is the answer to domination is too simplistic and misses Zhuangzi's point of criticizing the tyranny of Bo Le. This is what Guo Xiang is arguing against, too, when he says that these same people are those who say that "walking is not as good as lying down." So, going back to the point of determinacies (*xing*), and one's allotted determinacy/nature (*xingfen*), it is just as wrong to superimpose some regressively fixed "natural" state to someone or something just as it is wrong to superimpose moral standards on anyone and everyone. Trying to erase everything "unnatural" to go back to something "authentic" is just as essentialist as assuming an external truth or ideal to which we must aspire. Both standards are external to what is "internal" to one's nature (*xing*).

Thus, Guo Xiang also dismisses the realization of one's nature (*xing* 性) *via negativa* and instead advocates the active and creative nature of spontaneity and being true to what it is, at that moment and in that situation. Moreover, a large part of this commentary can be attributed to Guo Xiang's rejection of the primacy of *wu* in Wei-Jin thought before him. There is perhaps nothing more direct than this passage where Guo gives a complete rejection of nonbeing by showing how it necessarily leads to superimposing an artificial stillness into being. At the same time, this passage also shows how each being's "self-so" is not as simple as "anything goes," which is to simply release the horses; instead, being self-so means that one is in accord with one's lot or *fen*.

In other words, it is the deliberate initiative to change one's own self according to such fixed standards, whether it be a fixed idea or nonbeing itself, that will lead to a loss of one's self. The self in this case, however, is the polar opposite of a Cartesian self that is unchanging and separate from the world, but nor is it a Humean self that is merely the sum total of experiences and thoughts (for it uniquely transforms unto itself); rather, it is a dialectical self that finds itself and its uniqueness via an act of forgetting. Guo Xiang notes:

> In a state of sitting in oblivion, what could there be unforgotten? First one forgets all outer manifestations (*ji* 跡), then one also forgets that which causes the manifestations. On the inside, one is unaware that there is a self (*shen* 身), on the outside one never knows that there is heaven and earth. Thus one becomes *utterly empty and can unite with the changes*, leaving nothing unpervaded.[34]

> 夫坐忘者，奚所不忘哉！既忘其跡，又忘其所以跡者，內不覺其一身，外不識有天地，然後曠然與變化為體而無不通也。

This forgetfulness, therefore, leads not to a forgetfulness full-stop, but to a forgetfulness that is a kind of remembering; a kind of remembering that remembers the nothing, one's own contradiction, for it has always already been there. It is this remembering of the nothing as well as the forgetting of all causes and all manifestations that leads to one's being self-so. Remembering, in the sense of recalling the nothing that has always already been there thus is to simply be constantly adapting to the what *is* there, which is also constantly changing. As such, one never has no identity as such, but one has no *fixed* identity or natural allotment (*xingfen*), because what one is, is constantly changing. Moreover, it is only through this singular transformation from remembering nothing that one can have a sense of belongingness and unity in the world, and through it, a sense of agency. This is more evident in an earlier passage where Guo Xiang says:

I take each transformation, both life and death, as "me." Since all are me, how can I ever be lost? Since I've never been lost, what worries can I have? Because one makes no resistance, one cries when others cry. But because one has no worries, one cries but does not lament. There is nothing I fail to take as me, so inner and outer are invisibly unified, past and present strung together on one thread, constantly renewed along with all transformations—so how could anyone know where the "me" is once and for all? So I say there is nowhere that I am not self-realized.[35]

夫死生變化，吾皆吾之。既皆是吾，吾何失哉！未始失吾，吾何憂哉！無逆，故人哭亦哭；無憂，故哭而不哀。靡所不吾也，故玄同外內，彌貫古今，與化日新，豈知吾之所在也！言無往而不自得也。

Again, this passage can be read as another renunciation of non-being as stillness, which is ultimately a kind of fixation still. As such, not only does this passage show a clear refutation of the idea of a "fixed nature" for Guo Xiang, for the real self is always changing, but also, it shows that in spite of and because of all the differences and uniqueness of every thing, one takes everything that is encountered—every transformation that one experiences—as one's self. In doing so, one blurs the lines between inner and outer, and ultimately transforms everything to become inner, to become "me." This is what Guo Xiang means when he talks about forgetting oneself: he means finding one's self in everything, to be *wu* so as to be *ziran*. Because past and present are unified in a single thread, one does not lament (*ai* 哀)—an emotion that makes one stuck in the past, that makes one fixated on the idea of something already lost. Yet, one takes outer factors to become inner in a constant and dialectical transformation, not removed, because again, it goes back to causality instead of a fixed nature, or even idea. The irony here is that one *takes* everything else to be herself, so that ultimately, there is nothing that is herself. As such, one becomes united with a constantly changing moment instead.

Moreover, this is why it is precisely when one thinks one's self to be removed from others, that is, whether deliberately withdrawn or inherently different and essentially unique in substance (whether positively or negatively) while everyone else is the same, that one loses her own self and inner nature, because in reality, inner is outer and vice versa. However, if one acknowledges that we are all different, then one realizes that we are all the same in that we are all different, and in our own equally right, self-so, ways. One of the passages that captures this best is when Guo Xiang opens the story of the Peng and Kun, and how Zhuangzi uses these images in order to show the equality of our allotted natures, no matter how big the difference, and no matter how one might seem to be better than the other. Guo Xiang says:

> The real existence of the Peng or Kun is a question of which I have made no detailed studies. But Zhuang Zi's leading idea is that one is self-realized when far-reaching and unfettered, indulging in doing nothing. He therefore carries smallness and greatness to their extreme limits in order to show the appropriateness of one's allotted nature.[36]
>
> 鵬鯤之實，吾所未詳也。夫莊子之大意，在乎逍遙遊放，無為而自得，故極小大之致，以明性分之適。

This passage shows relativity not in such a way that anything goes, or anything can be right or true, but, similarly to the sentiment of Deleuze and Guattari, "the truth of the relative"[37] in that it is right for the Peng and only the Peng to have large wings in the way that it was for the Peng, and it was right for the small bird and only for the small bird to be small in the way that it was for the small bird.

They are, again, similar in being different. According to Tang Yijie, this means that "if seen from another angle, they are absolute not only in their difference, but also, everything, in their essence, exists and moves in absolutely independent self-sufficiency."[38] He continues, saying that Guo Xiang "recognizes, on one hand, that things have difference, but on the other hand, that they are still not different. So he recognizes that difference and having no difference is the same. This is significant in the history of Chinese philosophy."[39] Indeed, this is a significant turn not only for Chinese philosophy but philosophy as a whole for it introduces an innovative logic whereby necessity is merged with contingency, the one is merged with the many, difference is taken as sameness, and indeed, as Tang Yijie notes, it is where "each thing's relative existence is enough for its absolute existence, hereby abolishing the difference between relative and absolute."⁴⁰ This is why in the following passage, Guo Xiang merges the notion of a particular nature, and one that is related to a collective functioning. He says: "his inner allotted nature stays intact, and nothing more. Each exactly matches the allotment of endowed nature"⁴¹ (全其性分之內而已。各正性命之分也). Thus, keeping one's allotted nature intact simply means one's actions and deliberations match what is internal to the allotment of one's endowed nature. The particular and the distinct are, at once, part and member to an underlying order and whole by virtue of their endowed nature. The *ming* 命 in *xingming* 性命 now thus takes on a new meaning in that it is not something that is predetermined in a linear or fixed manner, because like everything else in the world, it too is malleable in its constant transformation, lending to its uniqueness.

Endowed Nature (*xingming* 性命)

Guo Xiang points to the self as the sole standard (*fa* 法)⁴² of the self. This is an important claim that highlights the singularity and spontaneity of one's identity—where a whole's parts are already whole in themselves because it contains all the other parts in it in dialectical unity. However, he also highlights the oneness of differences and sameness of our natures, owing to their mutual yet singular necessity in the whole, through the concept of endowed nature (*xingming* 性命). One would imagine that this would lead to a logical tension, but as already established, this is precisely what Guo's logic of convergence allows for. This is evident in the following passage through the concept of *xingming*:

> Because their forms are mutually opposed, Mt. Tai is larger than an autumn hair. But if each and every one depends on its allotted nature, if each merges with its own limits, then what is large in form has never been excessive and what is small in form has never been insufficient. As long as each is sufficient only within their nature, then the tip of a hair in autumn does not particularly deem its smallness as small, and the great mountain does not particularly deem its greatness as great. And if we take sufficiency of the nature to be greatness, then nothing under heaven is more sufficient (to itself) than an autumn hair. Whereas if sufficiency to their own nature is

not what we mean by great, then even Mt. Tai can be called small. Thus it is said that: "Nothing in the world is larger than the tip of a hair in autumn, and Mt. Tai is small."[43]

When a great mountain is deemed small, then nothing in the world is great; when the tip of a hair is deemed as big, then nothing in the world is small, There is no smallness nor greatness, there is no long or short life, therefore cicadas do not covet greater camellias, and are delightfully self-realized, rejected quails don't value the heavenly pond and are glorious and admirable by means of their sufficiency. If each finds sufficiency in its natural state and is at peace with its endowed nature, then even heaven and earth are not sufficient to be deemed (especially) long-lived, and are thus born together with me, and all things are not sufficient to be deemed (especially) different, and are thus attained together with me. And so in the life of heaven and earth, what is not equal? In the self-realization of the ten thousand things, what is not the same?[44]

夫以形相對，則大山大於秋豪也。若各據其性分，物冥其極，則形大未為有餘，形小不為不足。〔苟各足〕於其性，則秋豪不獨小其小而大山不獨大其大矣。若以性足為大，則天下之足未有過於秋豪也；（其）性足者（為）大，則雖大山亦可稱小矣。故曰天下莫大於秋豪之末而大山為小。

大山為小，則天下無大矣；秋豪為大，則天下無小也。無小無大，無壽無夭，是以蟪蛄不羨大椿而欣然自得，斥鴳不貴天池而榮願以足。苟足於天然而安其性命，故雖天地未足為壽而與我並生，萬物未足為異而與我同得。則天地之生又何不並，萬物之得又何不一哉！

Guo Xiang explains here how deeming things as large and small are only judgments when in relation to the other, so that these qualities are actually ultimately nonexistent and hold no truth in themselves, because it is only if they are contrasted that they have fixed sizes. Since each is its own uniqueness in its own difference, only its own self can be the standard for itself, each is "large" enough and thus all the same, which itself results in the mutuality of all things. Such mutuality is possible because each has taken on its own nature and own self as the sole standard. Thus, explaining Zhuangzi's last line in the passage, which says:

> . . . heaven and earth are generated alongside me, and the ten thousand things are one with me.[45]

> . . . 天地與我並生，而萬物與我為一。

Everything in heaven and earth is equal in its endowed nature, everything is capable of realizing its own full potential of its endowed nature. This is possible because there is no universal principle that governs existence. Natural patterns and endowments are simply spontaneous, and therefore, diverse yet self-organizing. This is why Guo Xiang explains:

> We do not know the reason for they're being so and yet they are so, we call this fate. But this seems to imply a meaning or intention behind it, so [we] must then go on to dispel the use the of the name fate so as to understand their self-so [or spontaneity]. Only then is the real principle of "fate" completely expressed.[46]

> 不知其所以然而然，謂之命，似若有意也，故又遣命之名以明其自爾，而後命理全也。

Moreover, Tang Yijie notes that Guo Xiang places an emphasis on the notion of fate (*ming* 命) "so that people can understand that things are originally generating and transforming in a spontaneous way (no reason why)"[47] and that "nothing tells them to be such—this is really the true meaning of '*mingli*'"[48] because the natural patterns of [fate's] endowment (*mingli*) is simply a manifestation of being simply-such or self-so (*zier* 自爾). This fate or "endowment" (*ming* 命)[49] of natural patterns (*li*) might seem to be something that pertains to a spiritual being, something that is higher than us and therefore has the capability to bless the creatures of the world, and by virtue of that capability alone, is otherworldly or religious. This is, however, not the case not only from what we know of natural patterns or coherence (*li*) as something that is simply spontaneous from our previous discussions, but also because Guo Xiang says:

> Natural patterns certainly correspond to each other, as if a god/gods are causing them. Natural patterns spontaneously correspond to each other, they mutually correspond not

because anything causes them to do so, so even though they mutually correspond, there is nothing divine [causing them].⁵⁰

理必有應，若有神靈以致之也。理自相應，相應不由於故也，則雖相應而無靈也。

What this means is that change and transformation is not from the top-down, but something that is dialectical, which makes the correspondences and mutual transformations spontaneous and without reason for being so, other than that they are so, for if each were not so, then everything else wouldn't be so either. Conversely, if everything else were not so, then this particular thing will not be so either. This is why each natural pattern or coherence (*li*), which is unique to any singular thing and thereby ironic (or having incoherence as coherence, as mentioned earlier), is necessarily so. They have no cause, yet are caused by everything else, yet everything else is always changing, so each thing is also always changing and contingent to that change. It is useful here to cite what Tang Yijie also says about this same passage, noting that "in this world, nothing is identical, so there is no need to strive for sameness, but rather, it is sufficient to simply agree to yield to all the natural activities of things accordingly."⁵¹ This is generally true, but one might notice the irony in Tang's language here, which is *striving* for sameness versus *yielding* to the natural activities of things, which he takes as contradictory, favoring the latter against the former. However, everything must indeed, all the same, *strive* in order to *yield*. This is a different kind of striving from striving for something that is external to one's lot—a conventional striving. At a more ultimate level, however, the strife is all the same a strife, but this time to yield, which is similar to the remembering of nothing that has always already been there, discussed in the previous passage. This dialectic of striving and yielding is again an instance of the logic of convergence applied. That is to say, that it is ultimately a kind of yielding because it is spontaneous but is nonetheless determined by one's own difference according to the difference of one's own circumstance, and so, though nonidentical, is also still the same in their difference, and is thus both self-so and a striving toward being self-so, or to adapt to one's own different circumstantial variables.

Guo Xiang's focus on the differences, while at the same time acknowledging sameness and mutual correspondence, leads to a convergence of universal and particular, concrete and abstract. This is why Guo Xiang also says:

All this [talk of death] above [in the *Zhuangzi* text], [means that] everything is without knowing their reason for being so and yet they are so, that is why it is said to be obscure. Now those who do not yet know all come to spontaneously know without knowing how they know; those who are born all are spontaneously born without knowing how they are born.

The ten thousand things are different from each other, but when it comes to life [they all] do not pursue knowledge [of why they are so], and so none of them are not alike. In all under heaven, thus, nothing is not obscure.⁵²

凡此上事，皆不知其所以然而然，故曰芒也。今未知者皆不知所以知而自知矣，生者〔皆〕不知所以生而自生矣。萬物雖異，至於生不由知，則未有不同者也，故天下莫不芒也。

This merging of contingency and necessity, of everything as cause of everything else, is what allows Guo Xiang to concretize fate (*ming*), which moves away from the mystical interpretations of the *Zhuangzi*. This is the logic of convergence at play, and is precisely why fate (*ming*) cannot be something that is assigned by a higher being or naturally so. In fact, it is precisely because each thing has its own nature at any given moment, and its own constantly changing allotment, that it is impossible to know how each thing operates in relation to everything else. Such nature and allotment is internal to an individual thing because something external would simply be another standard, so it only makes sense that each thing can manifest only its own internality in such a way that it allows for others to do the same, because an "other" will never be able to manifest another's nature or allotment. This is why the recurring use of the term "endowed nature" or "natural endowment" (*xingming* 性命) in Guo Xiang's philosophy can only reflect something that is internal. This "internality" is not static over time—what is internal at any given moment is just what is self-so and vanished, done without effort, and what one has adapted to at that time—constantly changing, yet "fixed" in the sense of being unchangeable by anything external at that moment in time.

The Spontaneity of Heaven's⁵³ Endowments

With all this emphasis on change and transformation, however, why then does Guo Xiang still say this nature of ours cannot be escaped from nor added to, and that we simply are where we should be? In a passage from the *Zhuangzi* about the death of Lao Dan, Zhuangzi rebukes those who mourn him excessively, going beyond their appropriate emotions, which is what they are endowed with. So Guo Xiang then comments to clarify that "heavenly-endowed nature is what [we] receive, each has an original allotment, which cannot be escaped [from], nor added to[54] (天性所受，各有本分，不可逃，亦不可加). What Guo means here, however, is that the deliberate acts of escaping and adding are superficialities that the mourners are forcing upon themselves. Guo Xiang does not mean that nature is static and fixed, but that it cannot be forced, and that how we act must be appropriate to the circumstance that, in this case, was not, since those who were excessively mourning were people who barely knew Lao Dan. On the contrary, our natures actually continually transform, but in their transformations, they are whole, singular, and therefore have what is appropriate for each moment in time. They change, but they cannot *be* changed, they mutually interact and form each other but cannot *be* formed, that is, not deliberately in a way that is essentially a motivational change in a linear manner. As such, they cannot exceed the very limit, which is changing deliberately, as one cannot deliberately change one's nature in order to achieve a specific end, even though it is bound to change in a spontaneous way when allowed to do so. As such, attempting to overstep one's limit happens when one superimposes a certain will toward one's own nature. One should not confuse nondeliberate with nonactivity, however. Guo Xiang makes it clear that it is not the same thing:

> **Ruo of the Northern Sea said, "That oxen and horses have four legs is the Heavenly. The bridle around the horse's head and the ring through the oxen's nose are the Human.**[55]

北海若曰：「牛馬四足，是謂天；落馬首，穿牛鼻，是謂人。

In the life of man, can we not use oxen and ride horses? When using oxen and riding horses, can we not pierce [the noses of oxen] and put yokes [around the necks of horses]?

Oxen and horses do not refuse this subjection, because it is suitable to the strength of their heavenly endowment. As long as it is in accord with the heavenly endowment, then even though the ornamentation [of nose rings and yokes] is men's doing, nonetheless, the source is from the heavenly.⁵⁶

人之生也，可不服牛乘馬乎？服牛乘馬，可不穿落之乎？牛馬不辭穿落者，天命之固當也。苟當乎天命，則雖寄之人事，而本在乎天也。

This is another instance of Guo Xiang responding to those who interpret the *Zhuangzi* as emphasizing nonactivity and primitivistic. Guo Xiang is saying that even though there are things that we can say are "heavenly" and things that are human, we must not misinterpret "human" to mean forced or automatically artificial. So, instead of endorsing a binary between the heavenly and human, as the original passage might look like, he blurs it, which is in fact more in line with the rest of Zhuangzi's general disposition. In this world, Guo Xiang is saying, we are inevitably interconnected and interlinked. There is no such thing as a hard reset for everything to go back to what is purely "heavenly" because no such purity exists. We all depend on each other for existence and life, and the best we can do is to make sure that whatever we do "is suitable to the strength of their heavenly endowment." Hence for Guo Xiang, one cannot simply abandon society and social relations altogether, inasmuch as one cannot get fixated on them. Thus, the overarching idea here is that there is no fixed and unchanging dialectic between what is heavenly or natural, versus what is human, because ultimately, we all need each other for the entire network of this world to function.

Of course, there are scholars who disagree with this interpretation. Tang Yijie, himself a Guo Xiang scholar, has a different take, insisting that it is a consequence of Guo Xiang's philosophy to superimpose on the nondominating philosophy of the *Zhuangzi*.⁵⁷ Jiang Limei, who considers the spiritual nature of heaven as an edifying force toward humans, even criticizes Guo Xiang for downplaying the possibility of transcendence that is supposedly originally found in Zhuangzi's philosophy.⁵⁸ Yuet-Keung Lo, however, goes as far as to claim that Guo Xiang "flattens" heaven, saying: "In the cosmic web of things, every member exists on its own and is equal in its own right; there is no master-servant relationship between things in which the master's existence justifies that of the servant. . . . More importantly, none can rise above the rest as the master because heaven is flat. In this sense, heaven is also egalitarian and the myriad things are all equal in their membership in heaven."⁵⁹ Furthermore,

Lo points out that this ontological flatness of heaven meant that there could not be any master cause that is external to all things, and that "lone-transformation also refers to an entity's interdependent evolution itself."[60] Lo's interpretation makes more sense and fits better into Guo Xiang's system. However, it is important to note that the result of this flatness is not the fragmentation of things, or rendering things as merely two-dimensional, but rather, is an elevation of things and their agency in the vast network of dynamic objects. For Guo Xiang, it is mutual dependence and intergrowth (*xiangyin* 相因) that allows for something to be lone-transforming (*duhua*). This is why Guo says:

> The efficacy of intergrowth is best manifested in perfect lone-transformation. What man relies on is heaven and what heaven engenders is lone-transformation. People all take heaven as their father, so they dare not dislike the change of day and night as well as the regulation of summer and winter; they follow heaven and live peacefully with these changes. How much more so for lone-transformation projecting into the realm of mysterious darkness such that one will not let it take its own course? Letting it take its own course, [one should follow] the transformation of life into death as if one would obey the command of fate.[61]

> 夫相因之功，莫若獨化之至也。故人之所因者，天也；天之所生者，獨化也。人皆以天為父，故晝夜之變，寒暑之節，猶不敢惡，隨天安之。況乎卓爾獨化，至於玄冥之境，又安得而不任之哉！既任之，則死生變化，惟命之從也。

In sum, Heaven is the term for the totality of things, and because it is composed of the myriad things, it is a collection of things that are mutually dependent and in intergrowth among each other and so are ultimately transforming unto themselves. Moreover, it is worth noting here that fate (*ming* 命) comes from Heaven (天 *Tian*), yet heaven, that which endows individuals with allotment and therefore nature, is not something that is fixed. Only if "heaven" is a fixed metaphysical entity would the apparent fatalism or essentialism of Guo Xiang be dangerous because at that point, nothing else changes. We know, however, that this is not the case. Guo Xiang says that "heavenly principle is self-so, knowledge does nothing in its midst"[62] (天理自然，知故無為乎其間).

It is "self-so," meaning it has no other cause and is simply spontaneous. Heaven, the objective reality of the world, is an ontological force that has nothing that shapes the universe in a fixed and linear manner, because it is empty.[63] Being spontaneous and self-so means it's always changing, and if this is what heaven is, then it must follow that the nature that it endows upon us must also be ever-changing. As Guo Xiang quite straightforwardly describes:

> "Heaven" is just a way of saying "what is so of itself, the self-so." For doing cannot be done by someone "doing" doing. Doing is spontaneously doing; it is self-so. Knowing does not know by someone "doing" knowing. Knowing is spontaneously knowing; it is self-so. As self-so knowing, knowing is not a result of knowing, is unknown, is itself a kind of nonknowing. Being always in this sense a nonknowing, what we call knowing emerges from nonknowing. As self-so doing, doing is not the result of doing, is undone, is itself a kind of nondoing. Being always in this sense a nondoing, what we call doing comes from nondoing. Since doing comes from nondoing, nondoing is always the master. Since knowing comes from nonknowing, nonknowing is always the source. Hence, the Genuine Human Being discards knowledge and thereby knows, does nothing and thereby does. Self-so, they come to life; sitting and forgetting, they find themself. It is only for this reason that they are described as eliminating knowledge and discarding doing.[64]

> 天者，自然之謂也。夫為為者不能為，而為自為耳；為知者不能知，而知自知耳。自知耳，不知也，不知也則知出於不知矣；自為耳，不為也，不為也則為出於不為矣。為出於不為，故以不為為主；知出於不知，故以不知為宗。是故真人遺知而知，不為而為，自然而生，坐忘而得，故知稱絕而為名去也。

Thus, we see heaven as a transformation, ironically, from the bottom up, instead of from the top downward. Such a bottom-up transformation allows the world to transform itself into itself, within itself, yet somehow, it is not the same as it was a moment ago, and will not be the same world in the next moment, because as discussed earlier transformation necessitates emergence, and vice versa.

Through this interpenetration and intergrowth (*xiangyin*) we can surmise that the self for Guo Xiang also interpenetrates the world and is constantly transforming and emergent from the world itself as well. Each self has its own unique nature and unifies with all others and thereby remains within its allotment (*fen*), despite such allotment being also in a constant flux. One's self is therefore never exclusive unto itself, and therefore never different. It is distinct, yet everything else is also distinct, therefore it is the same as everything and everyone else. It is unchangeable, in this exact moment, but it will inevitably change, and that is an eternal occurrence—change is constant, what is constant is change. Just as is the structure of Guo Xiang's notion of heaven and causality, so also here, self therefore, is shaped not by an inner agency that comes transcendentally from nowhere, but by things of the world, others that surround and influence it, yet since it is everything else that influences and penetrates the self, then it is ultimately shaped only by itself. Not only does linear causality break down, the very categories of self and other also break down. This is what ultimately allows for an innovative conception of freedom as seen in Guo Xiang's philosophy of *zide*.

4

Freedom as Autonomy

Independence and Dependence

We now understand how the self and its inherent connection to others and otherness, while it remains unique and singular. We know that natural tendencies and identities of things are shaped not by an external thing or an overarching source but are emergent from the interaction and interpenetration of unique selves, which are always in the process of change and transformation. Such change and transformation allows the self to interpenetrate other selves, while those other selves also interpenetrate selves that are other than them, and so ultimately transforms only within itself. In this manner, the epistemological binary between self and other breaks down. This breakdown is necessary as a significant step to one's own self-realization and freedom, which goes beyond dependence and independence, as well as Isaiah Berlin's formulations of positive and negative liberties.

In Berlin's seminal essay on the *Two Concepts of Liberty*, he provides a powerful critique against the notion of positive liberty on the basis that it superimposes ends on the human being and, hence, treats one as a means to an end rather than as ends in themselves. However, Berlin fails to recognize that no one is an "end" removed from all other means—in a network of both humans and nonhumans where our actions have consequences that affect each other, we are all ends and means—the dichotomy is moot. Berlin argues: "In the end, men choose between ultimate values; they choose as they do, because their life and thought are determined by fundamental moral categories and concepts that are, at any rate over large stretches of time and, space, a part of their being and thought and sense of their own identity; part of what makes them human."[1] But what if those ends, those moral categories and concepts have been predetermined by external factors?[2] Needless to say, it is naïve at best to assume that our thinking and the formation of these moral categories and concepts that every person has—even if one does not impose them on others—exist without conditions causing them to arise. Equally naïve is the implied assumption that rationality is removed from the circumstances that affect how we conceive of the values that we hold dear. For Berlin, autonomy means that we can govern ourselves and our decisions contra outside factors. This is why he criticizes those who "retreat to the inner citadel."[3] Since "heteronomy is dependence on outside factors,"[4] and they cannot control those outside factors, they thus simply choose to escape within and remove themselves from "the empirical, world of causality."[5] While it is not within our scope to provide a comprehensive analysis of Berlin's critique of these apparent mystics, it would suffice to note that his remark on heteronomy marks a clear distinction from autonomy. This further shows the dichotomous logic that governs his concept of autonomy, where the binary self is something other than the external world.

The following chapters on freedom, therefore, aim to show that freedom and autonomy can transcend such dichotomy between positive and negative liberty, or freedom to and freedom from, respectively. By drawing on the previous chapters' conception of the nondichotomous self, one might mistake Guo's concept of autonomy as similar to Berlin's "retreat to the inner citadel," for it seems to absorb the external into the internal. In this chapter and the next, we will see that it is actually quite contrary. While Guo Xiang's conception of the self emerges from a breakdown of (linear) causality, it is also a robust affirmation of the network of cause and effect—of dependence and interdependence. Freedom, in this sense, is a realization of the nondichotomous and nonessentialized self. For Guo Xiang, one who is free is capable of being both fully independent and dependent at the same time, precisely because such a self transcends the subject-object, or internal and external, divide. Although it is often claimed that self-determination is necessary for self-realization,[6] I show here how it is possible to turn this inside out, that is, how it is self-realization achieved through radical dependence that is actually necessary for self-determination and independence.

In sum, this chapter is a discussion on independence (*wudai* 無待) and dependence (*youdai* 有待), which argues that dependence is inexorably intertwined with achieving independence, as is consistent with Guo

Xiang's logic of convergence. The significance of this lies in the idea that a fundamental dependence is required for achieving independence and self-determination, and ultimately freedom. It is impossible for the self to exist in isolation, as was shown in the previous chapter. As such, its thinking and agency cannot arise from nowhere. However, this does not mean that one's self and agency will arise from a particular source either, as was shown in the first main chapter. Rather, one's own self, thought, and agency arise from the world itself, in a dialectical relationship of being released unto the world itself. In other words, freedom and therefore autonomy, or in Guo Xiang's articulation, self-realization (*zide*), is independence from one's environment inasmuch as it is, dialectically speaking, dependence on one's environment.

Independence (*wudai* 無待) and dependence (*youdai* 有待) are central concepts in Guo Xiang's philosophical enterprise. Scholars such as Liu Xiaogan, however, note that "the *Zhuangzi* does not have anything known as independence (*wudai*), and although there is dependence (*youdai*), it also still isn't a philosophical category. Taking dependence (*youdai*) and independence (*wudai*) as philosophical categories is not of the *Zhuangzi*, but of the commentary of Guo Xiang."[7] If, therefore, Guo Xiang felt the need to tease out these concepts from Zhuangzi's philosophical system, it is because they are core conceptions to hold together the philosophical enterprise of which he had conceived. Indeed, the *Zhuangzi* never mentions *wudai*, and there are only three passages where it mentions *youdai*. While two of these pertain to life and death, and one is directly about causality, it is as Liu Xiaogan claims: they aren't philosophical categories. Nonetheless, Guo Xiang's commentary posits a philosophical interpretation to these terms, and so if we are to understand Guo's systematic philosophy founded on the *Zhuangzi*, we ought to analyze them philosophically.

Let us begin by looking closely at one of the direct mentions of *youdai*, which pertains to the topic of life and death, not only for the sake of brevity, but also because it taps into the concept of having no deliberate heart-mind (*wuxin*) which is an integral concept for Guo Xiang's notion of self-realization (*zide*) and autonomy.

Radical Dependence

In the following passage, Yan Hui asks Confucius about how, even when he does the same things in the same way as Confucius does them, he cannot fathom why people are drawn to Confucius even when he does nothing. Here is Confucius's answer in the Zhuangzi text (in bold), followed by Guo Xiang's commentaries by the line:

"Ah," said Confucius, "we had best look into this! There is no grief greater than the death of the heart-mind—beside it, the death of the body is a minor matter.

仲尼曰：「惡！可不察與！夫哀莫大於心死，而人死亦次之。

Now the heart-mind regards death as death, so it immediately experiences its death; the immediacy of its death, is due to grieving the loss of itself. When there is no grief, one is himself. When there is grief, then it is the death of the heart-mind. So, [this] grief is greatest.

夫心以死為死，乃更速其死；其死之速，由哀以自喪也。無哀則已，有哀則心死者，乃哀之大也。

The sun rises out of the east, sets at the end of the west, and each one of the ten thousand things moves side by side with it.

日出東方而入於西極，萬物莫不比方，

All this can be seen.

皆可見也。

Creatures that have eyes and feet must depend on them to complete their labor.

有目有趾者，待是而後成功，

Eyes complete the labor of seeing, feet complete the labor of walking.

目成見功，足成行功也。

When it comes forth, they appear; when it sets, they disappear.

是出則存，是入則亡。

It is simply due to not being able to see it that it disappears, ultimately [meaning that] it does not disappear.

直以不見為亡耳，竟不亡。

For all the ten thousand things it is so. [Their] death is dependent on something, [their] life is dependent on something.

萬物亦然，有待也而死，有待也而生。

Depending on the hidden is called death, depending on the manifest is called life. Ultimately thus, nothing [really] dies or lives.

待隱謂之死，待顯謂之生，竟無死生也。

Having received this one complete physical form, I hold on to it, without changing, in this way waiting for the end [of my life].

吾一受其成形，而不化以待盡，

As [physical] being is unable to transform and become nonbeing, thus [as soon as] anything receives any complete physical form, there will be no time when its transformations are finished.[8]

夫有不得變而為無，故一受成形，則化盡無期也。

I move in conformity to all things,

效物而動，

He is spontaneously without a deliberate heart-mind,

自無心也。

day and night without break,

日夜無隙，

So he eternally changes anew.

恆化新也。

but I do not know what the end will be.

而不知其所終；

He does not regard death as death.

不以死為死也。

Like smoke, my bodily form takes shape.

薰然其成形，

Like smoke it spontaneously forms: How could any doing have to be added to this?

薰然自成，又奚為哉！

I understand that fate cannot be regulated beforehand; I proceed in this way, day after day.[9]

知命不能規乎其前，丘以是日徂。

He is not bound to the past, and follows along wherever transformations go, so [he lives and dies] day after day.[10]

不係於前，與變俱往，故日徂。

This passage is philosophically dense as it tackles many core concepts in Guo Xiang's philosophy. The heart-mind (*xin* 心), according to Guo Xiang, experiences death immediately. By this, he means that by recognizing death, it dies; it dies due to grieving its own loss. The death of one's heart-mind (*xin*), as that which exercises the act of cognition, is effectively the loss of oneself precisely because it is a contemplation of a lack that effectively makes that lack real because it goes beyond itself to look at itself, it goes beyond its allotment (*fen*).[11] Living, therefore, is all about complete dependence within the process of the system. We see this in the following line where Guo Xiang seems to strikingly touch on the theme of perception in its relation to reality. While the theme of dependence and causality is present even in the original *Zhuangzi* text, only in Guo Xiang's commentary do we see the dynamic of perception and reality being raised. Interestingly, Guo Xiang both affirms and denies perception as reality. He says that perception and action are what complete reality, because it is simply what we see or walk on that is real to us. Further than that, Guo here is denying a split between reason or perception and reality—it is the physical feet, the physical eye, that walks or sees, nothing more. In the same way, there is nothing, not even nonbeing, that is behind this material reality, which exists as we perceive it. As such, the logical consequence is also that things die only when we stop perceiving them. This then means that nothing ultimately ever perishes—we only feel and think that they do—for that death only exists in one's heart-mind. Once one's body is here, physically and materially, it does not become nonbeing but simply transforms into other things—other substances, other chemicals—and so never is there a point where what is already being, or materially here, becomes nonbeing. Each thing is thus *radically* and completely dependent on others for its existence and transformations. This is what Guo Xiang means when he says "there will be no time when its transformations are finished." He then goes back to Confucius and discusses how Confucius deals with this reality, going on to explain that Confucius doesn't deliberately change for any long-term or future goal and is a mere receptacle for the world's fleeting moments, therefore constantly transforming and dying every single day. He has no heart-mind (which is the ideal state, since grieving one's heart-mind acknowledges its existence and therefore in that instance, one loses oneself) that superimposes upon things, so he is able to move in conformity to all things. Since those things are constantly changing, then so does he. However, he does not regard death as death, unlike one who has a heart-mind, for one who has no heart-mind passes on no judgment on what is real or true. One who has no heart-mind does not ruminate for there is no linear and sensibly coherent explanation to ruminate on. His body forms spontaneously, so he follows that spontaneity, not being bound to the past by deliberately trying to change the future. Confucius thus simply follows along wherever transformations go. In this manner, he lives by the day, living and dying at each rising and setting of the sun. This is thus the image that Guo Xiang provides us in order to show what real dependence, complete dependence is: the complete lack of a deliberate heart-mind (無心 *wuxin*)—this lack is the complete embodiment of the world's change and transformation, of life and death.

Ultimately thus, having no heart-mind—being prisoner to no desire or external truth, becoming free of trouble, and thus independent—is all about dependence and causality. As was seen in the chapter on ontology, Guo Xiang maintains that nothing comes from nothing, and everything comes from everything (物生之自得; 自生; 獨生; 自化; 獨化). This is so with human agency as well—there is nothing in this world that can arise from absolute nothingness, or have no cause at all, for on the contrary, everything causes everything else, and precisely for this reason, that each thing is a convergence of all others, making each the cause for its own self: dependence and independence converged.

As I've mentioned earlier, Guo Xiang does not repeatedly mention these concepts over and over, and there are few passages where he discusses them in detail, but they are nevertheless philosophically charged. More specifically, in this next passage, we see him linking the notion of independence (*wudai*) to the text's mention of dependence (*youdai*), despite the text only using the latter, and as merely a normative rather than a philosophical term. The second retelling of the story of the Penumbra and Shadow in the *Zhuangzi* goes as follows:

> **Penumbra said to Shadow, "A little while ago you were looking down and now you're looking up, a little while ago your hair was bound up and now it's hanging loose, a little while ago you were sitting and now you're standing up, a little while ago you were walking and now you're still—why is this?"**[12]

> 眾罔兩問於景曰：「若向也俯而今也仰，向也括〔撮〕而今也被髮，向也坐而今也起，向也行而今也止，何也？」

Shadow said, "Quibble, quibble! Why bother asking such a petty question?

景曰：「搜搜也，奚稍問也！

Movement is self-so, there is no reason to inquire about such a petty question.

運動自爾，無所稍問。

I do them without knowing how or why.

予有而不知其所以。

Self-so, thus [are things for which we] cannot know the reason why.

自爾，故不知所'。

I'm the shell of the cicada, the skin of the snake—something that seems to be but isn't.

予，蜩甲也，蛇蛻也，似之而非也。

The Shadow resembles a form yet is not that form.

影似形而非形。

In firelight or sunlight I draw together, in darkness or night I disappear.

火與日，吾屯也；陰與夜，吾代也。

Is there not an other on which I depend?

彼吾所以有待邪？

And that other is further dependent on others!

而況乎以有待者乎！

It moves yet there is a limit to it. Thus, if this is what is said to be dependent, it follows that it is ultimately independent, and so the natural coherence (*li*) of lone-transformation is evident.

推而極之，則今之（所謂）有待者（率）（至）於無待，而獨化之理彰（矣）。

If that other comes, then I come with them; if they go, then I go with them; if they come with the Powerful Yang, then I come with the Powerful Yang. But this Powerful Yang—why ask questions about it?"[13]

彼來則我與之來，彼往則我與之往，彼強陽則我與之強陽。強陽者又何以有問乎？」

Since the power of Yang simply moves around spontaneously, they simply come and go in accordance with each other. There is no intention [behind this], so it cannot be inquired about.[14]

直自強陽運動，相隨往來耳，無意，不可問也。

The power of Yang is manifest in the shadow and umbra, and these, consequently, are also dependent on their source. But why the second retelling? Two things appear here for the first time: Guo's usage of dependence (*youdai*) as a philosophical category, and the concept of the "Powerful Yang." Yang also means sun, so this passage really tells us how, in this world, if the sun revolves and moves, it does so simply because it does so, there is no reason or motivation that causes it to move—that is simply how the world goes. So, the penumbra simply follows along according to how that sun moves, and if that sun moves along in a spontaneous way, it follows that the penumbra is also ultimately spontaneous, without cause, independent (*wudai*). According to Guo, sun, all that depends on it (which the penumbra itself depends on), penumbra, and shadow, these all spontaneously spring up and follow the emergence of the other. As such, if we trace the source on which the shadow depends, it will be a dependence ad infinitum, and if we inquire about the reason shadow does what it does, there will be reasons ad infinitum, all related to the others, so in the end, everything depends on everything, and everything is the reason for everything. Guo Xiang then takes the narrative to its natural logical consequence, that since everything follows everything, then all things are therefore lone-transforming (*duhua*). To lone-transform, thus, is to *completely* depend. Here, we again see the logic of convergence at work, not just in activity but also in composition. Since the shadow completely depends on the penumbra, which ultimately depends on the "Powerful Yang," something active and bright, something the shadow is not, it also contains within it that brightness—its own contradiction. Furthermore, notice also that the shadow explains how he can only do whatever he does by means of following or being in accordance with his source, hence dependent and limited. The penumbra then, in its relation and dependence to the shadow, also acts in accordance with that source. Yet that source on which the shadow and penumbra depend is further dependent on another, and so on and so forth. This is why Guo Xiang says that "if this is what is said to be dependent, it follows that it is ultimately independent." To move with a limit, and yet be in that constant movement, is to be infinitely and completely dependent, which Guo argues is what is meant by "independence," because it is not dependent on any one thing that moves it. In the end thus, there can be no difference between dependence (*youdai*) and independence (*wudai*). Complete dependence is complete independence, and vice versa. Ultimately, this causal interdependence is the very condition sine qua non of one's independence. However, this independence only emerges from an unknowing generativity, for it is precisely in performing and following one's role (one's own *fen* 分) at that given instant in the process of this systematic intercausation, without knowing why (because knowledge is capable of understanding mere linear narratives), that one fulfills perfect dependence and therefore spontaneous independence.

Although it is in Guo Xiang where we see this radical intercausality lead to "independence," that everything depends on everything is a major theme in the *Zhuangzi*. When the text says "hiding the world in the world, such that there is nowhere to escape to"[15] 藏天下於天下而不得所遯, Guo Xiang again highlights this for us, commenting:

> There is nowhere in which it is hidden, yet all relies on it. Thus, nothing does not vanish into things, nothing is not one in change. Therefore, there is no external and no internal,

no death and no life. The entire body of heaven and earth are one with change and transformation, so there is nowhere to escape to, or to not realize.[16]

無所藏而都任之，則與物無不冥，與化無不一。故無外無內，無死無生，體天地而合變化，索所遯而不得矣。

Zhuangzi is overtly prescriptive here, emphasizing how we must make everything the standard of everything (or each thing as the standard of itself), and thereby model ourselves, including how we feel about life and death, according to the transformations of the world itself: one must hide the world in the world. Guo Xiang then explains this with the same level of prescriptiveness, telling us that everything vanishes (*xuan* 冥) into everything, *depends* on everything, so if one wants to realize one's self, and if one wants to become independent–transforming only unto one's self—then one must depend on everything.

The Emergence of Independence

In order to further elaborate on how independence emerges from radical dependence, I will look at two more passages in the *Zhuangzi* and Guo's commentaries on them. In the following two passages from the first chapter of the *Zhuangzi*, Guo Xiang explains independence (*wudai*) and how dependence (*youdai*) precedes being far-reaching and unfettered[17] (*xiaoyao* 逍遙). Meanwhile, this term is often considered as the placeholder for the notion of freedom in the *Zhuangzi*. While more on this shall be discussed later, it is sufficient for now to note that in these two passages, Guo Xiang straightforwardly shows that dependence (*youdai*) is the first step toward achieving the independence (*wudai*), and indeed self-realization (*zide*), that is first necessary for one's agency and actions to become far-reaching and unfettered (*xiaoyao*).

In the commentary on Zhuangzi's differentiation of small and big consciousness, Guo Xiang elaborates on the epistemological nature of independence (*wudai*), and how one's own freedom depends on that epistemological comfort of becoming one with one's own lot (*fen*), or in this case, sphere (*fang* 方). The passage is as follows:

Each thing has its own nature, each nature has its own limits. They are like years and understanding, how could they be things one could match up to by striving and wishing! From here onward until we get to (the section about) Liezi, Zhuangzi successively shows how, according to whether his years and understanding are great or small, everyone trusts their own particular sphere, and how nobody so far has been able to get the better of another on this basis. *Zhuangzi then rounds it off with a description of the independent person who is lost unto other-ness, forgets about his own self, and vanishes into the multitude of differences [that is immediate to him]*; who, since the different spheres are all equally attained, has neither achievement nor name [for] himself. For this reason, he who unites small and great is one for whom there is neither small nor great. If one cares about small and great, then even when comparing the great Peng to the quail, the official to (Liezi) riding the wind, he is still to an equal degree entangled in things, simply. He who equates death and life is one for whom there is neither death nor life. If one cares about death or life, then even when comparing the great Chun-tree to the cicada, Peng Zu to the morning mushroom, they are still equal in dying prematurely, simply. Therefore, he who roams where there is neither small nor great is one who suffers no exhaustion. He who is unconscious of whether he is not dying or not living is one without limits. For, just as in being far-reaching and unfettered, if one is attached to certain spheres, then though one is released and free to roam, there will still be occasions when one suffers exhaustion. One is not yet capable of independence.[18]

物各有性，性各有極，皆如年知，豈跂尚之所及哉！自此已下至於列子，歷舉年知之大小，各信其方，未有足以相傾者也。然後統以無待之人，遺彼忘我，冥此群異，異方同得而我無功名。是故統小大者，無小無大者也；苟有乎大小，則雖有大鵬之與斥鴳，宰官之與禦風，同為累物耳。齊死生者，無死無生者也；苟有乎死生，則雖大椿之與蟪蛄，彭祖之與朝菌，均於短折耳。故遊於無小無大者，無窮者也；冥乎不死不生者，無極者也。若夫逍遙而繫於有方，則雖放之使遊而有所窮矣，未能無待也。

Guo Xiang highlights how each thing cannot deliberately become "great," as one's own nature, and therefore limit, is like years and understanding—they cannot be forced. While here it seems to simply explain what Zhuangzi meant when talking about the small being unable to force itself to become great, Guo Xiang takes a slight turn from this and says that, ultimately, there really isn't any difference between small and great, for whichever one it is, it is simply one's own particular sphere (*fang* 方). In this manner, all are equal in simply being unable to escape this particularity of situation and circumstance. As such, for the independent person (*wudai zhi ren* 無待之人) there is neither small nor great, simply a sphere (*fang*) that ought to be attained. Since all spheres (*fang*) are equally attained for him, depending on each one of them particularly and singularly, they ultimately unite themselves with the other, or others, and vanish into the multitude of differences. Notice here how Guo Xiang parallels the words that (*bi* 彼) and this (*ci* 此), far and near. What this seems to convey is that the independent person unites with both near and far, and by forgetting himself, reaches everywhere. They converge among them equally and, since there is an absence of deliberate effort, then neither do they deliberately strive for "greatness" such as fame or acclaim. What this means is that because there is no force of effort, they are not entangled in things that are external to his sphere (*fang*). This lack of attachment, however, is not to be confused as complete lack. As had already been discussed in the previous chapters, Guo Xiang unfailingly advocates attaching oneself simply to one's lot (*fen*) or sphere (*fang*) and completely detaching from that which is external to it. In this manner, comparison becomes impossible, and so difference between great and small, life and death, also disappears—difference itself disappears. Without such comparison or deliberate effort into something external to one's own sphere, then there is no exhaustion, no limits—just the sphere. In the end, this full epistemological dependence on one's own sphere is what it means to be an independent person (*wudai zhi ren* 無待之人), and if this is not granted, then becoming far-reaching and unfettered (*xiaoyao*) means nothing.

Yang Lihua takes this even more literally and notes: "From the perspective specific to survival, the 'independence' that Guo Xiang talks about is no different for all ordinary people, and the various needs of food, shelter, and clothes are also [things that] we cannot go a day without."[19] While seemingly overly simplistic, this analogy is quite apt, as it captures the theme of nonknowing that Guo Xiang repeatedly emphasizes. Because we do not think about these basic necessities as we depend on them, we go about our daily lives more freely. In one's hunger, lack of a home to rest in, or lack of any basic comfort, one cannot be "far-reaching and unfettered" (*xiaoyao*), or in a more basic scenario, one cannot be expected to go about as leisurely with what one ought to go about with in daily life.

The complexities of the logic of convergence aside, this description of independence by Yang Lihua is perhaps the closest description there currently is to Guo Xiang's notion of freedom. We often think about freedom as the height of independence, and indeed, in the sense of self-determination, it is so; but what is the self in that process of determination? Dependent, Guo Xiang would say. For Guo, not only are dependence and interdependence complementary or noncontradictory with independence, but they are also *necessary*. Moreover, the necessity of dependence for Guo Xiang does not come at the cost of, but is the means for, independence, as well as the spontaneity that comes with it, as is due to its nonknowing quality.

Guo Xiang elaborates more on this theme of nonknowing in the following passage, where he expounds on the notions of independence and dependence in greater depth for a second a time in the first chapter of the *Zhuangzi*. The passage is as follows:

> "Heaven and earth" is just a blanket term used to indicate all beings. It is all individual beings that form the very substance of heaven and earth, and it is each being's self-so that aligns true to itself. "Self-so" means what is so of itself, without being done by anyone or for any purpose. Thus, Peng's ability to fly high and the sparrow's ability to stay low, the great tree's ability to last long and the mushroom's ability to perish quickly, all these are done spontaneously, all are self-so; they are beyond the ability of anyone's particular activity. Because these are self-so capabilities not done by anyone or for any purpose, they are aligned true [to themselves]. Thus, to "chariot upon what is true both to heaven and to earth" means to follow along with the character of each thing. To ride "atop the back-and-forth of the six atmospheric breaths" means to wander in the paths of transformation and change. If you travel forth like this, where can you go that will bring you to a halt? If you can ride upon whatever you happen to encounter, what will you have to depend on? This is how the person of supreme force, who *vanishingly unifies self and other, wanders far and unfettered*. If you are depending on some particular conditions,

even if you have the grace and ease of a Liezi, you will still be unable to travel when there is no wind. Such people can only wander far and unfettered after they attain that which they depend on—and how much more so is this the case for Peng? It is only one who can vanish into things and follow along with the great process of transformation who can be truly free of dependence and thus constantly unobstructed. And is it only them who is thereby freed of obstruction? No! They also comply with all dependent things, allowing each to attain what it depends on. Since they do not lose what they depend on, they too are joined with the Great Openness. So although I cannot make the dependent and the independent the same as each other, the fact that each rests securely in its own character, its heavenly mechanism unfolding of itself, receiving it but not knowing how or why—this is something I cannot make different among them. And if even the independent is ultimately no different from the dependent, how much less could there be any difference between the larger and smaller among the dependent?[20]

天地者，萬物之總名也。天地以萬物為體，而萬物必以自然為正。自然者，不為而自然者也。故大鵬之能高，斥鴳之能下，椿木之能長，朝菌之能短，凡此皆自然之所能，非為之所能也。不為而自能，所以為正也。故乘天地之正者，即是順萬物之性也；禦六氣之辯者，即是遊變化之途也；如斯以往，則何往之有窮哉！所禦斯乘，又將惡乎待哉！此乃至德之人玄同彼我者之逍遙也。苟有待焉，則雖列子之輕妙，猶不能以無風而行，故必得其所待，然後逍遙耳，而況大鵬乎！夫唯與物冥而循大變者，為能無待而常通，豈獨自通而已哉！又順有待者，使不失其所待，所待不失，則同於大通矣。故有待無待，無所不能齊也；至於各安其性，天機自張，受而不知，則無所不能殊也。夫無待猶不足以殊有待，況有待者之巨細乎！

While Guo Xiang simply begins with an explanation of the term "heaven and earth" here, he goes on to explain the concreteness of this ontological system. Again, he reiterates that the natures of all beings are simply self-so (*ziran*) and that is why they align true to themselves (*weizheng* 為正). In other words they are beyond deliberate activity or purpose, they simply follow along their own characters, which give rise to the characters of others, each thing going with all changes and transformations. Guo here distinguishes between the kind of dependence that is a vanishing into things, and the kind of dependence that is linear, in order to clarify his point that it is the former kind that allows one to *follow along*, thereby depend on, the *great* transformations, which is to say, the transformations of all things. To vanish into things is to become those things, which are things that are made by other things. Thus, the person of supreme force (*zhi de zhi ren* 至德之人) simply relies on all this, hence unifying self with "other" (*bi* 彼). This reliance, this dependence, is the only way to truly becoming far-reaching and unfettered (*xiaoyao*) without exhaustion. Ultimately thus, there is no difference between independence (*wudai*) and dependence (*youdai*) for only through such dependence—being at rest with one's nature, letting it unfold itself, and receiving without knowing why—can one become truly independent. In this passage, Yang Lihua emphasizes the epistemological angle and notes:

> All are constrained by their own boundaries' limits, between each other they all live and understand things based on their respective natural lot (性分). They cannot communicate with each other, only those who have surpassed *discrimination* (分别) and *relative opposition* (对待) can reach the existential condition/realm of all beings. In real independence (无待) there is no difference between independence (无待) and dependence (有待) because if the independent (无待) cannot fully eliminate the boundary between independence (无待) and dependence (有待) then he (the independent) will still relatively oppose (对待) and discriminate (分别), thus becoming dependent (有待者).[21]

We see here two levels of being dependent. On one level, dependence means that one depends on a particular thing, as noted in the preceding original passage, and this is a kind of dependence that discriminates and differentiates—not because one acknowledges the singularity of his own lot, but because—he *compares*. This is a diachronic kind of dependence. On another and ultimate level, however, there is the ideal kind of dependence, which is what is referred to as vanishing into things, and this has no difference with independence, one that does not discriminate or differentiate, because there is only the singularity of his own lot, so he is therefore unconscious of any "other" and is ultimately united with his encounters of those "other" beings, since all change and transformation mean that encountering and intercausality is inevitable, as has been discussed. The absence of deliberate knowing, and hence comparison, is thus self-so, and is the beginning of true dependence, and ultimately, independence. For Guo Xiang, thus, knowing and understanding itself also has two kinds: deliberate and nondeliberate, and the latter is one that simply depends on whichever it encounters, hence becoming self-so.

While Guo Xiang rejects dependence, causality, and knowing, on a diachronic level, he acknowledges their existence on an absolutely synchronic level. By this, I mean a kind of synchronicity that has diachronic dependences, causalities, and knowledges implicit in it. Taking all the members of a whole as one's constitution, one becomes the whole itself, and becoming the whole itself, one becomes singular. Put differently, when Zhuangzi and Guo Xiang speak of "forgetting," they mean so diachronically, for it is in this level that deliberate action and linear causality exist. Synchronically, however, one becomes so fully aware of one's immediate circumstance that one merges with it, because one depends on it. Thus, ultimate independence springs forth from synchronic radical dependence. Knowledge for Guo Xiang is thus dependent on a singularity of circumstances, and because those circumstances are interconnected to all the others, it is always transforming, and hence always reemerging as spontaneous and self-so. This is also evident in the following passage of the *Zhuangzi* with Guo Xiang's comments:

Understanding has something that it depends on before it can be accurate, and that which it depends on is never fixed.[22]

夫知有所待而後當，其所待者特未定也。

He who understands nothing he [definitively] approves of, and nothing he [definitively] disapproves of,[23] therefore he must depend [on something]. But as for him who relies on heaven for a living, he encounters things and is in accord [with them]. This dependence therefore has no fixture.[24]

夫知者未能無可無不可，故必有待也。若乃任天而生者，則遇物而當也。有待則無定也。

What this means is that understanding has two levels as well. At a more basic level, knowledge has a direction of its actions, and knowing cannot but have a particular position that one can hold. However, there is another level where understanding is a kind of dependence that makes one able to be in accord with whatever one encounters: when dependence has no fixture. This latter kind is absolute because it depends not on any one thing, but on everything by means of depending on these ever-changing encounters. By being absolute, it has no linear predetermination, and there is no one thing that determines it or that it determines, but rather it is both dependent on and depended on by ever-changing moments that are ultimately interconnected with everything. That is why Guo Xiang says one who relies on heaven simply goes in accordance with everything he encounters, being dependent on whatever is appropriate for the circumstance.

We often think that one's true realization, that is, to be truly one's self, occurs when we are independent. Social psychologists often refer to this phenomenon as authenticity, the state of being one's true and core self. Guo Xiang, however, tells us that the true and core self is actually dependent on the factors around it. There is no inherent agency that is truly at the core of our identities, no fixed "I" (*wo* 我), but that does not mean that independence, which is integral to self-realization, is not possible. It simply means that in Guo Xiang's logic of convergence, independence *is* dependence in its radical or ultimate level, and vice versa. It is in this sense, and in the context of an ever-changing world, that Guo Xiang conceives of what I have called "dependence-based autonomy." In this manner, moreover, realization, as well as its rightness and truth, has no fixture—it is self-so (*ziran*). Indeed, to be self-so is to depend on things, thereby realizing one's vanishing into them. This is because it is impossible for anything, including one's own self, to exist in isolation. As such, its thinking and agency cannot arise from nowhere. However, this does not mean that one's self and agency will arise from a particular source either. Rather, one's own self, thought, and agency arise from the world itself, in a dialectical relationship of being released unto the world itself. In other words, freedom and therefore autonomy, or in Guo Xiang's articulation, self-realization (*zide*), is independence not from, but *through*, one's environment, and as such, is an emergent quality of radical dependence.

5

Freedom as Self-Realization

Dimensions of Zide 自得

This kind of self-so rightness that is dependent on whatever it encounters, finding its singular fulfillment in its singular and unique circumstance, is indeed the central theme of Guo Xiang's work. The historical background that we have discussed in this work earlier is testament to how consistent his methodological framework was with his philosophical enterprise. Indeed, his work was meant to be both a criticism and rehabilitation of the Confucian values in government, which were abused and used as an excuse for nepotism and corruption, as well as the growing trend of Daoist tendencies for seclusion and escapism, championed by the likes of Ji Kang and Ruan Ji who, as Wang Xiaoyi notes,[1] acted in arrogance and extravagance—promoting alcoholism and nudity—tendencies that were pervasive among upper-class intellectuals of the time. Guo does this through his logic of convergence that draws from his ontological framework, which combines being and nothingness, one and many, self and others, and indeed dependence and independence. This convergence is also a function of self-realization (zide 自得). In this chapter therefore, I argue that self-realization (zide) has two dimensions, being wuxin 無心 and xiaoyao 逍遙. In order to demonstrate this, I provide an account of the different dimensions of Guo Xiang's self-realization (zide 自得) or freedom. Here, I argue that there are mainly three dimensions, namely the positive state of wuxin 無心, which is necessary in order to achieve self-realization (zide), followed by a section highlighting the difference and sameness of self-realization (zide) itself as manifested by the equality of its differing varieties. I then tackle the notion of being "far-reaching and unfettered" (*xiaoyao* 逍遙) in the last section, and discuss how it is a practice of self-realization (*zide*), such that its limits are made apparent. Finally, I derive, from all this, Guo Xiang's notion of freedom: *freedom in*, to which I also refer as "dependence-based autonomy." I argue that this denotes a kind of autonomy that is based on depending on one's own environment in order to realize oneself (*zide*), be autonomous, and thereby become a self-determining agent. In particular, I focus on its epistemological nature as well as potential for a contemporary understanding of freedom and autonomy. By doing so, I demonstrate how Guo Xiang provides a holistic account of freedom by highlighting the emergent and singular nature of one's placement in the world's network of causality.

Having No Heart-Mind (*wuxin* 無心): Discarding the Discarding

An important concept in Daoist sagehood is *wuxin* 無心. Though it does not appear in the *Daodejing* and only appears five times in the *Zhuangzi*, it emphasizes the release from value judgments and even an identity or sense of self, as the heart-mind (*xin* 心) is often considered the seat of consciousness. While it is beyond the scope of this study to have a discussion on the nuanced notion of the heart-mind,[2] it is fair to say that this understanding of *wuxin* 無心 from the classical Daoist texts has an emphasis on heart-mind (*xin* 心), that is, on its harms and the need for its removal. While the concept was not as prominent in classical Daoist texts, however, Jia Jinhua argues[3] that it is likely due to the dialectical influences between Buddhism and Daoism that *wuxin* gained more prominence, and that Guo Xiang was definitely aware of the Buddhist texts that deal with it at the time. In spite of the similarities, however, Jia acknowledges that there is a difference between the two notions of *wuxin*. While the Buddhist *wuxin* is meant "to awaken all human beings to realize the empty nature of their existence and to transcend the mundane cycle of life and death,"[4] Jia says that Guo Xiang adds a new dimension because "his theory of liberation is never separated from sociopolitical concern."[5] Indeed, as we have previously noted as well, Guo's goals (like his peers during the Wei-Jin period) were primarily sociopolitical. In fact, Guo's work can be read *both* as a reappraisal and critique of Confucian and Daoist philosophy. He criticizes the abuses that can spring from both extremes and seeks to reinterpret them in profound unison. Thus, according to Jia, the meaning of *wuxin* for Guo Xiang is "to take up social responsibility and engage with political affairs while at the same time keeping a spontaneous and detached mind."[6] She further explains that "while the sage engaged in social affairs, governed the empire, benefited people, and established merits and virtues, he also understood that merit, fame, and power were just like floating clouds, and therefore he was able to keep a detached, liberated mind, or in Guo's words, 'no-mind' (*wuxin*). In this way, he reached the unification of officialdom and eremitism."[7]

In spite of being able to highlight Guo Xiang's two-pronged enterprise, however, Jia does not go far enough and ultimately does not appropriately capture Guo Xiang's logic of convergence. The loss of heart-mind (*wuxin*) in Guo is neither detachment nor liberation *from* anything but rather is more akin to an attachment to everything and no one single thing. It is not a movement away from but *into* something. As opposed to emphasizing the role of the heart-mind (*xin*), the key to understanding Guo's notion of *wuxin* is to understand his ontology of nothingness (*wu* 無).[8] Indeed, nothingness (*wu*) in Guo Xiang is related to all its other suffixes or all other 無-x (i.e., 無為, 無往, 無用, 無知, etc.) and to the ontology of nothingness itself, which is inexorably linked to self-so (*ziran*) or 自-x.[9]

> Having no deliberate mind . . . [means] not only to discard right and wrong, but also to discard this discarding. They are discarded and again discarded, until no-discarding is reached; only then do we have nothing discarded and nothing not-discarded, and right and wrong vanish of themselves.[10]

> [. . .] 莫若無心，既遣是非，又遣其遣。遣之又遣之以至於無遣，然後無遣無不遣而是非自去矣。

It is not just that nothing is true or absolute, but everything is true and absolute. To discard discarding itself means that nothingness is not absolute. It is a negation of negation, wherein one takes as true whatever one encounters at that given moment, not that one takes nothing as true. In this manner, the binaries of right and wrong, or true and false, naturally just vanishes of themselves. Again, this is not because everything is wrong, or everything is false, but exactly the opposite. In discarding the discarding, each thing is right, each thing is true. For instance, the following is a famed passage on emotion and mourning in the Confucian *Lunyu* that Guo Xiang comments on:

> When Yan Yuan [Yan Hui] died, the Master wailed with such profound grief that his disciples said, "How profoundly you feel!" "Do I feel such profound emotion? If I did not feel such profound feeling for this man, for whom would I feel it?"

> 顏淵死。子哭之慟。從者曰。子慟矣。子曰。有慟乎。非夫人之爲慟而誰爲慟。

> As others wailed, he too wailed, and as others felt profound emotion, he too felt it, for, utterly impartial, he transformed himself in step with others.[11]

> 人哭亦哭。人慟亦慟。蓋無情者與物化也。

Just as it is with truth, being impartial or having "no emotion" (*wuqing* 無情) simply means having no one emotion, and simply transforming oneself with others. Transforming himself with others, he feels every emotion that others feel, so as others wail, he too wails and feels just as profoundly as those others. This is what Guo Xiang ultimately means when he repeatedly mentions that the sage vanishes into (*xuanming* 玄冥) things. It is not complete detachment, but a complete and full attachment to whatever one encounters, and to then be attached to the next feeling just as fully. Just as with discarding right and wrong, as well as feeling profoundly as the definition of being or having "no emotion" (*wuqing*), Guo Xiang's notion of *wuxin* similarly cannot mean to simply be the detachment from this or that feeling but the detaching of detaching itself.

Guo Xiang also mentions *wuxin* several times in his commentary on the *Lunyu*. From what we know of the text, the following passage is perhaps the closest to a definition that we can get to his notion of *wuxin* as found in his commentary on the Confucian classic:

> The Master said, "In my relation to others, whom do I blame, whom praise? If there is any that may be praised,

> there is a way to verify it, that is, by recourse to the common folk, for it was by recourse to them that the Three Dynasties were conducted by the straight and proper Dao."

子曰:吾之於人。誰毀誰譽。如有可譽者。其有所試矣。斯民也。三代之所以 直道而行也。

Whereas to be free of conscious mind and so give oneself over to the world is to follow the straight and proper Dao, to be of self-conscious mind and try to make the world follow one is to pervert its method. This is why one should conduct things by the straight and proper Dao. Praise or blame should not be based on finicky personal views, for whether one is good or not should be verified by recourse to the common folk. Therefore, the text states, "In my relation to others, whom do I blame, whom praise? If there is any that may be praised, there is a way to verify it, that is, by recourse to the common folk, for it was by recourse to them that the Three Dynasties were conducted by the straight and proper Dao."[12]

無心而付之天下者。直道也。有心而使天下從己者。曲法者也。故直道而行者。毀譽不出於區區之身。善與不善。信之百姓。故曰:吾之於人。誰毀誰譽。如有所譽。必試之斯民也.

It is worth noting that Richard Lynn translates *wuxin* here as "to be free of conscious mind," which captures the fact that there is no single aim toward which it is directed, but perhaps it might not emphasize enough that it is indeed directed into an absolute singularity that captures all directions in any given moment through its interconnected transformations. This is why Guo Xiang says that to be *without a deliberate heart-mind* (*wuxin*) means to "give oneself over to the world," unto the rightness (or proper dao) of a given time or situation.

In all these passages we repeatedly see the theme of what I've called the logic of convergence, which is also the very methodology of Guo Xiang. As Richard Lynn notes, Guo's enterprise is far from the escapist connotation of a kind of "self-liberation" that *wuxin* 無心 is commonly related with. Lynn says that "Guo's promotion of the sage-ruler in Daoist terms was designed to serve as a catalyst for the regeneration of self and society and the foundation of a worldly utopia."[13] In other words, Guo

Xiang's nothingness is manifested as being, existence, action, and indeed society (名教 mingjiao), in all its transformations, interconnectedness, and ultimately, self-so (ziran). Perhaps the passages where this is the most evident, however, are the following, in which Lynn has taken on the work of placing parallels for us:

> **Confucius said, "Agreed. I shall take office."**
>
> 孔子曰:諾。吾將仕矣。
>
> The sage, free of self-conscious mind, in taking or not taking office, just complies with the ways of the world. When Yang Hu urged him to take office, since it was the right thing to do, he could not but agree. *If the world cannot use me, I have no use of my own* (無自用), for this is the way to follow the straight and proper Dao and resonate with others. However, the principle underlying "being stern" and "being conciliatory" is also implied herein."[14]
>
> 聖人無心。仕與不仕隨世耳。陽虎勸仕。理無不諾。不能用我。則我無自用。此直道而應者也。然危遜之理。亦在其中也。

Lynn continues, saying that "Guo Xiang's assertion that the sage is free of self-conscious mind also appears in his *Zhuangzi* commentary, in *Shanxing* 繕性 (chapter 16)":[15]

> The sage, free of self-conscious mind, allows the world to fulfill itself, and all attempts to fulfill it by recourse to the superficial aspects of purity have nothing to do with true sagehood. Since the sage does nothing but *allow the world to fulfill itself*, what can he have to do with making the world acquire sageliness! Therefore, though the footprints left by Heavenly Monarchs and Earthly Kings always kept changing from age to age, the Dao of the sage never fails to remain whole and intact.[16]
>
> 聖人無心，任世之自成。成之淳薄，皆非聖也。聖能任世之自得耳，豈能使世 得聖哉! 故皇王之跡，與世俱遷，而聖人之道未始不全也。

Although these two passages have different thrusts, we can still see the same two-pronged approach. In the first one where he comments about taking office, Guo Xiang insists that to be *wuxin* and to follow the straight and proper dao means to resonate with others, and this consists of allowing himself to be used by the world. Similarly in the second passage, or the one where Guo Xiang comments on the *Zhuangzi*, he insists that becoming *wuxin*, as it is with the sage, is to allow the world to fulfill itself (*zide*). This is why he says that even though the traces (跡 *ji*) of different sages are different, they are the same in that their dao remains intact, because they are all *wuxin*. In this passage, moreover, we are directly confronted with the constitutive link between *wuxin* and self-realization (*zide*)—a representation, if not a direct consequence, of Guo Xiang's ontology of nothingness that, by its nature, converges necessity with contingency as discussed in our earlier chapter on existence (chap. 2). There is another passage in the *Zhuangzhizhu* that resembles this *Lunyu* commentary of Guo Xiang's, as it also links *wuxin* to staying within society and serving its changing needs. Guo Xiang explains:

> He who is in accord with the various classes of men is unable to leave the society of men. This being the case, the reasons for society's changes, generation after generation, are different but suitable [for each generation]. Only he who has no deliberate heart-mind and doesn't use his own views (不自用)[17] can then conform according to what the changes indicate, and does not bear their burdens.[18]
>
> 與人群者，不得離人。然人間之變故，世世異宜，唯無心而不自用者，為能隨變所適而不荷其累也。

In other words, being *wuxin* means to conform to the different changes that society undergoes because though they may manifest differently, each is suitable to its time. The views that Guo Xiang refers to here when he tells us not to use one's own views are what he also calls "finicky personal views" (*qu qu zhi shen* 區區之身). This is because to rely on one's own views is to be blindsided,[19] since what is suitable always changes from moment to moment. Therefore, the real manifestation of *wuxin* is not escaping, but participating within and for society. That is, the discarding of discarding is the affirmation of spontaneous activity.

Ultimately, this participatory character of the logic of convergence is what it means "to allow the world to fulfill itself" (*zide*).

Self-Realization (*zide* 自得): Equalizing Assessments of Attainments

Zide 自得, as this work purports, is the central concept integral to understanding Guo Xiang's notion of freedom and/or autonomy. However, much has already been said on why this is so in the previous sections and chapters. A brief gloss over would perhaps simply be expressed by saying that becoming self-realized (*zide*) consists of *wuxin* and *xiaoyao*, which we shall discuss in the next section. For now, however, it would be sufficient for our purposes to note that one must first be *wuxin* in order to be *zide*, which is then necessary to practice *xiaoyao*. These, however, are not steps in achieving freedom, but a radical convergence of both the negative and positive features of freedom, resulting in the shift toward a *dependence-based autonomy* that is "freedom in." Self-realization (*zide*), therefore, is being comfortable in the act of shaping oneself, one's values and choices, to vanish into one's surroundings in order to achieve autonomy in an intercausal world. However, as previously mentioned in this chapter, this autonomous realization is not about "finding one's true self" for there is no such thing in Guo Xiang's philosophy. The "self" that is realized here is a product of intercausality, nevertheless realized by looking *into* one's self and its own environment, instead of transcending it, as can be seen in the previous section. This is why Guo Xiang says we should strive for what is internal to one's nature (性分之內 *xingfenzhinei*) and denounce traces of externality, as discussed in the previous chapter. In this sense, one is comfortable with depending on one's given lot instead of chasing traces. This is what *dependence-based autonomy* means—one's achieved capability to adapt and depend on the environment, in spontaneously shaping oneself according to changes.[20]

This is best shown in the following passage from the *Zhuangzi* wherein he describes the type of person who has found his proper place in the world:

> Fu Yueh attained it, and with it he became the prime minister of Wu Ting and controlled the whole empire. Then, charioting upon one constellation and drawn by another, he made himself equal to the stars of heaven.[21]

傅說得之，以相武丁，奄有天下，乘東維，騎箕尾，而比於列星。

It must be noted that the word *lie* 列 here has a sense of being arranged in order, connoting belongingness. So in *placing* himself among the stars, the Chinese text does give off a sense that Fu Yue is assuming his rightful place, where he was always meant to be, while also giving off a sense of spontaneous action, according to the correct dao. So what Guo Xiang does in his commentary here is to explain how finding one's rightful place in the world is spontaneously realized, which is itself the nature of attaining oneness with the world-force, the dao:

> The dao, has no capability. This says that attaining dao is from dao, so as to show its spontaneous realization. Spontaneously realized, the dao cannot be made to realize him; [if] his own self is not yet realized, then that self will also be incapable of realizing himself. As such then, all those who [attain] realization, externally it is not due to the dao, internally it is not produced from oneself. It is [rather] a sudden self-realization and lone-transformation. The difficulty of coming into being, is that it is [spontaneously] self-realized and lone-transforming. [But] once he has already realized his coming into being, how could he still be distressed over anything that his life has not realized, and then go do something about it?[22]

> 道，無能也。此言得之於道，乃所以明其自得耳。自得耳，道不能使之得也；我之未得，又不能為得也。然則凡得之者，外不資於道，內不由於己，掘然自得而獨化也。夫生之難也，猶獨化而自得之矣，既得其生，又何患於生之不得而為之哉！

What this means is that one cannot possibly *do* anything to *deliberately* change something.[23] That is to say that not only is there nothing external to something that can fulfill its self-realization, but that there is also nothing intrinsically that one can deliberately do in order to fulfill one's self-realization. The very simple acceptance that makes it seem easy is turned inside out, making it the very same thing that makes it difficult, and hence an attainment. Once this is attained, however, one attains not only oneself, but oneness with the movement of the world. Indeed, Fu Yue's complete and absolute dependence on his surroundings and environment is also true the other way around, he is independent because self and other are converged in complete harmony. These two (dependence and independence) happen simultaneously through attaining both the internal and external at once, in the same way the self-generativity, self-transformation, lone-generativity, and lone-transformation all happen simultaneously as well. This is why Guo Xiang also says that "one who is self-realized internally, is one whose affairs are complete externally"[24] (內自得者，外事全也). It is then that one realizes his inherent connection to everything else, as both effect and cause—his limit becomes his very potential, since everything is dependent on everything, all in oneness and unity, yet converging in their singularities. As Guo Xiang tells us: "the ten thousand things are ten thousand bodies, unified in self-realization, their realization becomes one"[25] (萬物萬形，同於自得，其得一也). What this implies, moreover, is that everything has a proper place and that all things, in their proper places, are sufficient in that, even though they are all bound to change in the flash of a moment. Guo says this directly in a comment on a passage in the sixth chapter of the *Zhuangzi*, saying:

> The previous me is not the present me. "Me" goes away together with the present moment. How then could the past be held onto? And yet, the people of the world are unaware of this, senselessly declaring that whatever they may presently have encountered can be tied down and kept there. Deluded, are they not?[26]

> 故向者之我，非復今我也。我與今俱往，豈常守故哉！而世莫之覺，橫謂今之所遇可係而在，豈不昧哉！[27]

To "try" and attain the dao, to "try" and hold on to an identity of "me," is, according to Guo, deluded because it tries to catch a moment in time and space that is inevitably fleeting and changing. This applies both internally, when superimposing actions onto things based on one's ideals and values, and externally, when trying to attain an external thing or ideal deliberately, such as trying to attain the dao. We then see that because the world itself lone-transforms and self-transforms, no deliberate action can possibly change the course of its lone-transformation. Everything is, in every fleeting moment in time, the way that it simply is and that is right inasmuch as that exists; as in the case of Fu Yue, not even the dao has any power to deliberately give anyone realization, because the dao is nothing but the spontaneous generation and transformation of everything and everyone in the world. Ultimately, Guo Xiang was trying to say that the dao is not a principle that shines down on us from a heavenly canopy as though the *logos spermatikos* of a grand narrative (as one might expect from an Abrahamic divinity), but that it is simply a spontaneous attainment that varies from moment to moment and being to being. This notion of self-realization is defined by the logic of convergence, wherein dependence is the condition for independence. Thus, Guo Xiang allows us to see a unique notion of freedom: one that is necessary and singular inasmuch as it is purely contingent in constitution and transformation, in relation to the necessity of everything else's contingency; one that is satisfied and at ease—this is what is meant by freedom.

This convergence of dependence and independence, and conversely emptiness and spontaneity, in the notion of self-realization (*zide*) inevitably leads to the convergence of self and other, as was discussed in the previous chapter as well. Not only that, but it ultimately discards the discarding by getting rid of any valuation or superimposition of judgments as to which is better than the other. This is best explained by Guo Xiang in the following passage:

> To consider oneself right and the other wrong is the constant condition of both self and other. Thus the other's finger, compared to my finger as the standard, distinctly fails to be a finger. This is "using [this] finger to show that a finger is not a finger." Conversely, my finger, compared to the other's finger as the standard, spectacularly fails to be a finger as well. This is "using not-this-finger to show that a finger is not a finger." To illuminate the absence of right and wrong, nothing is more effective than understanding "this" and "that" in terms of each other, which shows that they are the same in their self-affirmation and other-disapproval. Since all are seen as wrong, nothing in the world is right. Since all are seen as right, nothing in the world is wrong. How can this be shown? If right were really right, it would have to be such that there could be no one in the world who could consider it wrong. If wrong were really wrong, no one in the world could consider it right. But in reality there is no standard of right and wrong; they are in complete chaos. When you understand this, even though each one believes only in his own narrow viewpoint, you see the consistency between them,

their sameness. For it is the same wherever one looks, above and below. Thus, the Consummate Person knows that heaven and earth are one finger, and all things one horse. He finds everywhere only a vast overflowing tranquility, where every creature is exactly appropriate in its own allotment, all the same in their self-realization, free of right and wrong."[28]

夫自是而非彼，彼我之常情也。故以我指喻彼指，則彼指於我指獨為非指矣。此以指喻指之非指也。若復以彼指還喻我指，則我指於彼指復為非指矣。此（亦）非指喻指之非指也。將明無是無非，莫若反覆相喻。反覆相喻，則彼之與我，既同於自是，又均於相非。均於相非，則天下無是；同於自是，則天下無非。何以明其然邪？是若果是，則天下不得（彼）有非之者也。非若果非，〔則天下〕亦不得復有是之者也。今是非無主，紛然淆亂，明此區區者各信其偏見而同於一致耳。仰觀俯察，莫不皆然。是以至人知天地一指也，萬物一馬也，故浩然大寧，而天地萬物各當其分，同於自得，而無是無非也。

In this passage, Guo Xiang highlights the difference of sameness, and the sameness of difference. Referring to Gongsun Long's sophisticated arguments regarding set theory and the paradoxes such as the white horse not being a horse,[29] Guo Xiang (taking Zhuangzi even further) puts forth a powerful critique and introduces (or, at this point, reiterates) the concept of the sameness of difference, and conversely, the same singularity of all things. This is what it means for all things to be one finger and one horse; all are the same in their absolute uniqueness and singularity. To Guo Xiang, "white horse is not a horse" is not a dead-end paradox but a necessity to how reality itself is structured. All are lone-transforming and therefore all spontaneously transform among each other; all are lone-generating, and all spontaneously generate each other through transformation. Nothing is ever not existing, for it simply changes forms, vanishes into (*xuan*) things, and hence, all are one finger and one horse. If there is no fixed existence, then how can there be fixed truths? As such, nothing is right, nothing is wrong; all are right, all are wrong. For Guo, it is not enough to deny the existence of right and wrong, one must also deny that denial through affirming all as right and wrong in their own, lone-transforming and lone-generating, way. This is why Guo tells us that "one who relies on self-so and forgets right and wrong, their substance relies only on the genuineness of heaven and their own self. And oh how much they have!" (夫任自然而忘是非者，其體中獨任天真而已，又何所有哉！).[30] To forget right and wrong thus, is to become self-so (*ziran*) and rely on heaven or nature and one's self, all at once—for the self is none other than its heavenly endowed nature (*tianxing* 天性)—as this is what it means to become radically dependent on change and transformation. Similarly, in self-realization (*zide*), the realization of one's self only applies to the standards of one's self, and vice versa with the other. This discarding of the discarding takes relativism inside out and takes the singular as absolute, because it understands that each thing, each affair, and therefore action, can be right and wrong in different circumstances, and they are therefore "all the same in their self-realization." Instead of everything being wrong, or everything being true, everything is right and also wrong, and so relativity no longer applies as something is relative to nothing except only itself. This is what it means to discard discarding, to flatten out existence and knowledge. This idea of the equality and flatness of self-realization (*zide*) in one's allotment (*fen*), fate (*ming*), nature (*xing*), rightness (*dang*), generation (*sheng*), transformation (*hua*), independence (*wudai*), and so on, is the culmination of Guo Xiang's unique interpretation of self-so (*ziran*), which then allows us to understand that autonomy is dependent on all these factors.

It is thus no wonder that in Guo Xiang's commentary, following the Chinese composition style of stating the topic in the beginning, the following passage is how he opens his magnum opus:

> Though small and great are different, yet if they are released into the realm of self-realization, then things will acquiesce to their nature, and affairs will correspond to their ability, each is suitable to his own allotment, in leisurely ease they are one, so how can there appear to be any better or worse between them?[31]
>
> 夫小大雖殊，而放於自得之場，則物任其性，事稱其能，各當其分，逍遙一也，豈容勝負於其間哉！

In the end, Guo Xiang's enterprise can be understood to emphasize the radical convergence of difference, the equality, and the absolute singularity of all things. Guo Xiang shows how there is freedom in the simple and spontaneous unity of one's self with one's environment, basking in its own rightness.

One of the most well-known passages that encompasses this best is the Butterfly Dream. This passage has been a famous and contested passage in both Sinitic and Anglophone scholarship, yet Guo Xiang's original interpretation has largely been overlooked in Anglophone scholarship.[32] The passage is as follows:

Once Zhuang Zhou dreamed that he was a butterfly, a butterfly happy as can be, and himself felt how comfortably this suited him!

昔者莊周夢爲胡蝶。栩栩然胡蝶也。自喻適志與。

Happily self-realized,[33] he flutters about with pleasure.

自快得意。悅豫而行。

But he was not aware that he was Zhuang Zhou.

不知周也。

Just when he was dreaming that he was a butterfly and thus unaware that he was Zhuang Zhou is no different than if he had died. However, no matter which state he was in, it never failed to suit him comfortably. Therefore, as one when alive is attached to life, so when dead one has to love death. Looking at it from this point of view, we realize that to be distressed about death while one is alive is to be in error.

方其夢爲胡蝶而不知周。則與殊死不異也。然所在無不適志。則當生而係生者。必當死而戀死矣。由此觀之。知夫在生而哀死者誤也。

When he awoke suddenly, he was astonished to be Zhuang Zhou,

俄然覺。則蘧蘧然周也。

It is only because this is addressed from Zhuang Zhou's point of view that it is said that "he awoke." He was yet unsure that it had not been a dream.

自周而言。故稱覺耳。未必非夢也。

but he did not know whether he was Zhuang Zhou who had been dreaming he was a butterfly or a butterfly dreaming that he was Zhuang Zhou.

不知周之夢爲胡蝶與。胡蝶之夢爲周與。

His not being self-conscious of being a butterfly now is no different from his not being self-conscious of being Zhuang Zhou while he was dreaming. However, since each state suited him comfortably at the time, there is no way to be sure that he was not a butterfly now dreaming that he was Zhuang Zhou. It commonly happens in the world that someone takes a nap and dreams the experiences of a lifetime, so there is no way to be sure that one's present lifetime is not just something dreamed during a nap.

今之不知胡蝶。無異於夢之不知周也。而各適一時之志。則無以明胡蝶之不夢爲周矣。世有假寐而夢經百年者。則無以明今之百年非假寐之夢者也。

Between Zhuang Zhou and the butterfly there had to have been a distinction.

周與胡蝶。則必有分矣。

The distinction between being awake and dreaming is no different than the distinction between life and death. The reason why he is self-conscious that one state suits his aspirations is because it is set off from the other—and not because of a lack of differentiation between them.

夫覺夢之分。無異於死生之辯也。今所以自喻適志。由其分定。非由無分也。

And this is known as the transformation of things [*wuhua*].

此之謂物化。

> Since time does not stop even for an instant, we cannot preserve the present no matter how much we might wish to do so, which is why the dream last night was transformed into the present. As for the change between life and death, how could it be any different! Yet people worry so much about the gap between them! Just now one is in this state and thus unselfconscious of that state—which is what dreaming of being a butterfly signifies. And taking an example from human experience, throughout life one never knows now what might happen later—which is what the story of Concubine Li[34] signifies. However, the stupid think with absolute clarity that they know that life is delightful and death is painful—this is because they have never heard about the transformation of things.[35]

夫時不暫停。而今不遂存。故昨日之夢。於今化矣。死生之變。豈異於此。而勞心於其間哉。方爲此則不知彼。夢爲胡蝶是也。取之於人。則一生之中。今不知後。麗姬是也。而愚者竊竊然自以爲知生之可樂。死之可苦。未聞物化之謂也。

Although this passage is often cited to argue that Zhuangzi is a relativist, and sometimes an adherent to the even the more Buddhist approach of achieving enlightenment in waking,[36] Guo Xiang takes on an approach that would seem unique or even odd in Anglophone scholarship. Instead of dismissing the distinction as unimportant, he embraces it—as Lynn's translation highlights—as the significant characteristic of change and transformation. Likening the transformation from butterfly to Zhuang Zhou to life and death, this passage is significant because Guo Xiang says that the butterfly is "happily self-realized" (*zi kuai de yi* 自快得意),[37] meaning it is *free in* the dream, just as one is *free in* life, or *free in* death, because one embraces whichever circumstance one is in and unites with it as one. Notice, moreover, Guo Xiang's cautionary warning about how "time does not stop even for an instant, we cannot preserve the present no matter how much we might wish to do so," which emphasizes the infinity of movement and change. Zhuang Zhou existed in a moment that, to our eyes now, seems very different and almost counterintuitive to the reality that we *do* know, and yet he is "happily self-realized" (*zi kuai de yi* 自快得意), precisely because that moment represents a whole, a singular necessity that contains within it its own contradiction. This is what it means to be self-realized and free: that one is united with a singular moment that will inevitably change into the next, and the next, in an eternal and dynamic process, making one inherently connected to everything else.

In a later passage that has also been mentioned in the previous chapter's discussion on 性分 *xingfen*, Guo Xiang highlights the realms of life and death once again, and how one ought to be at home in each realm. He says: "I take each transformation, both life and death, as 'me.' Since all are me, how can I ever be lost? . . ."[38] So I say there is nowhere that I am not self-realized"[39] (夫死生變化，吾皆吾之。既皆是吾，吾何失哉！。。。言無往而不自得也). Guo Xiang thus treats each realm in the Butterfly Dream as distinct because that is at the core of change and transformation, which means that, in change and transformation, all of them are me—the same in their difference, necessary in their contingency—they are all me. This is how, in all these realms, one is self-realized (*zide*) and free.

While it is beyond our scope to delve into the thanatology of Guo Xiang's philosophy, suffice it to say his view on death reflects his view of life, and this applies to all aspects of his philosophical enterprise. One is not more important than the other, even though each is distinct and singular, and so, though death is different from life, it ought to not be an object or source of fear. While neither Zhuangzi nor Guo Xiang delude themselves into believing or arguing that death is part of life or that there is life after death, they both acknowledge that it is a necessary transformation that occurs in one's being, albeit distinct from life. As such, the realm of death, while distinct and unknown, is an inevitable necessity of life—one must depend on life when one is alive in order to be fully self-realized, acknowledging that life is what defines oneself—and one must depend on death when one dies, knowing that it defines oneself. Self-realization (*zide*), therefore, is defined by its dependence on whatever one encounters, and the lack of value judgment in giving importance to one over another, in acknowledging that all realms are equal in their singularity and difference, not because a single system cannot be wrong, but because a single system or entity is self-cohering and is a horse that can only be judged and assessed as its own horse, similar to all the other horses of the world. To achieve this ultimate dependence that makes independence possible, one needs to have achieved having no deliberate heart-mind (*wuxin*); one ought to "discard the discarding," in order to be self-realized (*zide*), and eventually be capable of exercising a "far-reaching and unfettered" (*xiaoyao*) kind of wandering.

Being Far-Reaching and Unfettered (*xiaoyao* 逍遙) within Bounds

Now, we can understand that the spontaneity of being self-realized (*zide*) is the precursor to expanding possibilities that being "far-reaching and unfettered" (*xiaoyao*) allows us to undertake—possibilities realized in our dependence on our environment. That is to say, the state of freedom is the capacity to make spontaneous decisions in the context of one's awareness of one's environment and hence dependence on it. As Yang Lihua puts it:

> As long as one can be self-sufficient, not overstepping the boundaries of one's own natural allotment (性分 *xingfen*) nor coveting external things, one can achieve being "far-reaching and unfettered" (逍遙 *xiaoyao*). But all the people and all the things, their state of being "far-reaching and unfettered" (逍遙 *xiaoyao*) are all "attached to certain spheres" (繫於有方[40]) and all must attain that which they are dependent on (得其所待[41]), for then and only then can they be "far-reaching and unfettered" (逍遙 *xiaoyao*).[42]

In this sense, self-realization (*zide*) is the realization of that on which we are dependent—as we have argued both in the previous chapter as well the previous parts of this section—and as such, the only way we can hope to exercise our possibilities in the state of being "far-reaching and unfettered" (*xiaoyao*). This is because for Guo Xiang, as had been reiterated time and again, everything has a limit and allotment. He argues that even those that we consider great, such as the vast ocean, have limits:

The limit of a hundred streams is boundless yet they are subsumed into rivers; rivers are subsumed into the ocean, and the ocean is subsumed into the world, therefore each has a limit.[43]

窮百川之量而縣於河，河縣於海，海縣於天地，則各有量也。

He later continues in the same passage:

... each know their limit, things are settled in their allotment. One who is leisurely at ease uses his original steps yet wanders in the realm of self-realization.[44]

... 各知其極，物安其分，逍遙者用其本步而遊乎自得之場矣。

Here, Guo Xiang reminds us that the real exercise of our *xiaoyao* is dependent on our limit and allotment, upon which self-realization (*zide*) is also dependent through adapting to one's changing and fleeting nature. Although, traditionally, *xiaoyao* is often regarded as the concept in the *Zhuangzi* and Guo Xiang as synonymous with the notion of freedom,[45] this is also the concept on which Zhuangzi and Guo Xiang most apparently diverge. This supposed divergence,[46] moreover, is key to understanding what such a notion of becoming far-reaching and unfettered (*xiaoyao*) is in Guo Xiang, as well as the misunderstandings that are often superimposed on Guo via an understanding of the *Zhuangzi* (as being faithful to it or not), rather than the other way around.

Perhaps prominently, Liu Xiaogan has argued that there are several key differences in Zhuangzi and Guo Xiang when it comes to their notion of becoming far-reaching and unfettered (*xiaoyao*). Nonetheless, he also says that Zhuangzi and Guo Xiang's notions of becoming far-reaching and unfettered (*xiaoyao*) share the same form with what Isaiah Berlin criticizes as the "retreat to the inner citadel."[47] We shall get back to this later, but for now, what Liu Xiaogan says are the six main differences in Zhuangzi and Guo Xiang's notions of becoming far-reaching and unfettered (*xiaoyao*) are, in sum:

1. Zhuangzi's *xiaoyao* is more outward whereas Guo Xiang's is more inward. Zhuangzi's is of spiritual transcendence

whereas Guo Xiang's has to do with contentment in one's individual life.

2. In terms of one achieving *xiaoyao*, Zhuangzi's *xiaoyao* can only be achieved by a select few, whereas Guo Xiang's *xiaoyao* consists simply of being self-sufficient in one's nature. In other words, Zhuangzi's *xiaoyao* is a special state achieved by "consummate and genuine men" (至人、真人) through rigorous self-cultivation, whereas Guo Xiang's *xiaoyao* is mainly a change in attitude, which is the result of being at peace with one's endowed nature (*xingming*).

3. The state of being in *xiaoyao* in Zhuangzi is more binary than that of Guo Xiang's. Whereas Zhuangzi's *xiaoyao* is the same freedom and ascension to spiritual transcendence for all kinds of people, Guo Xiang's has different types of *xiaoyao*, but since they are all based on an individual's singular reality, each is not the same as the other.

4. Because Zhuangzi's *xiaoyao* takes someone from reality to the beyond, it has a three-dimensional structure, whereas Guo Xiang's *xiaoyao* has a flatter structure due to the fact that it is all grounded simply in reality. While in Zhuangzi there is a specific structure to achieving *xiaoyao*, in Guo Xiang there is no difference between high and low, or first and last, all steps toward *xiaoyao* are on the same level as the other.

5. Zhuangzi's *xiaoyao* is purely spiritual, and even personal, in content. Guo Xiang's *xiaoyao* advocates social order and the individual's harmony with the whole.

6. Zhuangzi's unchangeable "fate" (*ming*) is an external natural phenomenon, whereas Guo Xiang's is rooted in one's natural allotment (*xingfen*) and endowed nature (*xingming*). As such, Zhuangzi's *xiaoyao* aims to break away from external fetters and shackles, whereas Guo Xiang's *xiaoyao* aims to achieve comfort and satisfaction in one's natural allotment (*xingfen*).[48]

While I do not think that this captures the nuances of Guo Xiang's philosophical enterprise as anything more than passive acceptance, it suffices as a concise but accurate enumeration of the supposed difference between Zhuangzi and Guo Xiang—sufficient for a surface-level understanding that allows us to follow Liu Xiaogan's argument that both these notions of *xiaoyao* are "only an adaptation, acceptance, or escape from reality."[49] In other words it does not have the power for social change and transformation. He continues:

> Of course, whether this unfortunate decision to avoid misfortune is correct and wise may be controversial. On the one hand, some people believe that it is better to fight and die than to give up freedom and evade violence; on the other hand, people cannot prove whether resisting really has no chance of success. If it is impossible to prove that resistance will inevitably fail, then there is no necessary or logical rationale for a premature retreat. Therefore, for many people, Zhuangzi's and Guo Xiang's approach is not worthy of sympathy, and their *xiaoyao* are not worth striving for nor upholding. This is in fact a question of choice and preference in values, not a question of whether spiritual and mental freedom is [philosophically] sensible.[50]

Here, however, Liu Xiaogan seems to be pointing at the fact that if an agent is consciously and fully aware of his motivations and actions, with values freely internalized, is it really unfree to go into a retreat into an inner citadel when social resistance proves to be futile? He continues: "If modern people cannot completely avoid fixed circumstances that cannot be changed, then they must reflect on how to live better, with more ease, and nobler, in this unpleasant but fixed circumstance. In this respect, Zhuangzi's and Guo Xiang's theory can happen to complement the deficiencies of modern Western political theory."[51]

He argues, finally, that "the pursuit of pure personal spiritual satisfaction should gain understanding or sympathy, or at the least, should not receive condemnation. This is an affirmation of the pluralism of values."[52] What is interesting to note here is that Liu Xiaogan is actually making a very logical argument that necessarily follows from Berlin's theory of "freedom from." If the values I have internalized shape my ultimate ends as living a nobler life with more ease, and I desire to achieve this through retreating into my inner self, is it not an exercise of my freedom to do so? While Berlin would counter by saying that "heteronomy is dependence on outside factors,"⁵³ whereas autonomy depends solely on the self, Liu Xiaogan points out the naïveté of this stance—all actions are based on circumstances, and the dualistic split between dependence and independence, heteronomy and autonomy, is simply untenable in the real world where the self is not a separate thing from its environment. While Liu Xiaogan, however, proposes that this retreat to the inner citadel simply be affirmed as a value among other values, or at the very least be spared of condemnation, what he ultimately shows, at least to my impression, is the inconsistency of Berlin's theory of "freedom from" when faced with a robust theory of mystical freedom. This is because although Berlin had aptly critiqued "retreat to the inner citadel" as an escape that cuts the self out from the empirical world of causality, his theory of "freedom from" ultimately does the same—supposing a notion of the self that is disconnected from its physical circumstances, transcending the causal networks that shape their values. If Liu Xiaogan is right, Guo Xiang's notion of freedom falls into the same dichotomous trap as Berlin's does.

Interestingly, Mercedes Valmisa has argued that while the aforementioned retreat is true for Guo Xiang, it is not for Zhuangzi. In fact, she argues that we only look at Zhuangzi's notion of freedom as psychologizing because of Guo's interpretation of it, and this is problematic because such an account "can be easily manipulated into discourses used to prevent much needed social transformation and attempts to restructure unjust power relations."⁵⁴ As such, Valmisa sought to reinterpret Zhuangzi's notion of freedom so as to derive a theory of self-determination from the Peng bird's story, among others.⁵⁵ Ultimately, she argues that for the *Zhuangzi*, freedom is where "the person exhibits psychological awareness and emancipation with the final goal of effecting a change in her sociomaterial conditions."⁵⁶ I agree with Valmisa here, at least with the reasons why a retreat to the inner citadel is a problematic account of freedom. Nonetheless, she misreads Guo Xiang. If we will recount Yuet Keung Lo's essay on lone-transformation (*duhua*) as self-determination, he says about Guo Xiang that "the philosophical import of lone-transformation lies in the negotiation of the tension and synergy between multitude and loneness."⁵⁷ Moreover, Lo clarifies that this means that "in realistic terms, intergrowth is essentially the most favorable outcome of one's negotiations with all possible contacts without compromising one's integrity and sacrificing one's life."⁵⁸ In other words, Guo Xiang is able to negotiate between the individual and multitude, as well as the dialectical relation between them. This much is a necessary outcome of his logic of convergence as well as the necessity of contingency, and contingency of necessity. I would argue, moreover, that Guo Xiang's "dependence-based autonomy" is more comprehensive and holistic than Valmisa's interpretation of autonomy and freedom in the Zhuangzi. Whereas the "final goal" for Valmisa is to effect sociomaterial change, for Guo Xiang, it is not so diachronic, and is instead both diachronic and synchronic. Guo Xiang's "dependence-based autonomy" is diachronic in the sense that there is movement toward self-determination in lone-transformation (duhua) and being far-reaching and unfettered (xiaoyao) but it is also synchronic in the sense that there is a double oscillation between dependence (youdai) and independence (wudai) in order to ultimately become self-realized (zide). Guo Xiang thus demonstrates the dialectical relation of the individual and her sociomaterial conditions, acknowledging that dependence is ultimately necessary for self-realization (zide), and thus the kind of self-determination worth wanting as well. Not only is the goal to change sociomaterial conditions, but those conditions must also be changed in order to achieve self-determination, in a dialectical and unending process.

Thus, going back to the concept of xiaoyao, we now understand that Guo Xiang does not really advocate for a retreat to the inner citadel, and Liu Xiaogan misses this exactly because taking xiaoyao as a concept on its own in Guo Xiang's philosophy does not suffice to address the nuances of what freedom and autonomy are, which is more closely captured by the concept of self-realization (zide), as complemented by being both wuxin as well as xiaoyao. We know this from Guo Xiang's conception of the nondichotomous self as previously discussed, but it nonetheless is important to note that, as we have previously mentioned, and which Liu Xiaogan himself acknowledges to a certain extent, Guo Xiang was a man of social and political engagement and advocated for this in his philosophy. This is why xiaoyao does not stand alone—it is merely a necessary consequence of self-realization (zide), which in turn is possible through the spontaneity afforded by wuxin. Perhaps the most pertinent passage that shows how Guo Xiang's xiaoyao is far from an inner retreat is the following passage regarding the pheasant of the marshes:

> "The marsh pheasant finds one mouthful of food every ten steps, and one drink of water every hundred steps, but he does not seek to be fed and pampered in a cage. For

> **though his spirit might there reign supreme, it does not do him any good."**[59]

澤雉十步一啄，百步一飲，不蘄畜乎樊中。神雖王，不善也。

> Qi [a dated word in Guo Xiang's time] means seeking. The cage is that which entraps the pheasant. [The pheasant] bends down and rises up in the midst of heaven and earth, at leisurely ease, it is self-realized in its designated area, it is secure in the pleasant place of nourishing life. How can it still seek to go into a cage, when it already undertakes [its own] nourishment?[60]

蘄，求也。樊，所以籠雉也。夫俯仰乎天地之間，逍遙乎自得之場，固養生之妙處也。又何求於入籠而服養哉！

> One who is exactly suitable and is never unsuitable, [is one who] forgets suitability.
>   [In the cage, the pheasant's] heart and spirit reigns long, its will and *qi* is filled with comfort; yet in spontaneous liberation among the clear and open earth, being unaware of goodness suddenly becomes [what is] good.[61]

夫始乎適而未嘗不適者，忘適也。雉心神長王，志氣盈豫，而自放於清曠之地，忽然不覺善（為）之善也。

This passage shows us that for Guo Xiang, there is no *xiaoyao* in a retreat to a life of spiritual comfort and ease, but rather one ought to always choose liberty even without the comfort of being pampered, for there is no greater comfort than the spontaneous forgetfulness of the kind of *xiaoyao* that allows one to be in the realm of self-realization (*zide*). This is because being far-reaching and unfettered (*xiaoyao*) never stands alone, as with most of Guo Xiang's concepts, but is merely the necessary consequence and praxis of self-realization (*zide*).

This is important to note because, as already discussed, to "retreat to the inner citadel" is narcissistic at best, since it is basically freedom deprived of its political subversiveness, prevented from manifesting its powerful ability for social transformation, which Guo Xiang, like most of the Wei-Jin scholars, had hoped for. Turning inward to escape from one's horrible external state not only distracts from social and political action, but it also splits one's inner world from that of the external, and this goes against the very core of Guo Xiang's philosophical enterprise as defined by his logic of convergence. Although one may argue that Guo Xiang's philosophy is largely mental or epistemic in nature, it is no stretch to claim that social transformation begins and is simultaneous with epistemology. More precisely, self-realization (*zide*) for Guo Xiang is ultimately epistemic, but it is conditioned by a radical dependence, and this is why self-determination for Guo Xiang is a "dependence-based autonomy."

From this, we are able to glean how Guo Xiang's freedom is able to provide us with a more holistic view than that of Berlin's simplistic positive and negative freedom dichotomy. Its virtue does not simply lie in being a useful framework for everyday life, but in political life, where we are ridden with epistemic baggage as we deal with differences and otherness.

Conclusion

"Freedom In" and Social Change

The philosophy of Guo Xiang is, ultimately, a philosophy of freedom. In this work, I have tried to explore exactly what this means in the context Guo Xiang's philosophical system. At the same time, I have attempted to provide a rehabilitation of freedom understood as self-realization. I aimed to achieve these through a more holistic and comprehensive approach to reexamining the concepts pertinent to Guo Xiang's philosophical account—binding the ontological and epistemological concepts that he introduced together with the sociopolitical aspects that ultimately motivated his work and goals.

In this work thus, we have engaged with Guo Xiang's philosophical system. Thus far, we have attempted to comprehend, unpack, and articulate what I called the logic of convergence, which, as I have argued, not only highlights the complementarity of opposites as well as myriad things, but further required their complete and radical convergence. I've demonstrated this through discussing the convergence of the concepts of nonbeing and being through the absolute nature of existence, and that existence is a network of beings rather than isolated atoms independent from each other. As such, the natures of emergence and transformation are both necessary and contingent. In Guo Xiang's system, the one pattern of being self-so (*ziran*) fuses with the many different natures of the multitude things. Through this radical intercausality where everything is caused by and through everything, all things are simultaneously both uncaused and radically caused.

We then looked through the framework of the "logical convergence" as a basis for the discussion of the nature of the self, and demonstrated a conception of the self that is neither split between a real and false one, nor radically independent of, or transcendent from, others. I applied the logic of convergence as the sameness of difference to my discussions on nature (xing 性) as framed by one's allotment (fen 分) and endowment (ming 命); whereas allotment highlights the particularity of the self, the endowment of one's nature highlights the self's connection to the whole. I then showed how one's nature can always be transforming by virtue of its spontaneous and emergent characteristics, despite having been provided by heaven (Tian 天), since heaven itself is self-so (ziran). Through an elaboration of these concepts, I have shown the interpenetration of the self that breaks down the dichotomy between subject and object, as well as self and others—an absolute and singular self that, through its radical interpretation, transforms only within itself. It is therefore this self that is realized when self-realization (zide) is achieved.

I have thus far attempted to explore the concept of freedom based on Guo Xiang's notions of causality as well as one's own nature. I followed several scholars in having attempted to argue that—like many of his peers and as is the practice of the Wei-Jin politicians and scholars—material life has shaped ideology rather than the other way around. As such, even though Guo Xiang talks at great lengths about ontological and epistemological concepts, his motivations and goals were, in the end, social and political in nature. This informed my discussions of independence (wudai) as being one and the same with dependence (youdai). From this, I reconstructed a notion of autonomy and called it a "dependence-based autonomy" wherein freedom is derived from radical dependence. I demonstrated this further by elaborating on the specific dimensions for achieving self-realization, equating having no heart-mind (wuxin) with a participatory urge of being self-so, as well as the uniqueness and singularity of that participation when one is self-realized (zide), since realization is dependent on one's environment. I also argued that, even though scholars have traditionally regarded "far-reaching and unfettered" (xiaoyao) as espousing freedom due to its libertarian nature, this is not the case in Guo Xiang, because to him, true freedom is unique to each and every creature, as we can see from the ironic phenomenon of xiaoyao as something that can only be truly achieved within bounds or limits.

Thus, I will finally introduce a reconstruction of the concept of freedom, which I argue ought to be understood as "freedom in." This notion of freedom is a better alternative to more dominant notions of freedom as presented by Isaiah Berlin, because unlike notions of freedom that aim to take the subject away from its environment, it allows us to deal more holistically with difference, otherness, and the reality of causality.

Furthermore, the historical context and methodological framework upon which Wei-Jin *Xuanxue* builds itself is undoubtedly political in nature, and Richard Lynn even goes as far as to say that "Wang's and Guo's readings have the *Laozi* and the *Zhuangzi* largely addressed to rulers."[1] In spite of this, however, the extant works on Guo Xiang both in the Sinophone and Anglophone worlds have largely been ontological and epistemological without addressing much of his sociopolitical thought. This is a shame, because Guo Xiang's work as commentary to the *Zhuangzi*, which is mostly what we know of his work, is ultimately a politicization of the text. He systematized Zhuangzi's ontological views so that they can be more overtly political, in such a way that he created a system of political ontology as well as social epistemology. This is the true feat of Guo Xiang's commentary, which, in turn, transformed the *Zhuangzi* into his own, and Guo Xiang thus into a philosopher in his own right. This is not to say that there are no extant works that recognize and engage Guo Xiang's commentaries as political in nature, but even when the sociopolitical aspects of Guo Xiang's philosophy are addressed, it is along the lines of a not too uncommon and bold criticism, which points out his hierarchical and thereby oppressive tendencies. Vincent Shen, for instance, accuses Guo Xiang of being contradictory and Janus-faced, saying that "his soul should have been swaying between *wuwei* that lets others be themselves and his manipulating others with power when he himself is well placed in a higher political position."[2] In contrast to the traditionally mystical interpretation of Guo Xiang as also seen earlier from Liu Xiaogan, Shen highlights the sociopolitical aspect of Guo Xiang's philosophy, noting that "Guo Xiang's idea of the truly real was imbued with empiricist overtone. Disliking any metaphysical and transcendentalist discourse of non-being and the theology of creator of the universe."[3] However, although he toys with the idea that Guo Xiang "could be seen as an early Chinese version of liberalism"[4] due to his emphasis on the individual, Shen eventually concludes:

> Finally, it's doubtful that Guo Xiang's system can safeguard the equality of all. On the one hand, each individual's allotted nature is different from each other's. Since each individual is invited to be satisfied, at least subjectively, with his/her own allotted nature, Guo Xiang's ontological individualism, in this

sense, belongs to equalitarianism. For this, Guo Xiang could be seen as a revolutionary. But the fact that he conceives the horse's nature in reference to its service to human beings; the servant's allotted nature in reference to his service to the lord; the allotted nature of the stupid in reference to his service to the wise, etc., and the idea that each, in doing so, can always do it in a self-satisfied way, all these depict a realistic picture of inequality and justification of a status quo caught within the framework of social hierarchy and political domination. In this sense, Guo Xiang is conservative.[5]

Naturally, this would be the conclusion that one would adopt if Guo Xiang's logic of convergence is ignored, also explaining how the interpretations of Shen and Liu are worlds apart.[6] As we have already discussed,[7] however, Guo Xiang's notion of one's nature is never fixed nor determined by truly or wholly external factors. This is why dependence is an intercausal requisite for independence, because in the end, the self is other, and the other is self. Therefore one's commitment to one's own lot, nature, or place in the world is a category of emptiness (*wu*) that takes on the principle of self-so (*ziran*) in manifesting one's self-realization (*zide*), in order to be far-reaching and unfettered (*xiaoyao*). This is why, in contrast to the interpretations of Liu and Valmisa, Guo Xiang's interpretation of nothingness (*wu*) is inexorably linked to being and spontaneity, as we have seen in the ontological chapter (chap. 2). In direct relation to the sociopolitical realm, however, Guo Xiang comments on the passage in the first chapter of the *Zhuangzi* where the sage-king Yao tries (and fails) to hand over his rulership to the hermit Xu You:

> Ruling derives precisely from not ruling, action from non-action. Yao is already a sufficient source, so what need is there to borrow from Xu You? If non-action follows from silently clasping hands in the mountains and forests, then this talk of Zhuangzi and Laozi should be abandoned by officials. This is because one who serves as an official must be within the realm of effortful action.

> 夫治之由乎不治，為之出乎無為也，取於堯而足，豈借之許由哉！若謂拱默乎山林之中，而後得稱無為者，此莊老之談所以見棄於當塗，當塗者自必於有為之域而不反者，斯之由也。[8]

Guo Xiang argues that government officials should be and need to be in the realm of effortful action, practicing spontaneity, as that is the true meaning of nonaction. The *Zhuangzi* passage does not give a value-judgment of whether this decision makes Xu You more honorable or wiser than Yao, but Guo Xiang does. Guo Xiang is basically telling us that Xu You knew he was less fit than Yao, because while he is "silently clasping hands in the mountains and forests," Yao is actually in the realm of effortful action. Guo further explains why Yao, due to the qualities he has, makes for a superior ruler than Xu You:

> One who is *with* things vanishes, which is why the myriad things are unable to depart from them. This is a case of having no heart-mind and [being able to] deeply resonate, so they follow upon contact; they float like an untethered raft, not trying to control whether they drift east or west. Thus, one who goes nowhere without sharing with the common people is also one who is ruler of the world wherever he goes. If one understands "rulership" like this, then the self-elevation of the world is truly the ruler's virtuosity.
>
> 夫與物冥者，故群物之所不能離也。是以無心玄應，唯感之從，汎乎若不繫之舟，東西之非己也，故無行而不與百姓共者，亦無往不為天下之君矣。以此為君，若天下自高，實君之德也。[9]

This passage is perhaps Guo's most direct way of inverting hierarchy, such that rulers and officials must be able to look at themselves as people who are in the service of people, only accomplishing their job when people become self-elevating. Further than that, Guo Xiang emphasizes that a good ruler must be able to share with and become one with the people—walking and mingling them, understanding them, listening to them—vanishing into them. To float like an untethered raft and have no control in this context means that this ruler must be able to move in accordance with the needs of the common people, and not his own desires, or a fixed bureaucracy according to certain ethical standards. This means that rulership equates to serving the changing needs of the people, not striving toward a fixed political ideal of kind, which might tend to warp present needs for the sake of future goals. This is what Guo means when he says that one must vanish into things, through having no heart-mind (*wuxin*) of one's own, and being sufficient in one's own allotment (*fen*); this is the means according to which one can transform with things and thereby the common people. Moreover, it is worth emphasizing that to understand this sociopolitical aspect in Guo Xiang means that we must take the onto-epistemological basis into consideration, because ultimately all actions and all relationships stem from what we understand as our selves. For Guo Xiang, this self is inextricably linked to the other, caused by everything and by nothing, both necessary and contingent. This is what it means to go beyond discarding, by discarding the discarding—to go beyond forgetting, by forgetting the forgetting. The constant transformation of one's allotment (*fen* 分) as discussed in the chapter On the Self is relevant again here: that means that one who is now a servant may later be lord. This means that he does not advocate that each must keep to his social role, but just that one's attitude toward whatever one's current role is at the time ought to be treated as currently operative. Nonetheless, a beautiful depiction of this is seen in the following passage in the *Zhuangzi*, where Guo Xiang also provides an insightful comment:

"When the springs dry up, the fish have to cluster together on the shore, gasping on each other to keep damp and spitting on each other to stay wet. But that is no match for forgetting all about one another in the rivers and lakes. Rather than praising Yao and condemning Jie, we'd be better off forgetting them both and transforming along our own courses."[10]

泉涸，魚相與處於陸，相呴以濕，相濡以沫，不如相忘於江湖。
與其譽堯而非桀也，不如兩忘而化其道。

Rather than be insufficient in loving one another, is it not better to be in abundance in forgetting each other? Now condemning and praising, in all cases, arise from insufficiency. Thus, the height of sufficiency, is to forget good and evil, to lose death and life, to take part in change and transformation as one, be in a state of openness that there is nowhere one does not reach, and so once again, how does one know where lies Yao and Jie?[11, 12]

與其不足而相愛，豈若有餘而相忘！夫非譽皆生於不足。故至
足者，忘善惡，遺死生，與變化為一，曠然無不適矣，又安知
堯桀之所在耶！

Gasping and spitting, we long for praise and condemnation, giving out praise and condemnation with hopes that it would be returned, so we can keep going and surviving. In his interpretation of the *Zhuangzi* passage, Ziporyn describes this as: "that righteous feeling of rectitude and belonging and approval we get when we say what is right and wrong, and who is right and wrong, when we feel justified and take it upon ourselves to justify ourselves and each other."[13] Yet, right and wrong, good and evil, judgments and values, all these are arbitrary to our time, place, and motivations. Guo Xiang thus shows how, in this arbitrariness, we simply praise the other for something that we *lack* and we condemn the other for something we think they *lack*. We feel good among brethren when we praise each other, because we are unlike those "bad" people. We feel good when we condemn others, because those "bad" people are beneath us. We praise life to feel that we belong here, that this is a purposeful existence, and condemn death because we do not know of it and must, therefore, fearfully shun it as "bad." Yet, life and death, self and other, is there a difference in their difference? Gasping and spitting might be acts of love and morality, which we think are done in good intention, yet they are ultimately wretched and bound to fail, because we aren't where we are actually, truly, in our place—forgetting all about each other in the abundance of water in the rivers and lakes. Love is insufficient, morality is insufficient, and the highest sufficiency lies in forgetting by means of participating in the oneness of the universe—of the rivers and lakes. In this way, we forget the forgetting, bask in openness such that we may be able to reach everywhere. Hence, rather than fixating on Yao and Jie, good and evil, this framework or that framework, even self and other, it is more useful to forget them all, and then forget that and take them all as one horse, one finger, one transformation. If, therefore, Vincent Shen had difficulty placing Guo Xiang as not a mystical escapist who rejects all that is external, but neither liberal nor politically "conservative," it is because he is none of these, and for good reason. Guo Xiang doesn't fit into the liberal framework, as Shen would have preferred, not because he has conservative tendencies, but because he has a different type of autonomy that is uniquely dependence-based, which means that he takes the oneness of our singular belongingness, and indeed intercausality, into account. The following passage, where Confucius is talking, most straightforwardly captures this:

> "In the days of Yao and Shun, no one in the world was a failure, but this was not gained due to any wisdom on their parts. In the days of Jie and Zhou, no one in the world was a success, but this was not because of any failure of their wisdom. It was just the circumstantial tendencies of the times that made it so.

> 當堯舜而天下無窮人，非知得也；當桀紂而天下無通人，非知失也；時勢適然。

> One should not belabor the heart-mind between failure and success.

> 無為勞心於窮通之間。

> **To travel over water without fearing the sharks and dragons is the courage of the fisherman. To travel over land without fearing rhinos and tigers is the courage of the hunter. To view death as no different from life even when the blades are clanging in front of one's face is the courage of the warrior.**

> 夫水行不避蛟龍者，漁父之勇也；陸行不避兕虎者，獵夫之勇也；白刃交於前，視死若生者，烈士之勇也；

> Each emotion has what it is at ease in.

> 情各有所安。

> **And to know that success depends on fate and failure on the times, to face great calamities without fear, this is the courage of the sage.**

> 知窮之有命，知通之有時，臨大難而不懼者，聖人之勇也。

The sage thus has nowhere where he is not at ease.

聖人則無所不安。

Relax, Zilu! My fate is already sealed."[14]

由處矣，吾命有所制矣。」

Fate is not something that he himself [and only himself] seals, therefore there is no [one] thing which he sets his heart upon.
    For him who is at ease in fate, there is nowhere where he is not "far-reaching and unfettered," therefore even though he sets forth from Kuang to Youli, there is no difference between being in the farthest depths of heaven and the idle imperial halls.[15]

命非己制，故無所用其心也。夫安於命者，無往而非逍遙矣，故雖匡陳羑里，無異於紫極閒堂也。

Although this passage would, at first sight, appear problematically fatalistic, we know from our discussions in the earlier parts of this work that this is far from being a shocking revelation in Guo Xiang's philosophy. From what we now know of his onto-epistemological foundations, we can understand that this is a call to acknowledge that our knowledge, self, the and results of our actions are arbitrarily caused by change and transformation. One does not and cannot deliberately, purposefully, get to *choose* one's fate, if simply because it is not in our power to predict the infinite changes and transformations of the future while we are in the present. Therefore he describes being far-reaching and unfettered (*xiaoyao*) as a spontaneous attainment that is both dependent and independent of its environment—an independence that cultivates being at ease wherever one is, through a fundamental dependency on its allotted environment. To have "no [one] thing which one sets his heart upon" (無所用其心), thus, is a spontaneous attainment that varies from moment to moment and being to being.

    This notion of being far-reaching and unfettered (*xiaoyao*), made possible by one's self-realization (*zide*) in one's given situation or fate (*ming*), and therefore freedom, is defined by the convergence of dependence and independence. Thus, it can only be counterproductive and oppressive if rightness or appropriateness is dictated by an external factor, whether it be the notion of some internal self that is ultimately problematic as it is in liberalism, or an outright external dominant authority. Such ideological dominance from an external authority is what Isaiah Berlin would refer to as positive liberty, which he critiques as "a deep and incurable metaphysical need; . . . to allow it to determine one's practice is a symptom of an equally deep, and more dangerous, moral and political immaturity."[16] Indeed such freedom that Berlin holds as oppressive, in contrast to the negative freedom of liberalism, is a false dichotomy of liberties; in the end, both ultimately come from a self that is withdrawn from its environment. In contrast, we are presented here with an alternative notion of freedom. This freedom derived from a self that is spontaneously emerging from moment to moment, determined not by constitution nor any particularly linear cause, but by everything else, that is, the transformation and movement of everything. As such, "freedom in": a freedom that is necessary and singular inasmuch as it is purely contingent in constitution and transformation, in relation to the necessity of everything else's contingency; one that is satisfied and at ease, not in spite of, but because of the *other*—that is, the convergence of subjectivity with objective order.

In other words, it is because the self doesn't arise from nowhere, that we are perpetually bound by all that caused how we know and understand ourselves, by what we think when we think of our own identities—each unique but also fleeting and inexorably linked to "others." We can never be sure of the consequences of our actions, especially when we deliberately seek their results just as gasping and spitting fish do, and we can always have good yet misguided intentions. However, to be aware that our actions, our "identities," or allotment and even fate are ultimately caused by everything and nothing, and to think of ourselves as agents in and of our environment, is freedom in its most autonomous sense. Guo Xiang's notion of freedom, as Liu Xiaogan has pointed out, is mental or epistemic in nature. However, this is not to say that it has no sociopolitical and moral implications. After all, the primary goal of Guo Xiang and his Neo-Daoist peers, as shown to us by Richard Lynn, was political reform. Guo Xiang's account merely shows us the underlying epistemic nature of our sociopolitical transactions, and that both of these philosophical aspects cannot be separated. If the self is the one doing the transacting, it matters how that self is formed. It matters, moreover, that we are liberated from a "self" not spontaneously formed, or not self-realized (*zide*), which is ultimately externally formed (*xingfenzhiwai* 性分之外). To be free is to is to be able to participate in change and spontaneity (*ziran*); the convergence of inner and outer, nature and sociality, is also the dissolution of their binaries. Everything that is possible is natural, everything is both inner and outer, and the interconnection of all aspects within this system is what allows for continual change and transformation—to be unfree, therefore, is to be stuck in space-time and in a fixed category or definition, whether forced or self-imposed. Unlike Isaiah Berlin's negative liberty, "freedom in" acknowledges that we are all means not ends-in-ourselves, but unlike positive liberty that is found in ideologies and religions, there is no end, no purpose, no goal—only means. Precisely, as Berlin proves, because there is a final goal to life that we must acknowledge that all we have are means, we are forever influenced and influencer. We do not have a "true" self that is born free. All we have is each other and our responsibility to each other; our responsibility to let each other swim in forgetfulness.

Guo Xiang's account of "freedom in" can thus serve as a more holistic alternative to Berlin's liberal "freedom from" and conservative "freedom to." This is a significant step in rehabilitating the concept to become truly intercultural and inclusive, because as we have seen, both of Berlin's types of liberties or freedoms are deeply ingrained in the "free will" pseudo-problem of Anglo-European philosophy. "Freedom in," in comparison, takes into account that in order to achieve the kind of self-determination where the self is not compromised, one must first achieve self-realization. As we have seen, self-realization is necessary to have a self-determining self-worth wanting. Moreover, it is necessary lest we fall into the trap of justifying any means for the worthy end of self-determination, "freedom from," which Berlin believes is the only end in itself, leading him to misguidedly proclaim that the search for realization is what "causes a member of some newly liberated Asian or African State to complain less today, when he is rudely treated by members of his own race or nation, than when he was governed by some cautious, just, gentle, well-meaning administrator from outside."[17] Yet this kind of liberalism, far from liberating states and peoples, colonizes them and justifies it. This, indeed, is the danger in positing a transcendent self as the stopgap where the buck stops, in assuming that there is a "natural" state of things, either waiting to be discovered or waiting to be returned to, as Rousseau might have it.

Guo Xiang, through his transformation of the *Zhuangzi*, allows us to conceive of a self that is already always within the concrete world, within the incompleteness of reality, where our very limitations allow us to produce and create infinite unforeclosed possibilities. It is in this dialectical process of interacting with the world around us, without superimposing fixed ideals or selves, that we collectively share the burden of continuously creating circumstances conducive to self-determination, and hence are able to possess what I have called a "dependence-based autonomy." More importantly, however, Guo Xiang's philosophical enterprise allows us to see that in order to achieve freedom, we must be able to adapt to the dialectical conditions that frame how we view ourselves and the others around us, as well as our place in the world as manufacturers and consumers of knowledge, knowledge that dictates how we transact with the world, and ultimately our political and moral autonomy. Guo Xiang's account of freedom is thus a powerful tool in dealing with the politics of difference—an issue that is pertinent now more than ever.

Freedom is situationally dependent. Dependence-based autonomy is an emergent quality of one who has successfully negotiated with the multitude for conducive conditions to self-realization, thereby achieving the kind of self-determination worth wanting. One of the most telling phrases that Guo Xiang tells us about what the *Zhuangzi* says is:

> If what we call "nonaction" follows from silently clasping hands in the mountains and forests, then this talk of Zhuangzi and Laozi should be abandoned by officials. This is because one who serves as an official must be within the realm of effortful action.
>
> 若謂拱默乎山林之中，而後得稱無為者，此莊老之談所以見棄於當塗，當塗者自必於有為之域而不反者，斯之由也。[18]

Nonetheless, it is what follows this that is more significant, where Guo says, "He who is self-confident forms an opposition with things, while those who go along with things have no such opposition . . . (夫自任者對物，而順物者與物無對 . . .)."[19] This shows how our actions should always depend on their contexts, but it tells us something deeper than that, too. It tells us that freedom is not self-determination in and of itself, whether within limits such that one does not overstep others' self-determinations, but rather that self-realization is something that we gain from acting. Acting in accordance with the needs of things and people, going along with them, in other words from fulfilling our ever-changing duties to other people, and that that is the only way we can have a self that is truly determining its own actions. To go along with things, one must first depend on them, and let them dictate our actions and constitute our own "selves." Ironically, this is the only way we can be truly self-determining in the sense that there is no external cause for our choices and actions, for we become radically contingent, not letting any single fixed thing (as either cause or effect) guide us. In this radical contingence, we become wholly singular, yet far from the individual as starting point, we see in Guo Xiang's *Zhuangzi* a contrary image of freedom. A kind of freedom that acknowledges how much we owe to each other, to the world, and how fulfilling that is within its proper context (albeit always changing), is what it means to be autonomous. In this manner, we do owe each other, but we also *make* each other, support each other, propel and empower each other—shape each other. We owe and we belong, but in changing circumstances, for a fixed belonging is an ideological danger. Instead, we must acknowledge that although we do owe each other, what we owe is never fixed, for our own selves are never fixed, and our identities are always contingent, but they are singular, and thereby necessary.

There is much work that is ahead of this new possibility in framing what freedom means, but for now, it would suffice to say that this alternative account of freedom goes beyond liberalism and its false dichotomization of liberty, precisely because far from being a mystic or a fatalist, Guo Xiang understood that "becoming one with nature" and "forgetting oneself in order to remember oneself" are not romantic ideals. There may be no such thing as absolute free will that is outside of causality, but this does not mean that we are mere puppets that are necessarily controlled. Autonomy or governing our own actions is possible, but acquiring it requires radical dependence. This kind of freedom, thus, is an encouragement to get back to the ground of our material practices and learn how the formation of our ideals can be reexamined through the singularity of our identities. *Freedom in* is freedom that is grounded, not relying on the "traces" (*ji*) of past models or sages, nor putting in deliberate effort (*youwei*) for a future ideal or value/s; it is the freedom of "vanishing into things" (*xuanming*). *Freedom in* arises from radical dependency because it relies on the circumstances, as well as people, that agents find themselves around. *Freedom in* has no blueprint for a future goal that we must strive toward but must spontaneously emerge from the real and concrete circumstances of our present condition. It is, therefore, revolutionary, both for its time and for today.

Throughout this work, my aim has been to show that freedom is something we achieve and realize. The notion that a subject is born with it, and that one can return to it by isolating oneself from others, would be a strange idea, not just to Guo Xiang but to most Chinese philosophers. Rather, freedom is frail, complex and fragile, and from our philosophical exposition, we see that—despite romantic ideations of individual libertarianism—only the kind of freedom that is collectively attained through radical dependence can be worth having. Self-cultivation, in as much as it focuses on the self, is something that cannot be achieved in isolation from others. Guo Xiang's intercausal account of the process of existence, as well as the epistemological silence that is required of us in order to be able to properly listen and interact with the world, are key to understanding our inherent connection to our cosmos, to each other, and ultimately our pursuit of freedom.

It is my hope that this humble exposition of the political contributions of Guo Xiang's *Zhuangzi*, and the importance of reading this work in a systematic and holistic way, can help current and future students of both Guo Xiang and Zhuangzi, as well as encourage philosophers to read nonmainstream accounts of contemporary issues that plague us. I have shown that concepts of freedom, autonomy, individualism, and even social change borne of onto-epistemic philosophies do exist in the Chinese philosophical tradition, which is a diverse and vibrant collection of differing philosophies. Most importantly, however, I have demonstrated how a concept of freedom, understood as "freedom in," and achieved through a "dependence-based autonomy," is a plausible and more comprehensive type of freedom than the purely political "freedom from," or purely metaphysical "freedom to." Though I recognize that many variations of these do exist in contemporary debates, what is unique to Guo Xiang is his dialectical approach, which starts from and is boldly within the social, yet is also deeply ingrained in ontological and epistemological concerns.

Indeed knowledge, and thereby Truth, is radically contingent upon material and concrete circumstances—Guo Xiang knew this—and so, social change, achieved via self-realization that allows for self-determination, can only be achieved through awareness of our material and concrete circumstances. The kind of self-realization that leads to self-determination, however, can only be brought about through allowing ourselves to vanish into, and depend on, the real conditions that emerge from moment to moment. This means that freedom cannot be brought about by first analyzing the concept in isolation from material conditions and then applying it outside. To achieve freedom means to transform in and with the conditions that shape us, to fundamentally and radically depend on the changes of our circumstances. Guo Xiang thus shows us how the only purpose of the hierarchy is to make the topmost transform in accordance with the bottom; that the analysis and superimposition of a self, separated from others, unto others in order to justify our own actions in accordance to supposedly universal values, is an illness we need to confront and contend with.

Looking at Guo Xiang's *Zhuangzi* and the philosophy of freedom found therein, we are thus made to understand that truly comparative and intercultural approaches can lead to truly distinct and unique arsenals of knowledge that are ripe, not only for shedding light onto our philosophical dispositions, but more importantly in leading us to understand the real and harmful consequences of fixating on our deeply held truths.

Notes

Chapter 1. The Question of Freedom

1. Genyou Wu, "On the Idea of Freedom and Its Rejection in Chinese Thought and Institutions," *Asian Philosophy* 16, no. 3 (2006): 219.

2. Jacques Lacan and Jacques-Alain Miller, *The Ethics of Psychoanalysis, 1959–1960: The Seminar of Jacques Lacan, Book VII* (London: Routledge, 2008).

3. Chenyang Li, Sai Hang Kwok, and Dascha Düring, *Harmony in Chinese Thought: A Philosophical Introduction* (Lanham: Rowman & Littlefield, 2021).

4. W. J. F. Jenner, "China and Freedom," in *Asian Freedoms: The Idea of Freedom in East and Southeast Asia*, ed. David Kelly and Anthony Reid (Cambridge: Cambridge University Press, 1998), 65.

5. Ibid., 65.

6. Ibid., 68.

7. Daniel A. Bell, *The China Model: Political Meritocracy and the Limits of Democracy* (Princeton: Princeton University Press, 2016), 56–57.

8. David Kelly, "Approaching Chinese Freedom: A Study in Absolute and Relative Values," *Journal of Current Chinese Affairs* 42, no. 2 (2013): 163.

9. Weiming Tu, *Way, Learning, and Politics: Essays on the Confucian Intellectual* (Albany: State University of New York Press, 1993), 6. Emphasis mine.

10. For a more comprehensive discussion, see Frederick Wakeman, "Rebellion and Revolution: The Study of Popular Movements in Chinese History," *Journal of Asian Studies* 36, no. 2 (1977).

11. Ying-shih Yü, "Individualism and the Neo-Daoist Movement in Wei-Jin China," in *Chinese History and Culture: Sixth Century B.C.E. to Seventeenth Century*, ed. Michael S. Duke and Josephine Chiu-Duke (New York: Columbia University Press, 2016).

12. Étienne Balazs, *Chinese Civilization and Bureaucracy: Variations on a Theme*, trans. H. M. Wright (New Haven: Yale University Press, 1964), 243.

13. Although little is known about Bao Jingyan, he has a surviving work entitled *No-Ruler Theory* 無君論 *Wujunlun*, which Balazs translates as "Neither

Lord nor Subject," quite possibly alluding to the anarchist slogan "Neither God nor Master" that had become prominent during the early twentieth-century anarchist movements, incidentally the same time when Balazs was writing. In this work, Bao criticizes the Confucian justification for the Mandate of Heaven and argues that this is an excuse used by those who benefit from it. Further, Bao points out the exploitation that arises from relationships that involve domination: "The fact is that the strong oppressed the weak and the weak submitted to them; the cunning tricked the innocent and the innocent served them. It was because there was submission that the relation of lord and subject arose, and because there was servitude that the people, being powerless, could be kept under control." For a translated version of the full text, see Bao Jingyan, "Neither Lord nor Subject," in Balazs, *Chinese Civilization and Bureaucracy: Variations on a Theme*, 243–46.

14. This would perhaps be more often referred to as metaphysical freedom, but at least in the context of Guo Xiang, there is no such thing as "beyond the physical" as is the case with what is metaphysical. Instead, as I will delve further into later, we simply have something that deals with causality and existence—as such, I refer to it as relating to ontology rather than metaphysics.

15. Jean-Jacques Rousseau, *A Treatise on the Social Compact, or, the Principles of Political Law* (London: D. I. Eaton, 1795), 4.

16. Daniel C. Dennett, *Elbow Room: The Varieties of Free Will Worth Wanting* (New York: Oxford University Press, 1984), 5.

17. For a more comprehensive discussion, see ibid.

18. Ibid., 169.

19. Democritus, III.17.39, quoted in C. C. W. Taylor, *The Atomists, Leucippus and Democritus: Fragments: A Text and Translation with a Commentary* (Toronto: University of Toronto Press, 1999), 34.

20. In Tim Whitmarsh's book about atheism and challenging divinities in the ancient Mediterranean, he says about Democritus that "in Democritus's material world, gods have become parasites rather than hosts." See Tim Whitmarsh, *Battling the Gods: Atheism in the Ancient World* (New York: Vintage, 2016), 68.

21. Pamela Huby, "The First Discovery of the Freewill Problem," *Philosophy* 42, no. 162 (1967): 361.

22. [F15] Aëtius [P I.25.4] S I.4.7c (67B2), quoted in Daniel W. Graham, *The Texts of Early Greek Philosophy: The Complete Fragments and Selected Testimonies of the Major Presocratics* (New York: Cambridge University Press, 2010), 553.

23. Huby, "The First Discovery of the Freewill Problem."

24. Ibid., 358.

25. Cicero, *On Fate*, 22–23, quoted in Brad Inwood and Lloyd P. Gerson, *Hellenistic Philosophy* (Indianapolis: Hackett, 1997), 47–48.

26. Cyril Bailey, *The Greek Atomists and Epicurus: A Study* (New York: Russell & Russell, 1964), 321.

27. According to this, Lactantius presents the traditional problem of evil and poses it thus: "And if this explanation [for the existence of bad things] . . . is true, then that argument of Epicurus is refuted. 'God,' he says, 'either wants to eliminate bad things and cannot, or can but does not want to, or neither wishes to nor can, or both wants to and can. If he wants to and cannot, then he is weak—and this does not apply to god. If he can but does not want to, then he is spiteful which is equally foreign to god's nature. If he neither wants to nor can, he is both weak and spiteful and so not a god. If he wants to and can, which is the only thing fitting for a god, where then do bad things come from? Or why does he not eliminate them?' I know that most of the philosophers who defend [divine] providence are commonly shaken by this argument and against their wills are almost driven to admit that god does not care, which is exactly what Epicurus is looking for." See Lactantius, *On the Anger of God*, 13.20–22, quoted in Inwood and Gerson, *Hellenistic Philosophy*, 94.

28. Epicurus, *Letter to Menoeceus*: Diogenes Laertius, [1–4] 10.121–135, quoted in ibid., 31.

29. Susanne Bobzien, "Did Epicurus Discover the Free Will Problem?," *Oxford Studies in Ancient Philosophy* 19 (2000).

30. Michael Frede, *A Free Will: Origins of the Notion in Ancient Thought*, ed. A. A. Long (Berkeley: University of California Press, 2011), 175.

31. Albrecht Dihle, *The Theory of Will in Classical Antiquity* (Berkeley: University of California Press, 1982), 123.

32. Epictetus, book I.I.12, quoted in W. A. Oldfather, *Epictetus: The Discourses as Reported by Arrian, the Manual, and Fragments* (Cambridge: Harvard University Press, 1925), 11.

33. Dihle, *The Theory of Will in Classical Antiquity*, 124.

34. See, for instance, Luke 10:15 and Matthew 11:23, where residents of the city of Capernaum (along with Bethsaida and Chorazin) are damned unto hell for their lack of faith in Jesus as the Messiah.

35. See, for instance, the Catechism of the Catholic Church, 1036. The logic behind deserving hell due to one's own choices also applies to the Problem of Evil in theodicy itself, as Alvin Plantinga argues in what he calls the "free will defense" where he expresses "the idea of being free with respect to an action. If a person is free with respect to a given action, then he is free to perform that action and free to refrain from performing it; no antecedent conditions and/or causal laws determine that he will perform the action, or that he won't. It is within his power, at the time in question, to take or perform the action and within his power to refrain from it." Alvin Plantinga, *God, Freedom, and Evil* (Grand Rapids: Eerdmans, 1977), 29. This defense, he says, "shows that the existence of God is compatible, both logically and probabilistically, with the existence of evil; thus it solves the main philosophical problem of evil" (64).

36. Dennett, *Elbow Room: The Varieties of Free Will Worth Wanting*, 5.

37. Ibid., 169.

38. Ibid., 169.

39. Immanuel Kant, *Immanuel Kant's Critique of Pure Reason*, trans. Norman Kemp Smith (London: Macmillan, 1929), 634.

40. Ibid., 411.

41. Ibid., 465. Kant here refers to external determination as coming from sensuous impulses because Reason is objective and universal, the Truth that is necessary and therefore free.

42. This sentiment is discussed comprehensively in Hegel's *Philosophy of History* and *Philosophy of Right*, among others.

43. Georg Wilhelm Friedrich Hegel, *Hegel: Elements of the Philosophy of Right* (Cambridge: Cambridge University Press, 1991), §15, 48.

44. Georg Wilhelm Friedrich Hegel, *Hegel's Lectures on the History of Philosophy*, trans. Elizabeth Sanderson Haldane and Frances H. Simson (London: Routledge & Kegan Paul, 1968), 401–02.

45. Isaiah Berlin, *Historical Inevitability*, in *Liberty: Incorporating Four Essays on Liberty*, ed. Henry Hardy (New York: Oxford University Press, 2002), 155.

46. Ibid., 164.

47. Ibid., 164–65.

48. Throughout Berlin's work, he most consistently cites Karl Marx and Auguste Comte as such examples, respectively. He discusses them as well in the same work. See ibid. More straightforwardly, however, Berlin explains this of Comte and says: "The same attitude was pointedly expressed by August Comte, who asked why, if we do not allow free thinking in chemistry or biology, we should allow it in morals or politics. Why indeed? If it makes sense to speak of political truths—assertions of social ends which all men, because they are men, must, once they are discovered, agree to be such; and if, as Comte believed, scientific method will in due course reveal them; then what case is there for freedom of opinion or action—at least as an end in itself, and not merely as a stimulating intellectual climate—either for individuals or for groups? Why should any conduct be tolerated that is not authorised by appropriate experts? Comte put bluntly what had been implicit in the rationalist theory of politics from its ancient Greek beginnings. There can, in principle, be only one correct way of life." See Berlin, "Two Concepts of Liberty," in *Liberty: Incorporating Four Essays on Liberty*, 197.

49. Berlin notes: "Sen, with admirable consistency and candour, does indeed explain that, when determinists use the language of moral praise and blame, they are like atheists who still mention God, or lovers who speak of being faithful 'till the end of time; such talk is hyperbolic and not meant to be taken literally—This does at least concede (as most determinists do not) that if these words were taken literally something would be amiss. For my part I see no reason for supposing that most of those who use such language, with

its implication of free choice among alternatives, whether in the future or in the past, mean this not literally, but in some Pickwickian or metaphorical or rhetorical way. Ernest Nagel points out that determinists, who, like Bossuet, believed in the omnipotence and omniscience of Providence and its control over every human step, nevertheless freely attributed moral responsibility to individuals; and that adherents of determinist faiths—Muslims, Calvinists and others—have not refrained from attribution of responsibility and a generous use of praise and blame." See *Liberty: Incorporating Four Essays on Liberty*, 9–10.

50. Berlin, "Two Concepts of Liberty," 169, emphasis mine.

51. Ibid., 169, emphasis mine.

52. Ibid., 190.

53. Ibid., 212.

54. Ibid., 195.

55. Ibid., 217.

56. Isaiah Berlin, *Russian Thinkers*, ed. Henry Hardy and Aileen Kelly (London: Penguin Books, 1994), xxiv.

57. Daniel C. Dennett, *Freedom Evolves* (New York: Viking, 2003), 306.

58. An exception, however, was Dong Zhongshu who anthropomorphized Heaven (天 *Tian*) with a will, as well as attributing to it the creation of humans, saying that "the creator of human beings is Heaven. . . . Heaven is also the supreme ancestor of human beings." See Zhongshu Dong, *Luxuriant Gems of the Spring and Autumn*, trans. John S. Major and Sarah A. Queen (New York: Columbia University Press, 2015), book 11, part 1, section 41.1.

59. A concept that Aristotle came up with in his *Metaphysics*. See Aristotle, *Metaphysics*, book 12. It was later adopted by the Scholastics, including Islamic philosophers, and in Christianity was popularized by Thomas Aquinas in his magnum opus, the *Summa Theologica*.

60. See, for instance, Chad Hansen, "Freedom and Moral Responsibility in Confucian Ethics," *Philosophy East and West* 22, no. 2 (1972); François Jullien, *Detour and Access: Strategies of Meaning in China and Greece*, trans. Sophie Hawkes (New York: Zone Books, 2000). Quoted in Christian Wenzel and Kai Marchal, "Chinese Perspectives on Free Will," in *The Routledge Companion to Free Will*, ed. Kevin Timpe, Meghan Giffith, and Neil Levy (London: Routledge, 2017). This is also seen in Erica Fox Brindley, *Individualism in Early China: Human Agency and the Self in Thought and Politics* (Honolulu: University of Hawai'i Press, 2010).

61. Wenzel and Marchal, "Chinese Perspectives on Free Will," 375.

62. Ibid., 374.

63. Ibid., 386.

64. Ibid., 375.

65. Hegel, *Hegel: Elements of the Philosophy of Right*, 21.

66. Tao Jiang, "Isaiah Berlin's Challenge to the Zhuangzian Freedom," *Journal of Chinese Philosophy* 39, no. 5 (2012): 86.

67. Ibid., 86.
68. Ibid., 83.
69. Ibid., 82–84.
70. Tao uses a story in the "Autumn Floods" as an example for this, when Zhuangzi compares those who serve the king to "an enshrined dead tortoise."
71. Bryan W. Van Norden, "Zhuangzi's Ironic Detachment and Political Commitment," *Dao* 15, no. 1 (2016): 13.
72. Ge Ling Shang, *Liberation as Affirmation: The Religiosity of Zhuangzi and Nietzsche* (Albany: State University of New York Press, 2006), 8.
73. Ibid., 148.
74. Ibid., 47.
75. Guoping Zhao, "Transcendence, Freedom, and Ethics in Lévinas' Subjectivity and Zhuangzi's Non-Being Self," *Philosophy East and West* 65, no. 1 (2015): 77.
76. Eske Janus Møllgaard, "Zhuangzi's Notion of Transcendental Life," *Asian Philosophy* 15, no. 1 (2005): 17.
77. Alan Fox, "Reflex and Reflectivity: *Wuwei* in the *Zhuangzi*," *Asian Philosophy* 6, no. 1 (1996): 61.
78. Ibid., 68.
79. Franklin Perkins, *Heaven and Earth Are Not Humane: The Problem of Evil in Classical Chinese Philosophy* (Bloomington: Indiana University Press, 2014), 177.
80. Ibid., 170.
81. Ibid., 183.
82. Xiaogan Liu, "Zhuangzi's Philosophy: A Three Dimensional Reconstruction," in *Dao Companion to Daoist Philosophy*, ed. Xiaogan Liu (Dordrecht: Springer, 2015), 205.
83. Ibid., 207.
84. Xiaogan Liu, "两种逍遥与两种自由 (Two Kinds of *Xiaoyao* and Two Kinds of Freedom)," *Journal of Huazhong Normal University (Humanities and Social Sciences)* (November 2007): 85.
85. Ibid., 86.
86. Ibid., 87.
87. We know little about Guo Xiang. However, we know that he was articulate. He held a high position in the government, and was favored by his benefactor, Sima Yue (d. 311, Prince of Donghai, regent of Emperor Hui of Jin, and throughout various periods during the Jin dynasty was a power behind the throne). This caused some to be jealous, since Guo Xiang, unlike many of his peers, was not born into a rich family. See 晉書 *Jin Shu*, 50.
88. See, for instance, Chenyang Li, "The Confucian Conception of Freedom," *Philosophy East and West* 64, no. 4 (October 2014); Sor-Hoon Tan, *Confucian*

Democracy: A Deweyan Reconstruction, SUNY series in Chinese Philosophy and Culture (Albany: State University of New York Press, 2012).

89. The term "Learning in the Profound" is a translation that has been suggested by Alan Chan, though he also suggests that perhaps *Xuanxue* should simply be retained, for the reason that the *Xuan* 玄 is difficult to fully capture in the English language. According to him, *Xuan* can refer to a specific color that is an almost black shade of red, or to something that is far and therefore dark, the vision of which only reaches us as a blur. See Alan Chan, "Neo-Daoism," in *The Stanford Encyclopedia of Philosophy*, ed. Edward N. Zalta (Summer 2019 edition).

90. Yü, "Individualism and the Neo-Daoist Movement in Wei-Jin China."

91. This is in consideration that the best representation of *Qingtan* is perhaps the image of *The Seven Sages of the Bamboo Grove*, which shall be discussed in more detail later in the volume.

92. I-ch'ing Liu, "Biographical Notices," in *Shih-Shuo Hsin-Yu: A New Account of Tales of the World* (Ann Arbor: University of Michigan Press, 2002), 578.

93. Richard Mather has authored an article that comprehensively discusses the tension between *mingjiao* 名教 and *ziran* 自然, which he translates as conformity and naturalness, respectively. According to Mather, the overarching aim of the Wei-Jin era is the attempt to synthesize both angles in light of combining both Confucian and Daoist thoughts. However, the attempt to synthesize these two, I believe, has a wider philosophical significance that can tell us something important about freedom and individuality, as shall later be demonstrated. See Richard B. Mather, "The Controversy over Conformity and Naturalness during the Six Dynasties," *History of Religions* 9, no. 2/3 (1969).

94. Cf. Michael Nylan, "Zhuangzi: Closet Confucian?," *European Journal of Political Theory* 16, no. 4 (2017).

95. William James, "Lecture IV: The One and the Many," in *Pragmatism* (New York: Dover, 1995), 76.

96. According to Berlin, there are two types of intellectuals: hedgehogs and foxes, or put simply, monists and pluralists. He discusses this at length in relation to Tolstoy, as one who was torn between the two, in a work entitled "Hedgehog and the Fox." See Berlin, *Russian Thinkers*, 22–82.

97. Rošker describes this as "a relational network of structurally connected concepts in which the meaning of every single notion is linked to other notions, and also to the entirety of relational semantic connotations included in this structural network of different, but mutually related meanings." Jana S. Rošker, "The Metaphysical Style and Structural Coherence of Names in Xuanxue," in *Dao Companion to Xuanxue* 玄學 *(Neo-Daoism)*, ed. David Chai (Cham: Springer International, 2020), 44.

98. Ibid., 55.

99. Ibid.

100. Xinzhong Yao, "Confucianism in the Wei-Jin Period," in *Routledge Curzon Encyclopedia of Confucianism*, ed. Xinzhong Yao (London: Routledge Curzon, 2013), 155.

101. Paul Demiéville notes: "The Ch'in and Han dynasties had made China into a unified empire. It had been necessary to introduce a method of centralizing power, and a system of order and authority based on a highly structured administrative and military machine; its ideology had to be essentially pragmatic, somewhat like that of imperial Rome. The metaphysical and mystical tendencies of Taoism and the varied speculations in which older schools of the pre-imperial era had indulged were laid aside in favor of Confucianism. Confucianism is a doctrine of this world, a sociology, and also a cosmology that links man to the universe through the heaven-earth-man triad, yet pays little attention to the ultramundane realms of the supernatural." Paul Demiéville, "Philosophy and Religion from Han to Sui," in *The Cambridge History of China: Volume 1: The Ch'in and Han Empires, 221 BC–AD 220*, ed. Denis Twitchett and John K. Fairbank (Cambridge: Cambridge University Press, 1986), 808.

102. For instance, Liu Shao's 劉劭 (early third-century) *Renwu zhi* 人物志 (Treatise on Personalities) was a famous text at the time.

103. See Yü, "Individualism and the Neo-Daoist Movement in Wei-Jin China."

104. Guo Xiang himself was a staunch supporter of Confucianism, also commenting on the *Analects*, but the same cannot be said of those before him. In fact, it may be said that he was partially reacting to the naturalism of those before him, most notably Ji Kang. Demiéville notes: "Hsi K'ang (223–262) [is] the rich Wei aristocrat married to a great-granddaughter of Ts'ao Ts'ao. At the end of the Cheng-shih period, he gathered around him a group of intellectuals later known as the Seven Sages of the Bamboo Grove. This sort of club included practicing believers in Taoist religion, which is sometimes called neo-Taoism. Some of these men cultivated the techniques of longevity, as for example Hsi K'ang himself, while for others, Taoist libertarianism turned to libertinism and *wu* to nihilism. The latter gave themselves up to drink, drugs, and—most scandalizing of all to the Confucian puritans—nudism, justifying these eccentricities by referring to Chuang-tzu's "naturism" (*tzu-jan*)." See Demiéville, "Philosophy and Religion from Han to Sui," 233. His connection to Cao Cao may have been the cause of his death, but throughout his work, he espoused a hostile attitude toward the "teaching of names" (名教 *mingjiao*). David Holzman, however, clarifies that the animosity between the Seven Sages of the Bamboo Grove, all of whom came from rich and noble families, toward the Sima clan, who encouraged Confucian moral codes borrowed from the Han, was not as straightforward as simply rebelling against the artificiality of Confucianism, but a variety of factors, mostly political. In fact, Holzman interestingly points out that while the Sima clan presented themselves as champions of Confucian orthodoxy, the Cao-Wei

family adopted a more legalistic tone as set by Cao Cao. This demonstrates that rather than a linear or one-way shaping of governmental policies from philosophical ideology, it was more dialectical and, more often than not, their reality and government shaped their ideological narrative rather than the other way around. See Donald Holzman, "Les Sept Sages de la Forêt des Bambous et la société de leur temps," *T'oung Pao* 44, no. 4/5 (1956). Furthermore, in the last main chapter, we see how Guo Xiang attempted to push back against the unfettered libertarianism of Ji Kang and his cohort as well. For a biography of Ji Kang, see 晉書 *Jin Shu*, 49.

105. See, for instance, Bao Jingyan's "Neither Lord nor Subject," in Balazs, *Chinese Civilization and Bureaucracy: Variations on a Theme*, 243–46. In this work, Bao questioned the concept of the Mandate of Heaven (*tianming*), which justified an emperor's rule, saying that it only serves to protect the few and the elite, while the common and innocent people do all the work and reap none of the benefits.

106. Étienne Balazs, "Nihilistic Revolt or Mystical Escapism: Currents of Thought in China during the Third Century A.D," in *Chinese Civilization and Bureaucracy: Variations on a Theme*, 226–54.

107. In Latour's article "Why Has Critique Run Out of Steam? From Matters of Fact to Matters of Concern," he shows how critique has now boiled down to two modes: either everything is simply mere projections of your mind, illusions, because there is no access to the things-in-themselves nor to Truth, or you are really nothing but the forces or determinations of natural and social sciences. Both discourses are the language of the critic: "the subject/object produces everything that," "the subject/object is nothing but." The reason for this, according to Latour, is because we treat nature and society as two separate entities, when they are, in fact, part of one and the same reality. In other words, objects and humans alike are what he calls actors in a network that contribute on their own. That is, we seem to mistake that either the subject or the object should be considered and studied on its own. Either the subject produces all, or objects produce all, creating a logical short circuit. See Bruno Latour, "Why Has Critique Run Out of Steam? From Matters of Fact to Matters of Concern," *Critical Inquiry* 30, no. 2 (2004).

108. I have shown here how this notion of the self has theological roots and hence becomes transcendent from social and material conditions that shape them. Although I have approached it from the Abrahamic point of view, several similar criticisms coming from different perspectives have previously been made against, more broadly, the Western ideas of the self. For instance, Gayatri Spivak tells us much of contemporary philosophy is hinged on classical philosophers such as Kant and Hegel, and yet we fail to realize "how Kant foreclosed the Aboriginal; how Hegel put the other of Europe in a pattern of normative deviations and how the colonial subject sanitized Hegel; how Marx negotiated

difference." See Gayatri Chakravorty Spivak, *A Critique of Postcolonial Reason: Toward a History of the Vanishing Present* (Cambridge: Harvard University Press, 1999), x. According to Spivak, this foreclosure is why "the field of philosophy as such, whose model was the merging of science and truth, remained untouched by the comparative impulse. In this area, Germany produced authoritative 'universal' narratives where the subject remained unmistakably European" (8). Spivak's criticism comes from an entirely different angle from ours, but it shows the problems of treating the "individual" with the sanctity with which the liberal framework does so, as well as touching on the causes for this sanctity. I have thus shown how what Spivak refers to as "European" has Abrahamic roots. A similar but more recent criticism comes from the camp of feminist epistemology. Among many others, Lorraine Code, for instance, criticizes what she calls the "perfectly autonomous man," which she says has not only been a cultural ideal in Western societies but also a primary influence in philosophical knowledge production. According to Code, "autonomous man is—and should be—self-sufficient, independent, and self-reliant, a self-realizing individual who directs his efforts toward maximizing his personal gains. His independence is under constant threat from other (equally self-serving) individuals: hence he devises rules to protect himself from intrusion. Talk of rights, rational self-interest, expediency, and efficiency permeates his moral, social, and political discourse. In short, there has been a gradual alignment of *autonomy* with *individualism*." See Lorraine Code, *What Can She Know? Feminist Theory and the Construction of Knowledge* (Ithaca: Cornell University Press, 1991), 77–78. Here I'd like to emphasize Code's remark that this individual's "independence is under constant threat from other individuals," as it is exactly what we find in Berlin's notion of the self, thus motivating his conception of freedom as "lack of *interference*."

Chapter 2. A Flattened Ontology and the Logic of Convergence

1. The usage of the term "logic" here may perhaps cause some confusion to Anglophone philosophers who are analytically inclined. As such, some clarifications are called for, the most important of which to note is that this term is not used in the formal sense, which is usually an exercise for mathematical or linguistic inference. I do not argue that Guo Xiang provides an alternative logic that can compete with classical or traditional logic. However, I do take philosophical precedence from the usage of this word in European philosophers, both classical and more contemporary, such as in G. W. F. Hegel and Gilles Deleuze, for instance. What I mean by "logic" here refers to Guo Xiang's pattern of thought that, in Hegel's definition, "coincides with metaphysics, i.e., the science of things captured in thoughts that have counted as expressing the essentialities of things." See Georg Wilhelm Friedrich Hegel, *Encyclopedia of the Philosophical*

Sciences in Basic Outline. Part 1: Science of Logic, trans. Klaus Brinkmann and Daniel O. Dahlstrom (Cambridge: Cambridge University Press, 2010), 58. This is the same type of logic that Deleuze refers to in his books *Francis Bacon: Logic of Sensation* and *The Logic of Sense*; both works contain the word "logic" in their titles but make no mention of any formal logical formulations. In fact, David Lapoujade goes as far as to claim that Deleuze is "first and foremost interested in logic." See David Lapoujade, *Aberrant Movements: The Philosophy of Gilles Deleuze*, trans. Joshua David Jordan (South Pasadena: Semiotext(e), 2017), 27, while also clarifying that logic in Deleuze "doesn't mean rational. We could even proclaim that for Deleuze a movement is all the more logical the more it escapes rationality" (27). In other words, my use of the word logic here is, in the same vein as said philosophers, simply a *means* to understand the general structure of being and reality, regardless of its rationality.

2. *Guo Xiang Commentary of the Zhuangzi: Coded Edition*, Chinese University of Hong Kong (CUHK), Research Center for Chinese Philosophy and Culture, 6.29.1G1–8. This text is from Guo Qingfan 郭慶藩, *Zhuangzi jishi* 莊子集釋 (Beijing: Zhonghua Book, 1961). All references in this volume to the Guo Xiang commentary are referred to as either *Zhuangzi* or *Guo Xiang Commentary* depending on whether it is the primary text or commentary, and in the CUHK markings; unless cited as translated by Brook Ziporyn, Feng Yu-lan, Alan Chan, or others, translations are my own.

3. *Zhuangzi*, in *Guo Xiang Commentary*, 2.14.9–10.

4. *Guo Xiang Commentary*, 1.(10.1–12.1)G1–3, trans. Birthe Arendrup, "The First Chapter of Guo Xiang's Commentary to Zhuang Zi," University of Copenhagen, 1964, 339–40, modified.

5. *Dao lun* in Alan K. L. Chan, "Sage Nature and the Logic of Namelessness: Reconstructing He Yan's Explication of Dao," in *Philosophy and Religion in Early Medieval China*, ed. Alan K. L. Chan and Yuet-Keung Lo (Albany: State University of New York Press, 2010), 25.

6. Wang Bi, *The Classic of the Way and Virtue: A New Translation of the Tao-Te Ching of Laozi as Interpreted by Wang Bi*, trans. Richard J. Lynn (New York: Columbia University Press, 1999), 52.

7. Wang Bi, *Laozi weizhi lueli* in ibid., 46.

8. Pei Wei, *Chong you lun* 崇有論 (Discourse on Esteeming Being), in Alan K. L. Chan, "Re-Envisioning the Profound Order of Dao: Pei Wei's 'Critical Discussion on the Pride of Place of Being,'" in *Dao Companion to Xuanxue* 玄學 *(Neo-Daoism)*, ed. David Chai (Cham: Springer International, 2020), 331.

9. Ibid., 331.

10. B. Ziporyn, *Zhuangzi: The Complete Writings* (Indianapolis: Hackett, 2020), 12.

11. *Guo Xiang Commentary*, 2.6.1G2–15, quoted in Wing-Tsit Chan, *A Source Book in Chinese Philosophy* (Lawrenceville: Princeton University Press, 1963), 328, modified.

12. Alan Chan calls this absolute lack the "Daoist Oblivion." See Alan K. L. Chan, "Embodying Nothingness and the Ideal of the Affectless Sage in Daoist Philosophy," in *Nothingness in Asian Philosophy*, ed. JeeLoo Liu and Douglas L. Berger (New York: Routledge, 2014), 221.

13. "Tzu-ch'i said, "The Great Clod belches out breath and its name is wind" 子綦曰：「夫大塊噫氣，其名為風。」See *Zhuangzi* 2.4.1, trans. Burton Watson, *The Complete Works of Chuang Tzu*, https://terebess.hu/english/chuangtzu.html.

14. Guo Xiang Commentary, 2.4.1G1–4.

15. Lihua Yang, 郭象 "庄子注" 研究 (*An Examination of Guo Xiang's Zhuangzi Commentary*) (Beijing: Beijing Daxue chu ban shu, 2010), 96.

16. Ibid., 96.

17. *Zhuangzi* 14.1.6, Burton Watson, *The Complete Works of Chuang Tzu*.

18. Guo Xiang Commentary, 14.1.6G.

19. Yang, 郭象 "庄子注" 研究 (*An Examination of Guo Xiang's Zhuangzi Commentary*), 26.

20. Guo Xiang Commentary 22.58.3G1–2, in Chan, *A Source Book in Chinese Philosophy*, 335, modified and supplemented.

21. Isabelle Robinet, "Kouo Siang ou le monde comme absolu," *T'oung Pao* 69 (1983): 77.

22. Ibid., 79–80, translated.

23. Ibid., 76, translated.

24. Ibid., 79, translated.

25. Pei Wei's philosophy can be found in his essay entitled 崇有論 *Chongyoulun*, which David Knechtges translates as "Disquisition on Esteeming the Existent," quoted in Chan, "Re-Envisioning the Profound Order of Dao." The essay itself can be found in *Jin shu*, *juan* 35. Here, Pei Wei can be seen as disputing the nihilistic tendencies of the time, which he attributed to "esteeming nothingness" (貴無 *guiwu*), deeming the trend of placing significance in the abstract notion of nothingness as dangerous due to the ethical decline it causes, though Étienne Balazs claims that Pei's motives were purely utilitarian and pragmatic in Balazs, "Entre révolte nihiliste et évasion mystique," 52. However, it is interesting to note that the first line in Pei's essay reads: "Now, it is certainly the case that the all-encompassing undifferentiated root of the multitude of things is the Dao of ultimate origins" (夫總混羣本，宗極之道也). See Pei Wei, quoted in Chan, "Re-Envisioning the Profound Order of Dao," 327. Chan, moreover, notes: "The noun phrase '*qunben*' has been taken to mean, for example, the totality of beings, the sum total of all there is. As such, the text is basically saying that the ultimate Dao is none other than the world of beings itself" (327). This interpretation can be seen as quite similar to Parmenides's totality of being, wherein he assumes all changes to be one, saying, "No was nor will; all past and future null; Since Being subsists in one ubiquitous Now—unitary and continuous." See Parmenides, lines 100–02, quoted in Martin J. Henn, *Parmenides of Elea: A Verse Translation with Interpretative Essays and Commentary*

to the Text (Westport: Praeger, 2003), 26. Chan, however, introduces a different interpretation wherein he points at the second line, which reads: "The myriad things are differentiated by the species to which they belong, which are of qualitatively distinct kinds" (方以族異, 庶類之品也). He takes this to mean that Pei Wei points to an "an undifferentiated source to differentiated kinds each with distinct qualities." See Chan, "Re-Envisioning the Profound Order of Dao: Pei Wei's 'Critical Discussion on the Pride of Place of Being.'" 327. In contrast, Guo Xiang highlights singularity and uniqueness and, as we shall later on see, the unique allotment (分 fen) of each and every being in the universe—that is, the manyness of the one.

26. Guo Xiang Commentary, 11.12.2G1.

27. Guo Xiang Commentary, 7.0G. A few other instances where he associates zihua with nothingness are: 理與物皆不以存懷, 而闇付自然, 則無為而自化矣。See 11.28.3G; 厲, 惡人也。言天下皆不願為惡, 及其為惡, 或迫於苛役, 或迷而失性耳。然迷者自思復, 而厲者自思善, 故我無為而天下自化。See 12.50.9G.

28. Guo Xiang Commentary, 11.32.14G.

29. Guo Xiang Commentary, 11.12.2G2–4.

30. Guo Xiang Commentary, 22.59.5G, quoted in Chan, A Source Book in Chinese Philosophy, 335, modified.

31. Guo Xiang Commentary, 22.59.6G.

32. Here I have modified Wing Tsit Chan's translations of 自然 ziran and 自爾 zier to read spontaneity and self-so, respectively, but I also use "self-so" for ziran. This is because the word "self-so" is apt for both terms, yet they are not interchangeable in Chinese. While the former emphasizes the process of a spontaneous flow of things, the latter places emphasis on the state of things being simply-such in themselves. Thus, I use different words when they are both present, but when the context does not require them to be distinguished from each other, I often use "self-so" for both ziran and zier, unless the context requires otherwise (such contextual translation for these words, however, is practiced in the rest of my translations to highlight the contextual nature of the language and the flexibility of the signifier rather than having fixed signified concepts).

33. Yijie Tang, 郭象与魏晋玄学 (Guo Xiang and Wei-Jin Xuanxue) (Beijing: Peking University Press, 2000), 229.

34. Robinet, "Kouo Siang ou le monde comme absolu," 112, passim.

35. It is important to note that Wang Xiaoyi also describes Guo Xiang's thought as the height of a parabola in the history of Chinese philosophy. See Xiaoyi Wang, "郭象命运论及其意义 (The Destiny Theory of Guo Xiang and Its Significance)," 文史哲 Journal of Literature, History, and Philosophy, no. 6 (2005).

36. Graham Priest, "Beyond True and False," Aeon, https://aeon.co/essays/the-logic-of-buddhist-philosophy-goes-beyond-simple-truth.

37. Graham Priest, In Contradiction: A Study of the Transconsistent (Oxford: Oxford University Press, 2006), 4.

38. Ibid., 4 n4.

39. Yasuo Deguchi, Jay L. Garfield, and Graham Priest, "The Way of the Dialetheist: Contradictions in Buddhism," *Philosophy East and West* 58, no. 3 (2008): 396.

40. Graham Priest, *One: Being an Investigation into the Unity of Reality and of Its Parts, Including the Singular Object Which Is Nothingness*, First edition (New York: Oxford University Press, 2014).

41. Francis Cook describes the Net of Indra as such: "Far away in the heavenly abode of the great god Indra, there is a wonderful net which has been hung by some cunning artificer in such a manner that it stretches out indefinitely in all directions. In accordance with the extravagant tastes of deities, the artificer has hung a single glittering jewel at the net's every node, and since the net itself is infinite in all dimensions, the jewels are infinite in number. There hang the jewels, glittering like stars of the first magnitude, a wonderful sight to behold. If we now arbitrarily select one of the jewels for inspection and look closely at it, we will discover that in its polished surface there are reflected all the other jewels in the net, infinite in number. Not only that, but each of the jewels reflected in this one jewel is also reflecting all the other jewels, so that the process of reflection is infinite." See Francis Harold Cook, *Hua-Yen Buddhism: The Jewel Net of Indra* (University Park: Pennsylvania State University Press, 1977), quoted in Priest, *One*, 179.

42. Priest, *One*, 175–81.

43. Ibid., 178.

44. Ibid., 179.

45. Ibid., 181.

46. Deguchi, Garfield, and Priest, "The Way of the Dialetheist: Contradictions in Buddhism," 400.

47. Ibid., 400.

48. *Guo Xiang Commentary*, 6.1.2G1–5, quoted in Brook Ziporyn, *Zhuangzi: The Essential Writings with Selections from Traditional Commentaries* (2009), 188.

49. Priest, *In Contradiction*, 4.

50. Graham Priest, "Dialectic and Dialetheic," *Science & Society* 53, no. 4 (1989): 388.

51. Georg Wilhelm Friedrich Hegel, *Hegel's Science of Logic*, trans. A. V. Miller (Amherst, NY: Humanity Books, 1998), 439.

52. Ibid., 440.

53. He is referring here to traditional or classical Aristotelian logic, which posits the law of noncontradiction, and writes this under a section entitled "The Law of Contradiction," turning this classical framework inside out.

54. Miller translates the German word *Vorstellen* into "ordinary thinking" here. This contrasts to speculative thinking (*begreifenden*) or the dialectical nature of philosophical exercise, which takes itself as the content of its own thinking process. As Paul Redding explains, Hegel refers to "the task of philosophy as that

of recognising the concept (*Der Begriff*) in the mere representations (*Vorstellungen*) of everyday life." See Paul Redding, "Georg Wilhelm Friedrich Hegel," *Stanford Encyclopedia of Philosophy* (Winter 2020 Edition), Edward N. Zalta (ed.), https://plato.stanford.edu/archives/win2020/entries/hegel/.

55. Georg Wilhelm Friedrich Hegel, *Hegel's Science of Logic*, trans. A. V. Miller (Amherst: Humanity Books, 1998), 439.

56. *Guo Xiang Commentary*, 6.29.1G1–8.

57. As in the Buddhist parable of using the Buddha's teachings simply as a "raft," to be discarded when its use is achieved.

58. *Guo Xiang Commentary*, 10.3.8G1–6, quoted in Brook Ziporyn, *The Penumbra Unbound: The Neo-Taoist Philosophy of Guo Xiang* (Albany: State University of New York Press, 2012), 134.

59. Ibid., 103.

60. *Zhuangzi*, 12.18.1–12, quoted in Burton Watson, *The Complete Works of Chuang Tzu*, modified.

61. *Guo Xiang Commentary*, 12.18.1G–12.

62. In an earlier passage in the *Zhuangzi*, Guo Xiang precludes this discussion by highlighting that what allows for self-transformation and self-realization is the nonaction as well as *wuxin* that are achieved through Innate Power. This ultimately allows one to converge in the transformations of heaven and earth, because one is self-so. See *Guo Xiang Commentary*, 12.1.2G–5 (一以自得為治。天下異心，無心者主也。以德為原，無物不得。得者自得，故得而不謝，所以成天也。任自然之運動。)

63. *Guo Xiang Commentary*, 2.6.1G2–15, quoted in Chan, *A Source Book in Chinese Philosophy*, 328, modified.

64. *Guo Xiang Commentary*, 6.24.4G1–2.

65. *Guo Xiang Commentary*, 6.24.4G3–4, quoted in Brook Ziporyn, *Zhuangzi: The Essential Writings with Selections from Traditional Commentaries* (Indianapolis: Hackett, 2009), 201, modified, interpolation mine.

66. Ziporyn, *The Penumbra Unbound: The Neo-Taoist Philosophy of Guo Xiang*, 100.

67. Ibid., 100.

68. Livia Kohn, *Early Chinese Mysticism: Philosophy and Soteriology in the Taoist Tradition* (Princeton: Princeton University Press, 1992), 71.

69. *Zhuangzi*, 22.20.1, quoted in Burton Watson, *The Complete Works of Chuang Tzu*.

70. *Guo Xiang Commentary*, 22.20.1G.

71. *Zhuangzi*, 2.33–34.1–4, quoted in Ziporyn, *The Penumbra Unbound: The Neo-Taoist Philosophy of Guo Xiang*, 101.

72. *Guo Xiang Commentary*, 2.34.2G, quoted in ibid., 101.

73. Ibid.

74. *Guo Xiang Commentary*, 2.34.4G4; 2.34.4G8–9, quoted in ibid., 101.

75. Ibid., 109–110.

76. It must also be noted that essences in *Zhuangzi* are in the plural because there is no one single substance, no one metaphysical absolute. This means that instead of universality, we have a confluence of pure individual substances that are different from each other in as much as one moment differs from all other moments, such that they all come together in order to form one organic whole, wherein each and every member of the whole fulfills a certain role that is significant to the flourishing of the whole.

77. Georg Wilhelm Friedrich Hegel, *Phenomenology of Spirit*, trans. A. V. Miller (Oxford: Oxford University Press, 2013), 181.

78. As a quick aside, it might be useful to remember here the distinction between formal and material truth in classical logic.

79. Paul J. D'Ambrosio, "Guo Xiang on Self-So Knowledge," *Asian Philosophy* 26, no. 2 (2016): 130.

80. Jeeloo Liu, *Neo-Confucianism: Metaphysics, Mind, and Morality* (Hoboken: John Wiley & Sons, 2018). 6.

81. For a more comprehensive discussion, see Brook Ziporyn, "Li in Wang Bi and Guo Xiang: Coherence in the Dark," *Philosophy and Religion in Early Medieval China* (2010).

82. Ibid., 113, interpolation mine.

83. Ibid., 128.

84. Up until this point, *li* 理 has mostly been translated as "principle." However, as is often the case with translation, one word is insufficient in this case to capture the meaning of such a loaded term such as *li*. As such, whenever it highlights a more epistemological angle (albeit retaining the ontological denotation, as the term has both), I translate it in accordance with Ziporyn's version, which is "coherence."

85. Ziporyn, "Li in Wang Bi and Guo Xiang: Coherence in the Dark," 118.

86. Ibid., 120, interpolation mine.

87. *Guo Xiang's Commentary*, 3.2.(1–2)G–3.5G, quoted in Richard John Lynn, *Zhuangzi: A New Translation of the Daoist Classic as Interpreted by Guo Xiang* (New York: Columbia University Press, 2022).

88. B. W. Van Norden, *Mengzi: With Selections from Traditional Commentaries* (Indianapolis: Hackett, 2008), 1A7.4.

89. Ibid., 1A7.8.

90. *Guo Xiang Commentary*, 22.22.6G.

Chapter 3. On the Self: Limits and Expanse

1. In his seminal work *The Wealth and Poverty of Nations: Why Are Some So Rich and Others So Poor*, David Landes argues that, even though it is a known

fact that China was, for a time, the leading nation in all matters of science and technology, not to mention its rich literary arsenal, Europe nonetheless overtook it because of cultural superiority. Landes argues that in Chinese culture, there is no sense of individuality, and this inevitably led to stagnation and isolation, uniformity and the death of critical thought. This is the reason, according to Landes, that China ultimately became poor. See David Landes, *The Wealth and Poverty of Nations: Why Some Are So Rich and Some So Poor* (New York: W. W. Norton, 1999). While Landes admits to a Eurocentric narrative, it is still not any less preposterous to make these claims about Chinese culture. Unfortunately, Landes is not alone, and to cite two examples among many, feminist French philosopher Julia Kristeva had remarked that "if Western metaphysics has difficulties comprehending the Chinese individual, it is because, for the Chinese, there is no individual." See Julia Kristeva, Vernon Cisney, and Nicolae Morar, "A European in China," *Critical Inquiry* 37, no. 3 (2011): 424. While we might think that it could not be worse from the analytic front where it is touted to be free of historical context, this is still, unfortunately, not the case. Famous philosopher of freedom Daniel Dennett notes that it is "an almost exclusively Western preoccupation." See Dennett, *Elbow Room: The Varieties of Free Will Worth Wanting*, 5.

2. *Guo Xiang Commentary*, 2.8.11G1–2.

3. Livia Knaul, "Kuo Hsiang and the Chuang Tzu," *Journal of Chinese Philosophy* 12, no. 4 (1985): 432.

4. In fact, Guo Xiang makes a similar point in a later chapter, where he supports the nonmingling of roles, allowing each body part to fulfill its own role contra micromanagement, resulting in a bottom-up mechanism that relies heavily on self-so (自然 *ziran*) and nondoing (無為 *wuwei*). He says: "When feet are able to walk, release them [into walking]. When hands are able to hold, rely on them [for holding]. Listen to what the ears hear, observe what the eyes see. For understanding, stop at what cannot be understood. For ability, stop at what is not possible. Use [things] according to their own spontaneous use, act [on things] according to their own spontaneous actions; let them lose themselves in what is internal to their nature and do not, in the tiniest bit, diverge into what is external to [natural] allotment. This is the ultimate transformation of nondoing" (足能行而放之，手能執而任之，聽耳之所聞，視目之所見，知止其所不知，能止其所不能，用其自用，為其自為，恣其性內而無纖芥於分外，此無為之至易也). See *Guo Xiang Commentary*, 4.43.5G1–4.

5. *Guo Xiang Commentary*, 4.10.3G.

6. The most immediate example that would come to mind is probably the Confucian or Ruist ideal of decadence during the Zhou, as well as the recurring characters, sages, of the olden times that are worth emulating, such Yao, Shun, and Yu. However, dominant Daoism and especially *Laozi* poses the poignant image of the 樸 *pu*, the uncarved block, a symbol of unspoiled sim-

plicity, and ultimately what we should go back to because it is in these days that man has lost his way.

7. *Guo Xiang Commentary*, 19.1.9G.

8. Arendrup, "The First Chapter of Guo Xiang's Commentary to Zhuang Zi: A Translation and Grammatical Analysis," 322–23, modified.

9. *Guo Xiang Commentary*, 1.3.1G1–4.

10. I translate the word *zhi* 至 differently depending on context, and it can sometimes appear as ultimate, height, supreme, but perhaps here it requires more explanation. Though "very precise" undoubtedly takes on a similar meaning to the previously mentioned words, here the emphasis is on the limit, that is, the furthest something can possibly go. Although it may perhaps be an idiosyncratic choice of words, they are (as we shall see) appropriate for how Guo Xiang views the notion of *fen* 分.

11. *Guo Xiang Commentary*, 17.1.4G.

12. *Guo Xiang Commentary*, 3.1.3G.

13. *Zhuangzi*, quoted in *Guo Xiang Commentary*. 2.14.12.

14. *Guo Xiang Commentary*. 2.14.12G1–2.

15. Richard Mather has authored an article that comprehensively discusses the tension between *mingjiao* 名教 and *ziran* 自然, which he translates as conformity and naturalness, respectively. According to Mather, the overarching aim of the Wei-Jin era is the attempt to synthesize both angles in light of combining both Confucian and Daoist thoughts. However, the attempt to synthesize these two, I believe, has a wider philosophical significance that can tell us something important about freedom and individuality. See Mather, "The Controversy over Conformity and Naturalness during the Six Dynasties."

16. For a more comprehensive discussion on traces, see Brook Ziporyn, "The Dangers of Traces," in Ziporyn, *The Penumbra Unbound: The Neo-Taoist Philosophy of Guo Xiang*.

17. *Guo Xiang Commentary*, 14.41.G(1–2)–3G, quoted in Lynn, *Zhuangzi: A New Translation of the Daoist Classic as Interpreted by Guo Xiang*.

18. This may sound counterintuitive but here I would like to remind the reader of the logic of convergence, and what Guo Xiang says about knowing in our earlier discussion on this. To recap, Guo Xiang says that "since knowing comes from nonknowing, nonknowing is always the source. Hence, the Genuine Human Being discards knowledge and thereby knows, does nothing and thereby does." See *Guo Xiang Commentary*, 6.1.2G1–5, quoted in Ziporyn, *Zhuangzi: The Essential Writings with Selections from Traditional Commentaries*, 188.

19. *Guo Xiang Commentary*, 2.14.25G1–3; this passage is part of a bigger excerpt that speaks of the "treasury of Heaven" that, if the reader recalls, also appeared in the previous chapter.

20. Referring to the dao, Guo Xiang said that "spontaneity is ordered in precedence and sequence" (自然先後之序也). See *Guo Xiang Commentary*, 13.7.2G.

21. Guo Xiang himself stresses this in his comments on the *Zhuangzi*. For instance, he says, "Although [the text] has the term, 'What makes things what they are' [物物者 *wu wu zhe*], this is meant merely to show that things make themselves what they are [物之自物 *wu zhi ziwu*]; ultimately there is no thing that makes things what they are. . . . Once we have understood that there is no thing that makes things what they are, we should also understand that neither can things make themselves what they are [物之不能自物 *wu zhi bu neng ziwu*]. But then who is it that does it? They are all unconsciously and abruptly thus and self-so" (雖有物物之名，直明物之自物耳。物物者，竟無物也，際其安在乎！既明物物者無物，又明物之不能自物，則為之者誰乎哉？皆忽然而自爾也). *Guo Xiang Commentary*, 22.35.10G–11 translated by and quoted in Brook Ziporyn, *Beyond Oneness and Difference: Li and Coherence in Chinese Buddhist Thought and Its Antecedents* (Albany: State University of New York Press, 2013), 162. Moreover, Ziporyn notes that "many scholars have taken these terms (性*xing*, 分 *fen*, and 極 *ji*) to have their more usual meaning here: a fixed nature, allotment, limit, or principle that serves as the determining underlying character of a thing, persisting over time and standing behind the phenomenal flux of appearances. This is then taken to be Guo's substitute for the Dao as determining creator, which all scholars admit he banishes from his thought" (164). Following the arguments from previous chapter, we know that such substituting would contradict Guo Xiang's ontology, and that the only plausible explanation is that since these categories are empty or *wu*, they are self-so.

22. Here, I translate *xing* 性 as nature. It is not only humans who have *xing*, but also animals or even things. In the following discussion, Guo Xiang refers to even the ten thousand things (*wanwu* 萬物), that is, everything, as having *xing*.

23. The demarcations refer to the *Zhuangzi* text, namely: 有左，有右，2.14.5 有倫，有義，2.14.6 有分，有辯，2.14.7 有競，有爭，2.14.8 此之謂八德.

24. *Guo Xiang Commentary*, 2.14.9G1–4.

25. *Guo Xiang Commentary*, 2.14.26G1–2.

26. Ziporyn, *Zhuangzi: The Essential Writings with Selections from Traditional Commentaries*, 65, modified.

27. *Guo Xiang Commentary*, 10.5.14G1–3.

28. *Guo Xiang Commentary*, 10.5.15G1–6.

29. Unlike the primitivist interpretations of Laozi and Zhuangzi, Guo Xiang takes on a contrary position wherein he believes that progress is good. In doing so, his goal was to have attempted to save the intellectual atmosphere of the Wei-Jin era from the threat of escapism and absolute retreat to mysticism, propagated by the likes of Ji Kang and Ruan Ji. See Xiaoyi Wang, "郭象历史哲学发微 (On Guo Xiang's Philosophy of History)," 文史哲 0, no. 2 (2002).

30. Guo Xiang comments on Zhuangzi's passage, that "the sages have benefited the world little and harmed the world much," and says: "How true this statement is! But although this statement is true, we still cannot do away

with the sages. Since all the knowledge in the world is not yet able to be completely obliterated, the way of the sages is still needed to subdue it. If everyone else's knowledge is allowed to exist and only the sages' knowledge is obliterated, this will harm the world even more than allowing the sages to exist. Thus although the harm caused by the sages is much, it is still better than the disorder of having no sages. But although it is better than having no sages, it is undeniably not as good as the total lack of harm there would be if all [the knowledge] were obliterated" (信哉斯言！斯言雖信，而猶不可亡聖者，猶天下之知未能都亡，故須聖道以鎮之也。群知不亡而獨亡於聖知，則天下之害又多於有聖矣。然則有聖之害雖多，猶愈於亡聖之無治也。雖愈於亡聖，故未若都亡之無害也。甚矣，天下莫不求利而不能一亡其知，何其迷而失致哉！). See *Guo Xiang Commentary*, 10.3.8G1–6, quoted in Brook Ziporyn, "Guo Xiang: The Self-So and the Repudiation-cum-Reaffirmation of Deliberate Action and Knowledge," in *Dao Companion to Daoist Philosophy*, ed. Liu Xiaogan (Dordrecht: Springer, 2014).

31. *Guo Xiang Commentary*, 9.1.2G1–7, quoted in ibid., 417.

32. Ibid., 417.

33. The following passage from Zhuangzi is what Guo is commenting on: "Here are the horses, able to tramp over frost and snow with the hooves they have, to keep out the wind and cold with their coats. Chomping the grass and drinking the waters, prancing and jumping over the terrain—this is the genuine inborn nature of horses. Even if given fancy terraces and great halls, they would have no use for them. Then along comes Bo Le, saying, 'I am good at managing horses!' He proceeds to brand them, shave them, clip them, bridle them, fetter them with crupper and martingale, pen them in stable and stall—until about a quarter of the horses have dropped dead. Then he starves them, parches them, trots them, gallops them, lines them up neck to neck or nose to tail, tormenting them with bit and rein in front and with whip and spur behind. By then over half of the horses have dropped dead." Ziporyn, *Zhuangzi: The Complete Writings*, 81.

34. *Guo Xiang Commentary*, 6.77.2G1–2, quoted in Livia Kohn, *Meditation Works:In the Daoist, Buddhist, and Hindu Traditions* (Magdalena: Three Pines Press, 2008), 1308.

35. *Guo Xiang Commentary*, 6.37.12G1–4–6.37.13–14, quoted in Ziporyn, *Zhuangzi: The Essential Writings with Selections from Traditional Commentaries*, 202, modified, last sentence mine.

36. *Guo Xiang Commentary*, 1.1.1G1–2, quoted in Arendrup, "The First Chapter of Guo Xiang's Commentary to Zhuang Zi," 314, modified.

37. The work of Deleuze and Guattari was a revolutionary turn in the history of Western philosophy and has stood strong amid the misrepresentations posed toward postmodern relativity. While Deleuze doesn't take it as far as Guo Xiang does, his work with Guattari nevertheless provides a valuable insight regarding the meaning of relativity and is thus noteworthy. Specifically speaking,

they say that "perspectivism, or scientific relativism, is never relative to a subject: it constitutes not a relativity of truth but, on the contrary, a truth of the relative, that is to say, of variables whose cases it orders according to the values it extracts from them in its system of coordinates." Gilles Deleuze and Félix Guattari, *What Is Philosophy?* (New York: Columbia University Press, 1994), 130.

38. Tang, 郭象与魏晋玄学 (*Guo Xiang and Wei-Jin Xuanxue*), 280.
39. Ibid., 280.
40. Ibid., 280–81.
41. *Guo Xiang Commentary*, 7.5.3G–4.
42. Recall Guo Xiang's discussion earlier on the standards we follow that are external to us in *Guo Xiang Commentary*, 10.5.14G1–3.
43. *Guo Xiang Commentary*, 2.13.12G1–6; *Zhuangzi* passage quoted in Ziporyn, *Zhuangzi: The Essential Writings with Selections from Traditional Commentaries*, 15.
44. *Guo Xiang Commentary*, 2.13.12G7–10.
45. *Guo Xiang Commentary*, 2.13.12.
46. *Guo Xiang Commentary*, 27.12.8G.
47. Tang, 郭象与魏晋玄学 (*Guo Xiang and Wei-Jin Xuanxue*), 274.
48. Ibid.
49. I interchangeably translate 命 *ming* as either "fate" or "endowment" throughout this work, depending on context. For instances where there is clearly no specific entity providing the 命 *ming*, I choose "fate." However for instances where there seems to be an "endower," usually heaven or 天 *tian*, then I translate this as endowment. Like the other words that I change the translation for whenever context deems it necessary, there is ultimately no difference in meaning between the two translations. This is especially the case in Guo Xiang where "heaven" is simply a natural entity and is "self-so" (自然 *ziran*), yet the English-language translations would appear less awkward if we interchange the words to flow more aptly with their contexts.
50. *Guo Xiang Commentary*, 27.12.9–10G.
51. Tang, 郭象与魏晋玄学 (*Guo Xiang and Wei-Jin Xuanxue*), 276.
52. *Guo Xiang Commentary*, 2.8.21G1–3.
53. Here, it is useful to recall another description of Heaven by Guo Xiang, which was also mentioned earlier. In this passage Guo says: "The term 'heaven' is used to explain that things are what they are spontaneously, and not to mean the blue sky. But someone says that the music of heaven makes all things serve or obey it. Now, heaven cannot even possess itself. How can it possess things? Heaven is the general name for all things. Heaven does not set its mind for or against anything. Who is the master to make things obey? Therefore each thing self-generates and thus has nothing that makes it emerge. This is the Way of Heaven （〔以天言之〕所以明其自然也，豈蒼蒼之謂哉！而或者謂天籟役物使從己也。夫天且不能自有，況能有物哉！故天者，萬物之總名也，莫適為天，誰主役物

乎？故物各自生而無所出焉，此天道也). See *Guo Xiang Commentary*, 2.6.1G11–15, quoted in Chan, *A Source Book in Chinese Philosophy*, 328, modified.

54. *Guo Xiang Commentary*, 3.12.3G.

55. *Zhuangzi* 17.16.1, quoted in Ziporyn, *Zhuangzi: The Essential Writings with Selections from Traditional Commentaries*, 73, modified.

56. *Guo Xiang Commentary*, 17.16.1G1–4.

57. Tang, 郭象与魏晋玄学 (*Guo Xiang and Wei-Jin Xuanxue*), 274.

58. Limei Jiang, "The Big and the Great: A Reconstruction of Zhuangzi's Philosophy on Transcendence," *Religions* 10, no. 1 (2019).

59. Yuet-Keung Lo, "Lone-Transformation and Intergrowth: Philosophy and Self-Justification in Guo Xiang's Commentary on the Zhuangzi," in *Dao Companion to Xuanxue* 玄學 *(Neo-Daoism)*, ed. David Chai (Cham: Springer International, 2020), 375.

60. Ibid., 376.

61. *Guo Xiang Commentary*, 6.9.3G2–6, quoted in ibid., 383. 命 "Fate" here is translated by Lo as fate, but lest we confuse this with fatalism, we must remember that it is that from which this fate comes, as discussed in the previous section. Thus, fate here must be understood as something that is also self-so.

62. *Guo Xiang Commentary*, 15.4.7G.

63. Recall here our discussion in the introduction of this work on the inherent difference of the notion of Heaven in Chinese philosophy. Here, specifically, Guo Xiang's notion of a spontaneous heaven is akin to a force that does not impose an ontologically determined and antecedent form onto nature, in contrast to a teleological force as in the Abrahamic traditions discussed in the introduction.

64. *Guo Xiang Commentary*, 6.1.2G1–5, quoted in Ziporyn, *Zhuangzi: The Essential Writings with Selections from Traditional Commentaries*, 188.

Chapter 4. Freedom as Autonomy: Independence and Dependence

1. Berlin, "Two Concepts of Liberty," 217.

2. While Berlin considers such network of causality and its resulting singularity of experience in passing, he is quick to dismiss the struggle for recognition (as unique and a standard of its own) as a "bitter longing for status," and the reason for why paternalism in Asian and African societies is rampant. See ibid., 203. There are now some apparent contradictions between this position and the advocacy for pluralism, which we shall delve more into in the latter part of this chapter.

3. Ibid., 181–87.

4. Ibid., 183.

5. Ibid., 183.

6. I have discussed this in the section on the problem of freedom in Chinese philosophy, but for a more specific discussion, see also Chenyang Li, "The Confucian Conception of Freedom," *Philosophy East and West* 64, no. 4 (October 2014): 902–19.

7. Liu Xiaogan quoted in Yang, 郭象"庄子注"研究 (*An Examination of Guo Xiang's Zhuangzi Commentary*), 136–37, parentheses mine.

8. What this means is that nothing goes out of existence but just transforms from one existence to another forever.

9. *Zhuangzi*, 21.20.1–11, quoted in Burton Watson, *The Complete Works of Chuang Tzu*, modified.

10. *Guo Xiang Commentary*, 21.20.1G(1–2)–11.

11. In a more political and social sense, this also implies that "playing the long game" or having an ideal that one *strives* to attain can justify many things in the present, including oppressive practices that deviate from one's *fen*.

12. *Zhuangzi*, 27.13, quoted in Burton Watson, *The Complete Works of Chuang Tzu*.

13. *Zhuangzi*, 27.14.1–7, quoted in ibid., modified.

14. *Guo Xiang Commentary*, 27.14.1G–7.

15. *Zhuangzi*, in *Guo Xiang Commentary*, 6.11.4.

16. *Guo Xiang Commentary*, 6.11.4G1–2.

17. Ziporyn, *Zhuangzi: The Essential Writings with Selections from Traditional Commentaries*, passim.

18. *Guo Xiang Commentary*, 1.5.1G1–7, quoted in Arendrup, "The First Chapter of Guo Xiang's Commentary to Zhuang Zi: A Translation and Grammatical Analysis," 329–31, modified.

19. Yang, 郭象"庄子注"研究 (*An Examination of Guo Xiang's Zhuangzi Commentary*), 142.

20. *Guo Xiang Commentary*, 1.7.13G1–9, quoted in Arendrup, "The First Chapter of Guo Xiang's Commentary to Zhuang Zi: A Translation and Grammatical Analysis," 339–40, modified.

21. Yang, 郭象"庄子注"研究 (*An Examination of Guo Xiang's Zhuangzi Commentary*), 143.

22. *Zhuangzi*, 6.2.2–3, quoted in Burton Watson, *The Complete Works of Chuang Tzu*, modified.

23. "無可無不可" is a phrase that Guo Xiang borrows from the *Analects*, 18:8.

24. *Guo Xiang Commentary*, 6.2.2G(1–2)–3.

Chapter 5. Freedom as Self-Realization: Dimensions of *Zide* 自得

1. Wang, "郭象历史哲学发微 (On Guo Xiang's Philosophy of History)," 142.

2. Rošker explains this term and says that "as ancient Chinese believed that the heart was the center of human cognition, the notion of *xin* is most commonly translated as 'heart-mind' in philosophical discourses. This understanding was determined by the absence of the contrast between cognitive (representative ideas, reasoning, beliefs) and affective (sensation, feelings, desires, emotions) states." See Jana Rošker, "Epistemology in Chinese Philosophy," in *Stanford Encyclopedia of Philosophy*, ed. Edward N. Zalta (Metaphysics Research Lab, Stanford University, 2018).

3. Jinhua Jia, "Redefining the Ideal Character: A Comparative Study between the Concept of Detachment in the Aṣṭasāhasrikā and Guo Xiang's Theory of Eremitism at Court," *Dao* 14, no. 4 (2015).

4. Ibid., 563.

5. Ibid., 563.

6. Ibid., 554.

7. Ibid., 554.

8. This is why although Jia adopts the more commonly Buddhist translation of "no-mind," I base my translation on Ziporyn's translation, into "having no deliberate heart-mind," or a parallel one of "being without deliberate heart-mind." That said, Lynn's translation of "being free of self-conscious mind" also emphasizes the lack of direction rather than the mind's emptiness itself, thereby being able to capture the meaning of this term in Guo Xiang. However, I do not follow Lynn's translation except when directly quoting him as the use of the term "free" might confuse the narrative in this chapter. Whenever translation into these phrases proves to be awkward, however, I have chosen to simply transliterate for the sake of contextual clarity.

9. Other than the aforementioned instances in earlier chapters where nothingness (無 *wu*) and self-so (*ziran* 自然) converge, the following are additional examples as to how Guo Xiang thinks this is the case both ontologically and epistemologically: 「實各自為，故無不為。」 See *Guo Xiang Commentary*, 25.49.11G;「今未知者皆不知所以知而自知矣，生者〔皆〕不知所以生而自生矣。」 See *Guo Xiang Commentary*, 2.8.21G2.

10. *Guo Xiang Commentary*, 2.13.1G5–6, quoted in Ziporyn, *The Penumbra Unbound: The Neo-Taoist Philosophy of Guo Xiang*, 117.

11. 論語體略 *Lunyu Tilue*, 2a–2b, quoted in Richard J. Lynn, "Guo Xiang's Theory of Sagely Knowledge as Seen in His 'Essentials of the Analects,'" in *Dao Companion to Xuanxue* 玄學 *(Neo-Daoism)*, ed. David Chai (Cham: Springer International, 2020), 401.

12. 論語體略 *Lunyu Tilue*, 3a–3b, quoted in ibid., 404–05.

13. Ibid., 393.

14. 論語體略 *Lunyu Tilue*, 4a, quoted in ibid., 407, modified, emphasis and parenthetical mine.

15. Ibid., 407, emphasis mine.

16. *Guo Xiang Commentary*, 16.4.4G1–3, quoted in ibid., 407–08.

17. Note the parallel here between 無自用 *wuziyong* as used in *Lunyu* commentary, and the 不自用 *buziyong* in the *Zhuangzi* commentary—signaling the synonymous meaning of nothing to an active refusal for deliberate action rather than a passive one.

18. *Guo Xiang Commentary*, 4.0G.

19. Guo Xiang talks about this to a large extent in the *Zhuangzi* commentaries, with one example being when he says: "Every creature without exception considers itself right and the others wrong praising itself and defaming others. It is in precisely this sense that, although each embraces a different definition of right and wrong, self and other are exactly equal" (夫自是而非彼 美己而惡人 物莫不皆然。然 故是非雖異而彼我均也). See *Guo Xiang Commentary*, 2.0G, quoted in Ziporyn, *Zhuangzi: The Essential Writings with Selections from Traditional Commentaries*, 135.

20. In her book *Adapting*, Mercedes Valmisa presents a similar notion of autonomy that she mainly draws from *Huainanzi*. She notes: "Freedom is an appropriation of what escapes me as a condition of possibility of my own becoming. In this way, freedom is constituted by non-freedom (fate—what lies beyond the person and cannot be avoided), agency is constituted by non-agency (the co-actions of others), joy is constituted by non-joy (nothing is to be prioritized as joyful), and, ultimately, the self is constituted by non-self (the world). The more world we integrate into our selves, the more heteronomous actions we appropriate as co-acting along with us, and the more of the unavoidable we reassign as enabling conditions of our becoming, the freer we become." See Mercedes Valmisa, "The Unifying Pattern," in *Adapting: A Chinese Philosophy of Action* (New York: Oxford University Press, 2021), 170. In Guo Xiang's understanding of the *Zhuangzi*, however, this in turn results in infinitesimal and strict boundaries instead of none, since this "co-acting" will look and act differently in each individual within each point in space and time.

21. *Guo Xiang Commentary*, 6.12.19, quoted in *Chuang-Tzu: A New Selected Translation with an Exposition of the Philosophy of Kuo Hsiang*, trans. Youlan Feng, China Academic Library (Heidelberg: Springer, 2016), 45.

22. *Guo Xiang Commentary*, 6.12.19G1–5.

23. The reason for this has generally been discussed in previous chapters. However, another passage where Guo Xiang qualifies this more directly is in a commentary on the tenth chapter of the *Zhuangzi*, where he says: "the eradication of the lips is not done in order to make the teeth cold, and yet teeth are cold. The wine of Lu was not made thin in order to bring about the siege of Han-tan, and yet Han-tan was besieged. The sages do not appear in order to give rise to the great robbers, and yet the great robbers arise. This is all self-so mutual generation (*xiangsheng*), a necessary tendency (夫竭脣非以寒齒而齒寒，魯酒薄非以圍邯鄲而邯鄲圍，聖人生非以起大盜而大盜起。此自然相生，必至之勢也).

Guo Xiang Commentary, 10.3.9G1–2, quoted in Ziporyn, *The Penumbra Unbound: The Neo-Taoist Philosophy of Guo Xiang*, 105.

24. *Guo Xiang Commentary*, 21.39.2G.

25. *Guo Xiang Commentary*, 2.13.13G1–2.

26. Guo Xiang, trans. Ziporyn, *Zhuangzi: The Essential Writings with Selections from Traditional Commentaries*, 195.

27. *Guo Xiang Commentary*, 6.11.2G5–7.

28. *Guo Xiang Commentary*, 2.10.12G1–14, quoted in Ziporyn, *Zhuangzi: The Essential Writings with Selections from Traditional Commentaries*, 147.

29. According to Gongsun Long, if one says "horse" then it should mean horses of all colors, but if one says "white horse" then obviously horses of other colors no longer belong to this category. Since "white horse" can be so singularly distinct from other types of horses, that is, opposite to them, then how can they all be the same horses? This seems to be an argument against the essential oneness of a category of beings. In other words, what Guo Xiang is pointing at here, as when he says that "the other's finger, compared to my finger as the standard, distinctly fails to be a finger," is that any standard according to which we strictly name and categorize truths is bound to contradict itself. For a more detailed discussion on Gongsun Long's argument as well as a proper introduction regarding its significance, see Yuolan Feng, "The School of Names," in *A Short History of Chinese Philosophy*, ed. Derk Bodde (New York: Free Press, 1966).

30. *Guo Xiang Commentary*, 2.1.2G2.

31. *Guo Xiang Commentary*, 1.0G, quoted in Arendrup, "The First Chapter of Guo Xiang's Commentary to Zhuang Zi: A Translation and Grammatical Analysis," 313, modified.

32. This is comprehensively discussed in an earlier work where I refer to Guo Xiang's interpretation as pluralistic monism. Though I have now come to understand Guo Xiang more clearly and think that this understanding doesn't go far enough in eliminating the middleman of nonbeing entirely, it is a helpful cursory survey of the different interpretations in Anglophone scholarship. See Christine Abigail Tan, "The Butterfly Dream and Zhuangzi's Perspectivism: An Exploration of the Differing Interpretations of the Butterfly Dream against the Backdrop of Dao as Pluralistic Monism," *Kritike: An Online Journal of Philosophy* 10 (2016).

33. Modified from "Happy and content with himself."

34. 麗之姬。艾封人之子也。晉國之始得之也。涕泣沾襟。及其至於王所。與王同筐床。食芻豢。而後悔其泣也。Concubine Li was the daughter of the Ai district border defense commandant. When the state of Jin first captured her, she cried so much that tears soaked the whole front of her garment, and it was only after she had arrived at the palace, shared his master bed with the ruler, and eaten his fine meats that she regretted she had ever cried. 一生之內。情變若此。當此之日。則不知彼。況夫死生之變。惡能相知哉。Throughout a

lifetime, one's emotions change as much as this. Since on any given day one never knows how he might feel on any other day, how much the less can one know what the change between life and death might bring! 予惡乎知夫死者不悔其始之蘄生乎。 **How do I know that the dead don't regret that they had ever first begged for life!** See Richard John Lynn, "Birds and Beasts in the Zhuangzi, Fables Interpreted by Guo Xiang and Cheng Xuanying," *Religions* 10, no. 7 (2019): 11.

35. *Zhuangzi*, 2.35.1–6; *Guo Xiang Commentary*, 2.35.1G–6, quoted in ibid., 10–11, modified.

36. Tan, "The Butterfly Dream and Zhuangzi's Perspectivism: An Exploration of the Differing Interpretations of the Butterfly Dream against the Backdrop of Dao as Pluralistic Monism," passim.

37. Lynn's apt but idiosyncratic translation here is perhaps noteworthy because it takes on a different kind of parallelism that juxtaposes the words *zikuai* 快意 and *zide* 自得, the former referring to a kind of elation, and the latter to self-realization. Combined, we arrive at "happily self-realized," meanwhile demonstrating the poetic quality of Guo Xiang's writings.

38. *Guo Xiang Commentary*, 6.37.12G1–2, quoted in Ziporyn, *Zhuangzi: The Essential Writings with Selections from Traditional Commentaries*, 202, modified.

39. *Guo Xiang Commentary*, 6.37.13–14G.

40. *Guo Xiang Commentary*, 1.5.1G1–7, cf. 118.

41. *Guo Xiang Commentary*, 1.7.13G1–9, cf. 120.

42. Yang, 郭象"庄子注"研究 (*An Examination of Guo Xiang's Zhuangzi Commentary*), 138.

43. *Guo Xiang Commentary*, 17.2.4G1.

44. *Guo Xiang Commentary*, 17.2.4G7.

45. For instance, see David Machek, "Is Freedom in Necessity or in Happiness? Guo Xiang's and Lin Xiyi's Controversial Readings of Zhuangzi's 'Free Rambling,'" *Studia Orientalia Slovaca* 9, no. 2 (2010). Machek, however, misses the philosophical nuances of freedom and takes it for granted in this simplistic equivalency. This ultimately leads to a two-dimensional understanding of freedom in both commentators, wherein he claims that for both, freedom is "absence of hindrances," that is closer to Berlin's negative liberty than a unique and innovative notion of autonomy and even free will that relies on the significance of an absolute dependency.

46. Although I acknowledge the divergence for the sake of argument here, Guo Xiang's faithfulness to the *Zhuangzi* is beyond the scope of this study. For my purposes of philosophical explication—an exploration of Guo Xiang's philosophy—it is more helpful to treat the *Zhuangzi* and Guo Xiang as one, and as how Guo interprets it.

47. Liu, "两种逍遥与两种自由 (Two Kinds of *Xiaoyao* and Two Kinds of Freedom)."

48. Ibid., 83–85.
49. Ibid., 85.
50. Ibid., 86.
51. Ibid., 87.
52. Ibid., 88.
53. Berlin, "Two Concepts of Liberty," 183.
54. Mercedes Valmisa, "The Happy Slave Isn't Free: Relational Autonomy and Freedom in the *Zhuangzi*," *Philosophy Compass* 14, no. 3 (2019): 5.
55. For a more comprehensive discussion of how this relates to our study, see the section on Guo Xiang in the introduction.
56. Valmisa, "The Happy Slave Isn't Free: Relational Autonomy and Freedom in the *Zhuangzi*," 9.
57. Lo, "Lone-Transformation and Intergrowth: Philosophy and Self-Justification in Guo Xiang's Commentary on the *Zhuangzi*," 389.
58. Ibid., 391.
59. *Zhuangzi*, 3.7.1–2, quoted in Ziporyn, *Zhuangzi: The Essential Writings with Selections from Traditional Commentaries*, 23.
60. Guo Xiang Commentary, 3.7.1G1–3.
61. Guo Xiang Commentary, 3.7.2G1–2.

Conclusion: "Freedom In" and Social Change

1. Richard John Lynn, "Reading Daoist Texts as Political Theory: Wang Bi on Laozi and Guo Xiang on Zhuangzi," *International Congress of Asian and North African Studies* (2000): 2.
2. Vincent Shen, "From Interpretation to Construction: Guo Xiang's Ontological Individualism," *Journal of Chinese Philosophy* 40, no. S1 (2013): 187.
3. Ibid., 172.
4. Ibid., 185.
5. Ibid., 187.
6. Interestingly, Chris Fraser has recently done work on Guo Xiang that places him in the middle of Shen and Liu. Although he highlights the independence of dao, and the important unique internal character in Guo Xiang's philosophy, he is careful to remind us, through the concept of *ming* 冥 or obscurity, of the distinctive emphasis on dependence in becoming a self-fulfilled agent. See Chris Fraser, "Metaphysics and Agency in Guo Xiang's Commentary on the *Zhuangzi*," in *Dao Companion to Xuanxue* 玄學 *(Neo-Daoism)*, ed. David Chai (Cham: Springer International, 2020). Drawing from Ziporyn, he says: "Guo Xiang's stance is that the good life—a life of intrinsic self-fulfillment and thus psychological freedom and ease—is to live according to how the dynamically developing dispositions, abilities, and resources we have at any one time interact

with the concrete situations we encounter. . . . A fascinating, profound feature of Guo's thought is how it grounds normativity in human self-fulfillment, albeit a distinctive conception of self-fulfillment achieved by adeptly and unselfishly adjusting our course to the shape of our circumstances" (364). Unlike Ziporyn, however, Fraser is more careful to acknowledge the possible limits of Guo Xiang's philosophy, questioning Guo Xiang's views on agency, and "to what extent the psychological state of 'joining in obscurity' with things is a practicable norm or only a vague theoretical ideal" (365), as well as the role of minded action in "non-minded responses" (365). These concerns, however, only come into play for Fraser because like Shen, and to some extent, Liu as well, he misses the role of the logic of convergence that we have pointed out. A self-realized or free person does not simply achieve such a state by "unselfishly adjusting our course to the shape of our circumstances" because her course is her very circumstance. This is made clear in Guo Xiang's account of causality. Moreover, the question of whether there is room for minded action, or whether one should "self-consciously step back and think about one's actions and ends, evaluating and revising them if needed" (362) is moot, as there is nothing according to which one can evaluate them correctly other than the circumstances around him, in which case it would then be self-so (ziran 自然), and by the dialectical necessity of his system, wuxin 無心.

7. The horse's nature as well as the concubines' and ministers' are passages discussed in the previous chapter.

8. Guo Xiang Commentary, 1.(8.1–9.1)G4–5.

9. Guo Xiang Commentary, 1.9.2G2.

10. Zhuangzi, 6.10.1–2, quoted in Ziporyn, Zhuangzi: The Essential Writings with Selections from Traditional Commentaries, 43.

11. Yao is often regarded as the epitome of virtue and goodness. A model for an emperor should strive to be, and "Jie is his traditional antipode, the last emperor of the Xia dynasty, which ended in the sixteenth century B.C.E. He is a legendary symbol of tyranny, cruelty, and all-around wickedness, and his excesses were used to justify the Shang dynasty's overthrow of the Xia." See ibid., 43.

12. Guo Xiang Commentary, 6.10.1G–2.

13. Brook Ziporyn, "Why Love and Morality Are the Best and the Worst Things We Do: Zhuangzi and the Spitting Fishes," *HuffPost*, 2017.

14. Zhuangzi, 17.25.2–5, quoted in Ziporyn, Zhuangzi: The Essential Writings with Selections from Traditional Commentaries, 74.

15. Guo Xiang Commentary, 17.25.2G–5(1–2).

16. Berlin, "Two Concepts of Liberty," 217.

17. Ibid., 204–05.

18. Guo Xiang Commentary, 1.[8.1–9.1]G5.

19. Guo Xiang Commentary, 1.9.2G1.

References

Arendrup, Birthe. "The First Chapter of Guo Xiang's Commentary to Zhuang Zi: A Translation and Grammatical Analysis." University of Copenhagen, 1964.

Bailey, Cyril. *The Greek Atomists and Epicurus: A Study*. New York: Russell & Russell, 1964.

Balazs, Étienne. *Chinese Civilization and Bureaucracy: Variations on a Theme*. Translated by H. M. Wright. New Haven: Yale University Press, 1964.

———. "Entre révolte nihiliste et évasion mystique: Les courants intellectuels en Chine au IIIe siècle de notre ère." *Asiatische Studien* 2, no. 1–2 (1948): 27–55.

Bell, Daniel A. *The China Model: Political Meritocracy and the Limits of Democracy*. Princeton: Princeton University Press, 2016.

Berlin, Isaiah. "Historical Inevitability." In *Liberty: Incorporating Four Essays on Liberty*, edited by Henry Hardy, 94–165. New York: Oxford University Press, 2002.

———. *Liberty: Incorporating Four Essays on Liberty*. Oxford: Oxford University Press, 2002.

———. *Russian Thinkers*. London: Penguin Books, 1994 [1978].

———. "Two Concepts of Liberty." In *Liberty: Incorporating Four Essays on Liberty*, edited by Henry Hardy, 166–217. New York: Oxford University Press, 2002.

Bi, Wang. *The Classic of the Way and Virtue: A New Translation of the Tao-Te Ching of Laozi as Interpreted by Wang Bi*. Translated by Richard J. Lynn. New York: Columbia University Press, 1999.

Bobzien, Susanne. "Did Epicurus Discover the Free Will Problem?" *Oxford Studies in Ancient Philosophy* 19 (2000): 287–337.

Brindley, Erica Fox. *Individualism in Early China: Human Agency and the Self in Thought and Politics*. Honolulu: University of Hawai'i Press, 2010.

Chan, Alan. "Neo-Daoism." In *Stanford Encyclopedia of Philosophy*, edited by Edward N. Zalta. Summer 2019 Edition.

Chan, Alan K. L. "Embodying Nothingness and the Ideal of the Affectless Sage in Daoist Philosophy." In *Nothingness in Asian Philosophy*, edited by JeeLoo Liu and Douglas L. Berger, 243–59. New York: Routledge, 2014.

———."Re-envisioning the Profound Order of Dao: Pei Wei's 'Critical Discussion on the Pride of Place of Being.'" In *Dao Companion to Xuanxue* 玄學 *(Neo-Daoism)*, edited by David Chai, 325–41. Cham: Springer International, 2020.

———. "Sage Nature and the Logic of Namelessness: Reconstructing He Yan's Explication of Dao." In *Philosophy and Religion in Early Medieval China*, edited by Alan K. L. Chan and Yuet-Keung Lo, 23–52. Albany: State University of New York Press, 2010.

Chan, Wing-Tsit. *A Source Book in Chinese Philosophy*. Lawrenceville: Princeton University Press, 1963. doi:10.2307/j.ctt7smn1.

Chuang-Tzu: A New Selected Translation with an Exposition of the Philosophy of Kuo Hsiang. Translated by Youlan Feng. China Academic Library. Heidelberg: Springer, 2016.

Code, Lorraine. *What Can She Know? Feminist Theory and the Construction of Knowledge*. Ithaca: Cornell University Press, 1991.

D'Ambrosio, Paul J. "Guo Xiang on Self-So Knowledge." *Asian Philosophy* 26, no. 2 (2016): 119–32.

Deguchi, Yasuo, Jay L. Garfield, and Graham Priest. "The Way of the Dialetheist: Contradictions in Buddhism." *Philosophy East and West* 58, no. 3 (2008): 395–402.

Deleuze, Gilles, and Félix Guattari. *What Is Philosophy?* New York: Columbia University Press, 1994.

Demiéville, Paul. "Philosophy and Religion from Han to Sui." In *The Cambridge History of China: Volume 1: The Ch'in and Han Empires, 221 BC–AD 220*, edited by Denis Twitchett and John K. Fairbank, 808–72. Cambridge: Cambridge University Press, 1986.

Dennett, Daniel C. *Elbow Room: The Varieties of Free Will Worth Wanting*. New York: Oxford University Press, 1984.

———. *Freedom Evolves*. New York: Viking, 2003.

Dihle, Albrecht. *The Theory of Will in Classical Antiquity*. Berkeley: University of California Press, 1982.

Dong, Zhongshu. *Luxuriant Gems of the Spring and Autumn*. Translated by John S. Major and Sarah A. Queen. New York: Columbia University Press, 2015.

Feng, Yuolan. "The School of Names." Chaps. 87–92 in *A Short History of Chinese Philosophy*, edited by Derk Bodde. New York: Free Press, 1966.

Fox, Alan. "Reflex and Reflectivity: *Wuwei* in the *Zhuangzi*." *Asian Philosophy* 6, no. 1 (1996): 59–72.

Fraser, Chris. "Metaphysics and Agency in Guo Xiang's Commentary on the *Zhuangzi*." In *Dao Companion to Xuanxue* 玄學 *(Neo-Daoism)*, edited by David Chai, 343–66. Cham: Springer International, 2020.

Frede, Michael. *A Free Will: Origins of the Notion in Ancient Thought*. Edited by A. A. Long. Berkeley: University of California Press, 2011.

Graham, Daniel W. *The Texts of Early Greek Philosophy: The Complete Fragments and Selected Testimonies of the Major Presocratics*. New York: Cambridge University Press, 2010.

Hansen, Chad. "Freedom and Moral Responsibility in Confucian Ethics." *Philosophy East and West* 22, no. 2 (1972): 169–86.

Hegel, Georg Wilhelm Friedrich. *Encyclopedia of the Philosophical Sciences in Basic Outline. Part 1: Science of Logic*. Translated by Klaus Brinkmann and Daniel O. Dahlstrom. Cambridge: Cambridge University Press, 2010.

———. *Hegel: Elements of the Philosophy of Right*. Cambridge: Cambridge University Press, 1991.

———. *Hegel's Lectures on the History of Philosophy*. Translated by Elizabeth Sanderson Haldane and Frances H Simson. London: Routledge & Kegan Paul, 1968.

———. *Hegel's Science of Logic*. Translated by A. V. Miller. Amherst: Humanity Books, 1998.

———. *Phenomenology of Spirit*. Translated by A. V. Miller. Oxford: Oxford University Press, 2013.

Henn, Martin J. *Parmenides of Elea: A Verse Translation with Interpretative Essays and Commentary to the Text*. Westport: Praeger, 2003.

Holzman, Donald. "Les Sept Sages de la Forêt des Bambous et la société de leur temps." *T'oung Pao* 44, no. 4/5 (1956): 317–46.

Huby, Pamela. "The First Discovery of the Freewill Problem." *Philosophy* 42, no. 162 (1967): 353–62.

Inwood, Brad, and Lloyd P. Gerson. *Hellenistic Philosophy*. Indianapolis: Hackett, 1997.

James, William. "Lecture IV: The One and the Many." In *Pragmatism*. New York: Dover, 1995.

Jenner, W. J. F. "China and Freedom." In *Asian Freedoms: The Idea of Freedom in East and Southeast Asia*, edited by David Kelly and Anthony Reid, 65–92. Cambridge: Cambridge University Press, 1998.

Jia, Jinhua. "Redefining the Ideal Character: A Comparative Study between the Concept of Detachment in the Aṣṭasāhasrikā and Guo Xiang's Theory of Eremitism at Court." *Dao* 14, no. 4 (2015): 545–65.

Jiang, Limei. "The Big and the Great: A Reconstruction of Zhuangzi's Philosophy on Transcendence." *Religions* 10, no. 1 (2019): 30.

Jiang, Tao. "Isaiah Berlin's Challenge to the Zhuangzian Freedom." *Journal of Chinese Philosophy* 39, no. 5 (2012): 69–92.

Jullien, François. *Detour and Access: Strategies of Meaning in China and Greece*. Translated by Sophie Hawkes. New York: Zone Books, 2000.

Kant, Immanuel. *Immanuel Kant's Critique of Pure Reason*. Translated by Norman Kemp Smith. London: Macmillan, 1929.

Kelly, David. "Approaching Chinese Freedom: A Study in Absolute and Relative Values." *Journal of Current Chinese Affairs* 42, no. 2 (2013): 141–65.

Knaul, Livia. "Kuo Hsiang and the Chuang Tzu." *Journal of Chinese Philosophy* 12, no. 4 (1985): 429–47.

Kohn, Livia. *Early Chinese Mysticism: Philosophy and Soteriology in the Taoist Tradition*. Princeton: Princeton University Press, 1992.

———. *Meditation Works: In the Daoist, Buddhist, and Hindu Traditions*. Magdalena: Three Pines Press, 2008.

Kristeva, Julia, Vernon Cisney, and Nicolae Morar. "A European in China." *Critical Inquiry* 37, no. 3 (2011): 419–33.

Lacan, Jacques, and Jacques-Alain Miller. *The Ethics of Psychoanalysis, 1959–1960: The Seminar of Jacques Lacan, Book VII*. London: Routledge, 2008.

Landes, David. *The Wealth and Poverty of Nations: Why Some Are So Rich and Some So Poor*. New York: W. W. Norton, 1999.

Lapoujade, David. *Aberrant Movements: The Philosophy of Gilles Deleuze*. Translated by Joshua David Jordan. South Pasadena: Semiotext(e), 2017.

Latour, Bruno. "Why Has Critique Run Out of Steam? From Matters of Fact to Matters of Concern." *Critical Inquiry* 30, no. 2 (2004): 225–48.

Li, Chenyang. "The Confucian Conception of Freedom." *Philosophy East and West* 64, no. 4 (October 2014): 902–19.

Li, Chenyang, Sai Hang Kwok, and Dascha Düring. *Harmony in Chinese Thought: A Philosophical Introduction*. Lanham: Rowman & Littlefield, 2021.

Liu, I-ch'ing "Biographical Notices." Translated by Richard B. Mather. In *Shih-Shuo Hsin-Yu: A New Account of Tales of the World*, 533–641. Ann Arbor: University of Michigan Press, 2002.

Liu, Jeeloo. *Neo-Confucianism: Metaphysics, Mind, and Morality*. Hoboken: John Wiley & Sons, 2018.

Liu, Xiaogan. "两种逍遥与两种自由 (Two Kinds of *Xiaoyao* and Two Kinds of Freedom)." *Journal of Huazong Normal University (Humanities and Social Sciences)* (November 2007).

———. "Zhuangzi's Philosophy: A Three Dimensional Reconstruction." In *Dao Companion to Daoist Philosophy*, edited by Xiaogan Liu, 193–219. Dordrecht: Springer, 2015.

Lo, Yuet-Keung. "Lone-Transformation and Intergrowth: Philosophy and Self-Justification in Guo Xiang's Commentary on the Zhuangzi." In *Dao Companion to Xuanxue 玄學 (Neo-Daoism)*, edited by David Chai, 367–92. Cham: Springer International, 2020.

Lynn, Richard J. "Guo Xiang's Theory of Sagely Knowledge as Seen in His 'Essentials of the Analects.'" In *Dao Companion to Xuanxue 玄學 (Neo-Daoism)*, edited by David Chai, 393–410. Cham: Springer International, 2020.

Lynn, Richard John. "Birds and Beasts in the Zhuangzi, Fables Interpreted by Guo Xiang and Cheng Xuanying." *Religions* 10, no. 7 (2019), doi:https://doi.org/10.3390/rel10070445.

---. "Reading Daoist Texts as Political Theory: Wang Bi on Laozi and Guo Xiang on Zhuangzi." *International Congress of Asian and North African Studies* (2000).

---. *Zhuangzi: A New Translation of the Daoist Classic as Interpreted by Guo Xiang*. New York: Columbia University Press, 2022.

Machek, David. "Is Freedom in Necessity or in Happiness? Guo Xiang's and Lin Xiyi's Controversial Readings of Zhuangzi's 'Free Rambling.'" *Studia Orientalia Slovaca* 9, no. 2 (2010): 111–28.

Mather, Richard B. "The Controversy over Conformity and Naturalness during the Six Dynasties." *History of Religions* 9, no. 2/3 (1969): 160–80.

Møllgaard, Eske Janus. "Zhuangzi's Notion of Transcendental Life." *Asian Philosophy* 15, no. 1 (2005): 1–18.

Nylan, Michael. "Zhuangzi: Closet Confucian?" *European Journal of Political Theory* 16, no. 4 (2017): 411–29.

Oldfather, W. A. *Epictetus: The Discourses as Reported by Arrian, the Manual, and Fragments*. Cambridge: Harvard University Press, 1925.

Perkins, Franklin. *Heaven and Earth Are Not Humane: The Problem of Evil in Classical Chinese Philosophy*. Bloomington: Indiana University Press, 2014.

Plantinga, Alvin. *God, Freedom, and Evil*. Grand Rapids: Eerdmans, 1977.

Priest, Graham. "Beyond True and False." *Aeon*. https://aeon.co/essays/the-logic-of-buddhist-philosophy-goes-beyond-simple-truth.

---. "Dialectic and Dialetheic." *Science & Society* 53, no. 4 (1989): 388–415.

---. *In Contradiction: A Study of the Transconsistent*. Oxford: Oxford University Press, 2006.

---. *One: Being an Investigation into the Unity of Reality and of Its Parts, Including the Singular Object Which Is Nothingness*. First edition. New York: Oxford University Press, 2014.

Robinet, Isabelle. "Kouo Siang Ou Le Monde Comme Absolu." *T'oung Pao* 69 (1983): 73–107.

Rošker, Jana. "Epistemology in Chinese Philosophy." In *Stanford Encyclopedia of Philosophy*, edited by Edward N. Zalta. Metaphysics Research Lab, Stanford University, 2018.

Rošker, Jana S. "The Metaphysical Style and Structural Coherence of Names in *Xuanxue*." In *Dao Companion to Xuanxue 玄學 (Neo-Daoism)*, edited by David Chai, 33–54. Cham: Springer International, 2020.

Rousseau, Jean-Jacques. *A Treatise on the Social Compact, or, the Principles of Political Law*. London: D. I. Eaton, 1795.

Shang, Ge Ling. *Liberation as Affirmation: The Religiosity of Zhuangzi and Nietzsche*. Albany: State University of New York Press, 2006.

Shen, Vincent. "From Interpretation to Construction: Guo Xiang's Ontological Individualism." *Journal of Chinese Philosophy* 40, no. S1 (2013): 171–88.

Spivak, Gayatri Chakravorty. *A Critique of Postcolonial Reason: Toward a History of the Vanishing Present*. Cambridge: Harvard University Press, 1999.

Tan, Christine Abigail. "The Butterfly Dream and Zhuangzi's Perspectivism: An Exploration of the Differing Interpretations of the Butterfly Dream against the Backdrop of Dao as Pluralistic Monism." *Kritike: An Online Journal of Philosophy* 10 (2016): 100–21.

Tan, Sor-Hoon. *Confucian Democracy: A Deweyan Reconstruction.* SUNY series in Chinese Philosophy and Culture. Albany: State University of New York Press, 2012.

Tang, Yijie. 郭象与魏晋玄学 (*Guo Xiang and Wei-Jin Xuanxue*). Beijing: Peking University Press, 2000.

Taylor, C. C. W. *The Atomists, Leucippus and Democritus: Fragments: A Text and Translation with a Commentary.* Toronto: University of Toronto Press, 1999.

Tu, Weiming. *Way, Learning, and Politics: Essays on the Confucian Intellectual.* Albany: State University of New York Press, 1993.

Valmisa, Mercedes. "The Happy Slave Isn't Free: Relational Autonomy and Freedom in the *Zhuangzi*." *Philosophy Compass* 14, no. 3 (2019): e12569.

———. "The Unifying Pattern." In *Adapting: A Chinese Philosophy of Action.* New York: Oxford University Press, 2021.

Van Norden, B. W. *Mengzi: With Selections from Traditional Commentaries.* Indianapolis: Hackett, 2008.

Van Norden, Bryan W. "Zhuangzi's Ironic Detachment and Political Commitment." *Dao* 15, no. 1 (2016): 1–17.

Wakeman, Frederick. "Rebellion and Revolution: The Study of Popular Movements in Chinese History." *Journal of Asian Studies* 36, no. 2 (1977): 201–37.

Wang, Xiaoyi. "郭象历史哲学发微 (On Guo Xiang's Philosophy of History)." 文史哲 0, no. 2 (2002): 141–46.

———. "郭象命运论及其意义 (The Destiny Theory of Guo Xiang and Its Significance)." 文史哲 *Journal of Literature, History, and Philosophy*, no. 6 (2005): 19–24.

Watson, Burton, trans. *The Complete Works of Chuang Tzu.* https://terebess.hu/english/chuangtzu.html.

Wenzel, Christian, and Kai Marchal. "Chinese Perspectives on Free Will." In *The Routledge Companion to Free Will*, edited by Kevin Timpe, Meghan Giffith, and Neil Levy, 374–88. London: Routledge, 2017.

Whitmarsh, Tim. *Battling the Gods: Atheism in the Ancient World.* New York: Vintage, 2016.

Wu, Genyou. "On the Idea of Freedom and Its Rejection in Chinese Thought and Institutions." *Asian Philosophy* 16, no. 3 (November 2006): 219–35.

Yang, Lihua. 郭象"庄子注"研究 (*An Examination of Guo Xiang's Zhuangzi Commentary*). Beijing: Beijing Daxue chu ban shu, 2010.

Yao, Xinzhong. "Confucianism in the Wei-Jin Period." In *RoutledgeCurzon Encyclopedia of Confucianism*, edited by Xinzhong Yao. New York: Routledge Curzon, 2013.

Yü, Ying-shih. "Individualism and the Neo-Daoist Movement in Wei-Jin China." In *Chinese History and Culture: Sixth Century B.C.E. to Seventeenth Century*, edited by Michael S. Duke and Josephine Chiu-Duke, 134–65. New York: Columbia University Press, 2016.

Zhao, Guoping. "Transcendence, Freedom, and Ethics in Lévinas' Subjectivity and Zhuangzi's Non-Being Self." *Philosophy East and West* 65, no. 1 (2015): 65–80.

Ziporyn, B. *Zhuangzi: The Complete Writings*. Indianapolis: Hackett, 2020.

Ziporyn, Brook. *Beyond Oneness and Difference: Li and Coherence in Chinese Buddhist Thought and Its Antecedents*. Albany: State University of New York Press, 2013.

———. "Guo Xiang: The Self-So and the Repudiation-cum-Reaffirmation of Deliberate Action and Knowledge." In *Dao Companion to Daoist Philosophy*, edited by Liu Xiaogan, 397–423. Dordrecht: Springer, 2014.

———. "Li in Wang Bi and Guo Xiang: Coherence in the Dark." *Philosophy and Religion in Early Medieval China* (2010): 97–134.

———. *The Penumbra Unbound: The Neo-Taoist Philosophy of Guo Xiang*. Albany: State University of New York Press, 2012 [2003].

———. "Why Love and Morality Are the Best and the Worst Things We Do: Zhuangzi and the Spitting Fishes." *HuffPost*, 2017.

———. *Zhuangzi: The Essential Writings with Selections from Traditional Commentaries*. Indianapolis: Hackett, 2009.

Index

Agency, 4, 8, 9, 14, 67, 75, 82, 92, 94, 97, 102, 106, 113, 161n60, 181n20, 184–185n6. See also autonomy
Analects, 164n104, 179n23, 180n11
Anarchism, 4, 158
Authenticity, 52, 81, 113
Autonomy, 15, 20, 50, 69, 95–97, 113, 116, 122, 127, 136–137, 139, 142, 147, 152–154, 166n108, 181n20, 183n45, 184n54, 184n56. See also agency

Bao Jingyan, 4, 157–158n13, 165n105
Berlin, Isaiah, 11, 12, 13, 16–21, 95–96, 133, 135–136, 139, 142, 150–151, 160n48, 160n49, 163n96, 166n108, 178n2, 183n45
Buddhism, xi, xv, xvii, xviii, 39–42, 56, 116, 130, 169n36, 170n39, 171n57, 180n8

Causality; causation, xx, 4–5, 9–1, 13, 20, 23, 25, 32–34, 39, 44, 51–54, 57, 65, 69, 83, 94, 96–97, 101–102, 105, 112, 116, 122, 136, 142–44, 148, 153–154, 158n14, 159n35, 178n2, 185n6

Confucius; Confucian, xi, xv, xvi, xvii, 2, 3, 4, 14, 16–17, 20–22, 25–27, 30, 42, 56, 64–65, 97–98, 101–102, 115–116, 118–120, 148, 158n13, 163n93, 164n101, 164n104, 173n6, 174n15

Dao, xii, 30, 38, 46–47, 56–58, 70, 119–121, 123t, 125, 168n25, 174n20, 175n21, 184n6
Dependence-based autonomy, 20, 113, 116, 122, 137, 139, 142, 147, 152
Duhua (lone-transformation), 33, 36, 44, 48, 51–54, 57, 92, 105, 136–137
Dusheng (lone-generation), 44, 48, 54, 57

Emergence, 4, 9, 34, 44, 53–55, 73, 93, 104, 106, 141
Emptiness, 28, 29, 30, 41, 45, 60, 125, 144, 180n8
Epistemology; epistemological, xix, 5, 20, 23, 71, 73–74, 77, 95, 106, 108, 111, 116, 139, 141–143, 146, 149, 154, 166n108, 172n84, 180n9
Equality, 68, 79, 84, 115, 127, 143

Ethics; ethical, xiv, 2, 3, 8, 10–11, 17, 22–23, 68, 145, 168n25. *See also* morality

Fatalism, 67–68, 92, 149, 153, 178n61
Forgetting; forgetfulness, 26–27, 46, 72, 82, 83, 93, 107, 108, 112, 126–127, 138, 146–147, 151, 153

Harmony, 1–3, 28, 58, 63, 124, 134
He Yan, 21, 30, 34
Heaven, xiv, xvi, xvii, 3–4, 14, 18, 30–31, 45–47, 72t, 78, 82, 85–87, 89, 91–94, 106, 109–110, 112–113, 122, 126–127, 138, 142, 149, 158, 161n58, 164n101, 165n105, 171n62, 174n19, 177n49, 177n53, 178n63
Hierarchy, 68, 143, 144, 145, 155

Independence; independent, 4, 9, 10, 21, 23, 34, 44, 50, 51, 52, 54, 67, 84, 95, 96, 97, 102, 104–113, 115, 123, 124–125, 127, 132, 136–137, 141–142, 144, 149, 150, 166n108, 184n6. *See also* autonomy
Individualism, 20, 22, 143, 154, 166n108

Ji (traces), xix, 26, 42, 57, 62, 64, 74, 77, 79, 104, 121–122, 153, 174n16
Ji Kang, 21, 115, 164n104

Laozi, xvii, 29, 30, 36–37, 143–144, 152, 173n6
Li (coherence, principle, pattern), xvii, 22, 27–28, 55–57, 63–66, 70, 71, 74, 79, 87–88, 104, 172n84
Liberalism, 2–4, 11, 13, 143, 147, 150–151, 153, 166n108

Liberty, 10, 12–13, 16, 18, 20, 95–96, 138, 150–151, 153, 183n45
Logic of convergence, xiii, xx, 20, 23, 25, 28, 33, 38–39, 43–44, 47–49, 56, 69–70, 85, 88–89, 97, 105, 109, 113, 115, 117, 119, 122, 125, 137, 139, 141, 142, 144, 174n18, 185n6

Ming (fate), 15, 52, 85, 87, 89, 92, 127, 134, 142, 149, 177n49, 184n6
Mingjiao (teaching of names), 21, 25, 74, 120, 163n93, 164n104, 174n15
Morality, xii, xiv, xvi, 11, 12, 17, 46, 74, 147. *See also* ethics
Mysticism, xii, xiii, xiv, xv, xvii, xx, 16, 89, 96, 136, 143, 147, 153, 164n101, 175n29

Network, 14, 22, 49, 53, 91–92, 95–96, 116, 141, 163n97, 165n107, 178n2
Nihilism, xiv, xvii, xx, 6, 17, 22, 30, 164n104, 168n25
Nonbeing, 22, 29, 30, 33–35, 37–38, 42–47, 51, 53, 56, 82, 83, 99, 101, 141, 182n32

Oneness, 21–22, 36, 47, 54, 85, 123, 124, 147, 148, 182n29.
Ontology, xvi, 4–6, 10, 20–23, 25, 27–30, 32–33, 36, 39–44, 66–70, 73–74, 77, 92–93, 102, 110, 115, 117, 121, 141–144, 154, 158n14, 172n84, 175n21, 178n63, 180n9

Pei Wei, 21, 30, 34, 36, 168n25
Purpose, xiii, xvii, xix, xx, 9–10, 32, 44, 68, 109–110, 122, 147, 149, 151, 155

Relativism; relativity, 84, 127, 130, 176n37
Ruan Ji, 21, 115, 175n29

Self-determination, 4–5, 10, 15, 49, 96–97, 109, 136–137, 139, 151–152, 154, 155
Social change, 19, 135, 141, 154

Truth, 10, 11, 13, 41–42, 77, 81, 84, 86, 102, 113, 118, 154, 160, 165n107, 177n37

Value, xiii, xvi, xx, 2–4, 11, 13, 16–19, 30, 42, 65, 75, 79, 86, 95–96, 115–116, 122, 131, 135–136, 145, 147, 153, 155, 177n37
Virtue, xiii, 3, 22, 49, 78, 79, 117, 139, 185n11

Wang Bi, xv, 21–22, 30, 34, 56
Wuwei (non-action, non-activity), 18, 73, 143, 173n4
Wuxin (having no heart-mind), 37, 46–47, 97, 102, 115, 116–121, 122, 132, 137, 142, 146, 171n62, 185n6

Xiaoyao (free and leisurely wandering), 17, 19, 106, 108, 109, 111, 115–116, 122, 132–139, 142, 144, 149
Xing (nature), 15, 46, 71, 75–77, 81, 82, 85, 89, 122, 127, 131–132, 134, 142, 151, 175n21, 175n22
Xuanming (vanishing into things), 52, 54, 118, 153
Xuanxue (Dark Learning, Neo-Daoism), xv, 21–22, 143, 163n89

Zidang (self-rightness), 67
Zide (Self-realization), 4, 45–46, 64, 94, 97, 106, 113
Zihua (self-transformation), 44, 47–49, 64–65, 94, 97, 106, 113, 115–139, 142, 144, 149, 151, 183n37
Ziran (self-so, spontaneity), xvii, xix, xx, 21, 25, 32, 35, 38, 54, 64–65, 74–75, 77, 110, 113, 117, 120, 127, 141–142, 144, 151, 169n32, 173n4, 177n49, 180n9, 185n6
Zisheng (self-generation), 33, 36–37, 44, 47–48, 54, 57